D1651790

# Foreword

$A$t the beginning of this new millennium, regional economies are confronting momentous changes. The globalisation of trade and economic activity is increasingly testing their ability to adapt and maintain their competitive edge. There is a tendency for income and performance gaps to widen between and within regions, and the cost of maintaining social cohesion is increasing. On the other hand rapid technological change and greater use of knowledge are offering new opportunities for local and regional development but demand further investment from enterprises, reorganisation of labour and production, more advanced skills and environmental improvements.

Amid this change and turbulence, regions continue to follow very different paths. Some regions are doing well and are driving growth. Others are less successful at capturing trade and additional economic activities. Many territories with poor links to the sources of prosperity, afflicted by migration, and lagging behind with respect to infrastructure and private investment are finding it difficult to keep up with the general trend.

These new patterns of population settlement, relationships between urban and rural areas and persisting or increasing territorial disparities are raising new issues. At the same time central governments are no longer the sole provider of territorial policy. The vertical distribution of power between the different tiers of government needs to be reassessed as well as the decentralisation of fiscal resources in order to better respond to the expectations of the public and improve policy efficiency. In that context public authorities need to weigh up current challenges, evaluate the strategies pursued in recent years and define new options.

Responding to a need to study and spread innovative territorial development strategies and governance in a more systematic way, in 1999 the OECD created the Territorial Development Policy Committee (TDPC) as a unique forum for international exchange and debate. The TDPC has developed a number of activities, among which are a series of national reviews. These studies, such as this one, follow a standard methodology and a common conceptual framework, allowing countries to share their experiences and disseminate information on good practices. This series is intended to produce a synthesis that will formulate and diffuse horizontal policy recommendations.

# Acknowledgements

*T*he OECD would like to thank the Polish authorities at the national and sub-national levels for their co-operation and support during the reviewing process. Special thanks are given to Mr. Piotr Zuber, Director of the Structural Policy Co-ordination Department in the Ministry of Regional Development, Mr. Robert Dzierzgwa, Ms. Lucyna Przybylska, Mr. Stanislaw Sudak, Mr. Stanislaw Bienias and Ms. Sylwia Nowak in the same ministry; as well as Professors Jacek Szlachta and Janusz Zaleski. The OECD would also like to thank the Polish authorities in the regions of Dolnoslaskie and Lubelskie, as well as the municipalities of Wroclaw and Lublin, for hosting and organising OECD missions. The support from the Polish Delegation to the OECD, including Mr. Ambassador Jan Woroniecki and Mr. Stefan Krecisz, is also gratefully acknowleged.

The Review was written and co-ordinated by Mrs. Dorothée Allain-Dupré, under the direction of Mr. Mario Pezzini and Mr. Roberto Villarreal. Substantial inputs were provided by Mr. François Bafoil, Senior Research Fellow CNRS at CERI (CNRS/Sciences Po). Mr. Don Christiansen, senior consultant, also contributed to the preparation of the report. Other contributions were provided by Mr. Javier Sanchez-Reaza (econometric and statistical analysis of Chapter 1); Mr. Patrick Dubarle (innovation policy); Ms. Soo-Jin Kim; Ms. Lee Mizell; Ms. Claire Charbit and Mr. Edouard Turkisch. The inputs provided by Mr. Rafal Kierzenkowski and Mr. Andrzej Kwiecinski are gratefully acknowledged.

Peer reviewing countries (Korea and The Netherlands) were represented by Mr. Junghun Kim, Director, Department of Public Finance Research, Korea Institute of Public Finance and Mrs. Willy Bruinsma, Senior Adviser, Ministry of Economic Affairs, The Netherlands.

Ms. Doranne Lecercle edited the final manuscript and Ms. Sophia Katsira prepared the Review for publication.

## Country profile of Poland

- **Area (sq kilometres):** 312 679.
- **Population**: 38.2 million people (6th largest population in the European Union).
- **Form of state:** unitary state.
- **Structure of government:** parliamentary republic.
- **Sejm membership (lower house):** 460; Senate membership (upper house): 100 ; Number of political parties in Sejm: 6.
- Member of NATO (1991), OECD (1996), EU (2004).

## Economic trends (2007)

- **GDP** (Zl billion, current prices): 1 166.7.
- **GDP per capita** (USD, market exchange rate): 11 069.
- **Labour force survey unemployment** (% of labour force): 9.6.

## Public finance

- **General government budget balance** (% of GDP): –2.0.
- **General government revenues** (% of GDP): 40.4.
- **General government expenditures** (% of GDP): 42.4.
- **State treasury debt** (end-year, % of GDP): 52.9.

## Currency

- **Monetary unit:** zloty
- **Currency units per:** USD EUR – Average: 2007 USD 2.7653/€ 3.7824 – April 2008: USD 2.1859/€ 3.4418.

## Territorial and institutional framework of Poland

- Poland has a three-tier governmental system: 2 478 municipalities (*gminas*), 314 counties (powiats); and 16 regions (voivodships).
- Administrative authority at voivodship level is shared between a government-appointed voivod (governor), an elected regional assembly (sejmik) and an executive elected by that assembly (marshal). Major cities normally have the status of both gmina and powiat: 65 cities have a powiat status.

## Names of the 16 voivodships and capital city

| Voivodship | Capital |
|---|---|
| Lower Silesian (Dolnosląskie) | Wroclaw |
| Kuyavian-Pomeranian *(Kujawsko-pomorskie)* | Bydgoszcz[1] Torun[2] |
| Lublin *(Lubelskie)* | Lublin |
| Lubusz *(Lubuskie)* | Gorzow Wielkopolski[1] Zielona Gora[2] |
| Lodz *(Lodzkie)* | Lodz |
| Lesser Poland *(Malopolskie)* | Krakow |
| Masovian *(Mazowieckie)* | Warsaw |
| Opole *(Opolskie)* | Opole |
| Subcarpathian *(Podkarpackie)* | Rzeszow |
| Podlachian *(Podlaskie)* | Bialystok |
| Pomeranian *(Pomorskie)* | Gdansk |
| Silesian *(Sląskie)* | Katowice |
| Swietokrzyskie *(Swiêtokrzyskie)* | Kielce |
| Warmian-Masurian *(Warminsko-mazurskie)* | Olsztyn |
| Greater Poland *(Wielkopolskie)* | Poznan |
| West Pomeranian *(Zachodniopomorskie)* | Szczecin |

1. Seat of voivod.
2. Seat of voivodship regional council.

OECD TERRITORIAL REVIEWS: POLAND – ISBN 978-92-64-04926-0 – © OECD 2008

# Table of Contents

## Tables

## Figures

**Maps**

ISBN 978-92-64-04926-0
OECD Territorial Reviews: Poland
© OECD 2008

# Assessment and Recommendations

## Poland: one of the fastest growing OECD countries, with regional development high on the political agenda

Poland's average annual growth rate was above 4% between 1995 and 2005 and growth of GDP exceeded 6% in 2006 and 2007, the second-best performance among OECD countries. It had a strong drop in unemployment, from 18% in 2005 to less than 10% at the end of 2007. Poland stands out as a relatively successful example of a transition from a partially state-directed economy to a primarily privately owned market economy, with above 75% of total output now produced in the private sector. Over a short period, it has diversified towards services (in particular business services) and more labour-intensive manufacturing. It has retained its position as a world leader in manufacturing and has specialised in rapidly growing sectors such as pharmaceuticals and electronic components. Poland has also become a very attractive location for foreign direct investment (FDI) and is now among the top ten OECD countries in terms of FDI flows as a proportion of GDP. Its FDI rose from 2.9% to 4.1% of GDP between 1996 and 2006. Owing to its geographical position – at the heart of the European continent and surrounded by Belarus, Czech Republic, Germany, Lithuania, Russia, the Slovak Republic and Ukraine – Poland has the potential to play a strategic role between western and eastern Europe, with Russia and Asia and within the Baltic Sea Region.

However, the growth of GDP is not distributed evenly throughout the country. Poland has one of the OECD area's greatest territorial disparities in terms of GDP per capita at TL3 level. Moreover, the disparities have *increased* since 1995, as the growth dynamics have been concentrated in certain locations. Three sets of disparities are visible: i) a persistent gap between eastern and western Poland; ii) a gap between Warsaw and the rest of the country; iii) rising intra-regional disparities, among the highest in the OECD, in particular in the regions of Warsaw (Mazowieckie), Poznan (Wielkopolskie) and Cracow (Malopolskie), which are largely due to rising disparities between large urban areas and rural ones. Like many OECD countries, Poland must seek to achieve an appropriate balance between support for poles of growth and the development of lagging regions, particularly its eastern peripheral regions, which are among the poorest in the European Union.

Poland offers a practical illustration of a country that benefits from a large window of opportunity for regional development policies, owing to high political commitment at the different levels of government as well as very strong financial support from the EU in 2007-13 (EUR 67 billion for cohesion policy), complemented by a significant national co-financing effort. In recent years, attention has largely concentrated on improving the quantity and quality of the regional physical infrastructure (particularly transport). Investment in human capital, innovation and entrepreneurship has also gained in importance since 2004. The Review recommends better tailoring the policy mix to various territories' specific needs, better co-ordinating regional and rural development strategies, and developing a specific policy approach for large urban areas. It also recommends taking a forward-looking perspective to strengthening the Polish multi-level governance system, as most Polish regions will not benefit from the same level of external support after 2013.

*The growing metropolitan-rural gap presents*
*a major challenge for balanced territorial*
*development and sustained competitiveness*

In terms of growth of GDP, the gap is widening fastest between large cities and rural areas. The growth rate in Polish urban areas has been among the OECD leaders for 1998-2003, behind Ireland, Korea and Hungary. Urban areas' share of national GDP has increased constantly since 1995, while that of rural and intermediate areas has decreased. Warsaw has been one of the fastest growing of all OECD metropolitan regions over the past few years. In addition, urban areas have per capita GDP that is more than double the average in predominantly rural areas; the differential between Warsaw and the national average was 263% in 2005. The role of services in the economy of large urban areas has risen significantly since the mid-1990s; they offer employment opportunities for more diverse skills and attract knowledge workers and FDI (essentially in Warsaw, Katowice and Poznan). Urban areas are 20% more productive (both labour and multi-factor productivity) than the average Polish sub-regions. This points to the need to strengthen agglomeration economies in a sustainable way in order to enhance productivity growth and transfers of knowledge. Large urban areas also face the challenge of managing the adverse consequences of very high growth rates, particularly the urban sprawl that has resulted from the 10 to 20% annual rise in housing prices since 2003. Increased commuting flows to and from large cities call for specific attention to urban-rural linkages in terms both of transport and housing.

Rural areas have benefited less from Poland's economic development, and many rural areas, in particular in eastern Poland, are caught into a vicious circle of low attractiveness, low infrastructure development and low educational attainment. Only 5.4% of the population living in rural areas has a higher education degree, compared to 17.5% in urban areas. Overall, employment in the agriculture sector remains high (17% of the total labour force), but labour productivity is low, as agriculture only accounts for 4.6% of GDP. Agriculture is fragmented, with mainly small and very small farms. More than 60% of Polish farms have fewer than 5 hectares, and 34% have less than 1 hectare. There is an important east-west divide, as the 20% of farms of over 15 hectares (mostly located in the west) account for more than 80% of agricultural output. The most important challenge for lagging rural areas is to enhance their links to urban areas and to diversify their economy to non-agricultural activities. This requires readier access to education, access to capital and information, and improved transport and telecommunications infrastructure. The challenges facing rural areas are national challenges, as a more diversified rural economy and improved mobility out of the agriculture sector would have a significant impact on the national output.

*Other challenges for territorial development are to advance the move to the knowledge economy, to improve the transport infrastructure, and to hasten the development of eastern Poland*

While some challenges are specific to urban or rural areas, the need to hasten the move to the knowledge economy and to improve the transport infrastructure is common to all regions.

- *The poor transport infrastructure is a major obstacle to economic development.* It has three major shortcomings: i) the development of roads at the functional scale of large cities is insufficient (lack of ring roads, bad connections with surrounding municipalities); ii) the connections between large cities (capital regions) are weak; iii) north-south connections are not well developed as east-west links had priority during the Communist era. In fact, the major infrastructure (road, railways, seaports, aviation) is either underdeveloped or in poor condition and in urgent need of repair, upgrading and extension. With only 663 km of motorways, Poland has the most limited network in Europe. There are 94.8 km of road network per 10 000 inhabitants (the EU25 average is 145 km). Besides, while Poland's rail system is the third largest in Europe, the capital stock is obsolescent.

- *All regions need to accelerate the move to the knowledge economy, focusing on human capital development and innovation.* Although attainment of tertiary education has improved considerably, the percentage of the population with tertiary attainment was still only 15.6% in 2004 (the OECD average was 25.2%). There is a large urban-rural gap. Moreover, since the 1990s, Poland's human capital has been affected by out-migration, particularly since EU accession. Outside of Warsaw, Poznan and Wroclaw, innovation does not yet play a strong role in regional growth, as evidenced by relatively low levels of patenting, for example. The links between Higher Education Institutes (HEI) and research centres with the entrepreneurial environment are weak, resulting not only in few patents, but in relatively few improvements to productive processes or new products going into the market. In 2004, Poland spent 0.58% of GDP on R&D, well below the OECD average (2.3%). The transition to the knowledge economy is also affected by the limited development of information and communication technologies (ICTs). In 2005, Internet access was only available to 23% of Polish households (29% urban, 11% rural) compared with the EU average of 43%.

- *The knowledge and infrastructure challenges are even greater for the five eastern regions* situated along Poland's eastern and northern borders, as they have the lowest growth rates and are the smallest contributors to national GDP (less than 3% each). The east-west divide, often referred to as "Poland A" and "Poland B", has proven quite resistant over the past decades. The slow development of eastern regions is mainly linked to historical legacies, the predominance in regional economies of agricultural activities with low productivity (30.2% of the total employment of the five regions) and their peripheral situation, bordering weakly developed countries (Ukraine and Belarus). Unlike most western regions, which have significantly reduced unemployment since 2004, unemployment has risen in the eastern border regions.

*Regional development is high on the Polish political agenda and benefits from one of the largest budgets among OECD countries*

Partly under the influence of the European Union, regional development has become a key issue on Poland's political agenda. Before 1999, Poland's territorial policy consisted essentially of support for industrial regions that were undergoing restructuring, for example with the development of special economic zones after 1994. A more proactive regional policy has emerged in the 2000s from two closely linked institutional processes: the creation of the 16 Polish regions (*voivodships*) in 1999 with elected regional assembly; and accession to the European Union in 2004 followed by support from EU structural funds. EU regional policy (cohesion policy) has helped to provide a new context for regional policies, as regions have become the building blocks of a competitive Europe and are in charge of implementing regional development strategies and of EU funds. Since 2004, EU funds have represented the bulk of

Poland's budget for regional policy complemented by significant national co-financing (a minimum of 15% is required). All regions have been eligible under the "objective 1" or newly defined "convergence" objective for 2007-13, although the region of Warsaw (Mazowieckie) has now passed the threshold of 75% of the average EU GDP per capita. Polish regions will therefore receive EUR 67.3 billion in cohesion funds for 2007-13; this represents 20% of total cohesion funds, making Poland the all-time leading recipient of support under the cohesion policy. These amounts add to the funds that Poland will receive under the European Agricultural Rural Development Fund (EUR 16.5). Together with EUR 22.4 billion from national sources, the national development strategy for 2007-15 foresees total funding of EUR 108 billion. The Ministry of Regional Development was created in 2005 to co-ordinate policies and EU funding, signalling also the political commitment to improve territorial development and multi-sector co-ordination.

The learning process has been rapid, although Poland has had little time to create a regional development policy framework, owing to time constraints on the absorption of EU funds (N+2 rule). Poland has benefited from the experience of other EU countries. It has adopted since 2004 a balanced policy mix for regional development co-financed with EU structural funds targeting infrastructure development, human capital, innovation, and rural development. In the 1970s and 1980s, 80% of cohesion policy funds in the EU went for investment in infrastructure, but strategies developed by Poland for 2004-06, and now for 2007-13, are more balanced. For the new period, the Polish National Strategic Reference Framework (NSRF) forecasts spending 41% of EU funds on infrastructure development, 14% on human capital, 10% on innovation, 3% on development of eastern Poland. 25% of the funds are decentralised and managed by regions directly to finance their own development strategies. The Polish NSRF largely reflects the priorities of EU regional policy, with a focus on so-called Lisbon objectives (i.e. growth-oriented activities: innovation, human capital, intelligent transport systems, multimodal transport, environmental protection, etc.). In fact, 64% of investments have been earmarked for Lisbon-related expenditure, among the highest rates in the ten new EU member states. The Ministry of Agriculture also has a separate rural development strategy. The balanced policy mix adopted at the central government level creates a challenge for effective multi-sectoral co-ordination of the various pillars and for tailoring the policy mix to meet different territorial needs.

*Regions are increasingly empowered to implement their own regional development strategies*

Although the central government has played the most important role in the design of regional development strategy and programming of use of EU funds,

Polish regions play an increasing role in the process. Poland has introduced an extended decentralisation process, especially compared to the other countries in Central and Eastern Europe. Municipalities (*gminas*) have since 1990 significant responsibilities and large budgets, while regions (*voivodships*), created in 1999, increasingly play the role of strategic partners with the central and local governments, to decide the priorities for local development, and the use of EU funds. Regional contracts, partly inspired by the French state-regions contracts, were introduced in Poland in 2001 and have helped to foster dialogue between regions and the state. They are co-financed by central and local governments for investments in transport, education, tourism and health care. In 1999, 314 districts (*powiats*) were also created with a more limited role than regions and municipalities; their main responsibilities are secondary schools and public health services. After almost a decade of existence, this decentralised policy framework is perceived as a success even if important challenges remain. Poland's efforts to establish an adequate sub-national system have facilitated the absorption and allocation of EU and national resources for regional development by improving the articulation of top-down and bottom-up initiatives for regional development.

For 2007-13, one-quarter of EU cohesion funds have been decentralised and the 16 regions have been named managing authorities responsible for elaborating and implementing regional operational programmes (ROPs). This is a further step towards increased decentralisation, as in 2004-06 the allocation of EU funds was entirely decided at the central level, with an "Integrated Regional Operational Programme". In total, regions are now in charge of managing 24.6% of the cohesion funds, i.e. more than EUR 16 billion. In addition, the operational programme Human Capital (14% of funding) is largely regionalised. In total, around 34% of funding is decentralised in Poland for 2007-13. The Ministry of Regional Development has provided regions guidance on the elaboration of ROPs, recommending that a minimum of 40% of expenditures should be devoted to Lisbon objectives. At the end of 2007, 24% of total ROP funding was allocated to innovation and entrepreneurship projects, and 25% to transport infrastructure projects. Regions should work to develop more place-based integrated approaches and to avoid piecemeal approaches.

*Major investments in transport infrastructure*
*are planned, but attention to cost-benefit*
*analysis, intra-regional needs and environmental*
*challenges should be improved*

The first priority of the Polish policy mix for regional development, at both central and regional levels, is the development of transport infrastructure. It is a priority, both for Poland and for the European Union, to improve labour mobility, which lags behind most other OECD countries, to enhance urban-rural linkages, to improve international accessibility and access to eastern markets. The Infrastructure and Environment programme, developed by Poland and co-financed with EU funds, is the largest ever funded by the European Commission (EUR 28 billion). EUR 20 billion is allocated to transport development, and other priorities include water and sewage management. Poland will also dedicate EUR 9.6 billion to the programme. Given the limited time frame for absorption of EU funds, it will be a challenge to carry out the programme. Moreover, the European soccer championship, which Poland will co-host with Ukraine in 2012, imposes an additional time constraint on many investment projects. Careful governance of infrastructure investments will be crucial to making the most of such large sums. Poland has to watch carefully to avoid the various obstacles that can hinder implementation, such as imperfect spatial planning, macroeconomic constraints or staff shortages in construction. Besides, it is critical for all levels of government to keep in mind that infrastructure does not by itself provide the conditions for long-term competitiveness. Transport investments have twofold effects on regional economies: they improve access to more distant labour and goods markets, and they increase competition in local markets. Therefore, along with building infrastructure, policies to improve local competitiveness must be adopted: education, support to small and medium-sized enterprises (SMEs), technology, provision of public goods, etc., particularly in eastern regions.

The main focus of transport policy since 2004 has been road development (expressways, motorways, national roads). The main priority has been to establish links between the major urban centres, in particular the 16 regional capitals. Although access to regional capitals is important to facilitate mobility of workers and goods and for political and equity reasons, care must be taken not to focus on inter-city linkages to the detriment of improving the underdeveloped connections between large cities and their surrounding municipalities (gminas). Greater investment in regional/metropolitan roads, including ring roads, which do not exist in most cities, not even Warsaw, might generate strong economic outcomes. In addition, the right balance between roads and public transport has yet to be found, especially in large urban areas. Urban public transport represents only 13.9% of the allocation at the central level; compared to 51% for roads and 4.7% for regional operational programmes, a sign of its comparatively low priority, yet Poland's originally well developed public transport systems have deteriorated over the past decade, owing to inadequate spatial planning and limited investment by local governments. In their regional programmes, central and local governments should carefully assess the economic advantages of investing in new roads as compared to other transport modes.

Overall, cost-benefit analyses of the proposed transport infrastructure investments seem insufficiently systematic. In their absence, it is difficult to prioritise the various investments and modes of transport. Long-term objectives are not stated precisely, and an overall spatial scheme for transport (after 2013) has not been developed. Besides, many road investment projects conflict with the EU's Natura 2000 programme, which covers 18% of Poland's territory, as many of the approved road investment projects fail to bypass protected areas. There may be as many as 100 potential conflict zones. There is a risk that payments for programmes and projects to be financed in 2007-13 may be blocked. Poland's tardiness in completing strategic environmental assessments for all projects has resulted in this situation. It is essential to ensure that Polish environmental legislation complies with EU legislation and to undertake environmental impact assessments for all projects.

There is also a danger that projects will be carried out at maximum cost, particularly given the rising price of materials (particularly steel and cement) and the shortage of labour in the construction sector owing to out-migration. The short time for absorption of funds is an even greater challenge given inflationary pressures. With an increase in interest rates that may negatively affect exports and private investment, Poland has to manage the risk of crowding out public investment in the short term. Additional measures should be taken to reduce these macroeconomic pressures, for example, measures to increase the labour supply in the construction sector, to further ease foreign workers' access to the labour market, and to intensify competition, not only among local construction firms but also with international firms, through better regulation and improved calls for tender in public works.

## Deficiencies in spatial planning are an obstacle for infrastructure development

Insufficient spatial planning creates problems for infrastructure development, particularly for transport and housing. Although municipal spatial planning is in principle a legal requirement, many local governments do not have proper planning systems. Only 20% of the territory has spatial plans and these focus on municipalities' administrative borders rather than on functional areas and rarely involve co-operation among municipalities. Upper levels of government (region, central government) are unable to enforce the implementation of strategic decisions. As a result, planning does not enough play the role of co-ordinating and giving spatial articulation to policies. The lack of adequate functional spatial planning has adverse consequences for both urban and rural areas. In large cities, it hinders the development of integrated transport systems and contributes to a rapid increase in the use of cars to the detriment of public transport, thereby increasing congestion and pollution. It has also slowed the development of housing, and Poland now faces a shortage of some 1 million dwellings, particularly for social housing, which again reduces labour mobility and reinforces growing urban sprawl. Poor spatial planning also adversely affects rural areas. With the increased price of land since EU accession, rural *gminas* tend to speculate on land rather than develop a strategic long-term vision on its best use.

## It is necessary to focus on endogenous resources and understand innovation in a broad sense

The second key dimension of the regional development policy mix is the focus on human capital, innovation and entrepreneurship. Although infrastructure development will improve accessibility and mobility, essential pre-conditions for regional development, enhanced competitiveness over the longer term will mainly require a focus on endogenous resources, *i.e.* development of human capital and innovation. The challenge for Poland and its regions is to understand innovation in its broader sense: even if Lisbon objectives are very broad, there is a risk of interpreting them narrowly in some cases, by focusing mainly on research and technological development for example. This may not be the most appropriate choice for all regions, with their different assets and needs. It is important to adjust programmes and strategies according to an in-depth assessment of regional and local needs and to understand Lisbon objectives as all types of policies that help to enhance knowledge transfers (whether education, support to medium-technology industries, or knowledge transfer between SMEs). The point is to establish an appropriate place-based policy mix for different types of territories so as to consolidate local or regional innovation systems. The challenge is huge, but conditions are favourable for change, owing to growing recognition in the Polish administration that innovation is important for future economic growth and that the regions will play a crucial role.

The elaboration of regional innovation strategies (RIS) by voivodships has helped them to identify their assets and challenges. However, apart from a few exceptions, RIS could be more focused, more based on regional comparative advantages, and discussed with private actors from the early stages of the process. The Ministry of Regional Development could help regions to develop their RIS with the use of specific analytical and methodological tools. France has recently developed such a toolkit to help regions elaborate their innovation strategies.

## Human capital development must be a priority

Human capital development is a key explanatory variable for regional competitiveness and disparities in Poland. Lower educational levels in rural populations limit labour mobility and contribute to inadequate economic diversification. In rural areas, the priority is to improve attendance at pre-school, as only 18% of children aged 3-5 went to kindergarten in the school year 2004-05 in rural areas, compared to 55% in urban areas. The overall rural-urban gap in pre-school access in Poland has a negative impact on women's work, their participation in the labour market and the overall educational attainment of rural children, in view of the link between attendance at pre-school and overall attainments of tertiary education. The Mexican programme *Oportunidades*, which links family support and the obligation to send children to school and provide health care, could serve as a model in Poland. It is also important to facilitate rural students' access to tertiary education, as they face significant financial obstacles. Besides, to help better match labour market needs and the supply of students, local employment agencies should be more closely associated with secondary and tertiary education institutions. This will allow them to inform young people and to better match supply and demand. Finally, improving adult training beyond initial training is a key priority, especially in regions with high unemployment, which are also those with the lowest participation in adult training (such as Warminsko-Mazurskie and Swietokrzyskie). Another crucial challenge for Poland is to retain skills, given the scale of out-migration since 2004, even if there are recent indications of a slowdown. Staff shortages are particularly severe in the health and construction sectors, but they are also serious in the services sector in large cities (Poznan, Wroclaw, Cracow, etc.).

*Attention should be given to the diffusion of knowledge and its use by SMEs, greater knowledge spillover from FDI, as well as better involvement of universities in marketable and industry-relevant research*

As in many other OECD countries, the diffusion of knowledge and its use by SMEs is not optimal, even though SMEs play a crucial role in innovation. Polish SMEs represent more than 99% of all enterprises (45.9% of total employment), among which 95% are micro-enterprises (fewer than ten employees). The number of SMEs has increased by 330% since 1990. This level of entrepreneurship can be a valuable spur to innovation if other necessary conditions are met, such as the capability to absorb knowledge and technologies, proper links between R&D centres and universities and SMEs, as well as financial support for innovation. It seems that major challenges remain for facilitating access to information and external funding and improving advisory and consulting assistance. Although SMEs receive somewhat more information since 2004, less than 0.5% have benefited from EU funding (in 2007). SMEs have not played an important role for funds related to innovation *per se*, as demand for EU innovation funds comes essentially from large enterprises, particularly the former state-owned enterprises (SOEs).

A priority for 2007-13 is to involve SMEs more in innovation and to ensure that information gaps and market failures are minimised. This requires, for instance, the creation of agencies or "brokers" specialised in support services for industries in the local productive system. Knowledge vouchers have also been a success in a number of countries (*e.g.* the Netherlands, Italy), and Poland might consider introducing them. More marketable and industry-relevant R&D could be carried out in the tertiary education sector. The decreasing importance of industry in funding research in higher education (11.4% in 1994 and only 6.3% in 2003) is a trend that needs to be reversed. Deregulating some university activities would also facilitate co-operation with the business sector, as Poland does not allow business representatives on university boards.

Foreign direct investment can play an important role in enhancing the competitiveness of local firms and in increasing employment and exposure to overseas innovations and methods. Since the early 2000s, more greenfield foreign capital (a share of 58% in 2004, up from 37% in 2002) has been invested and has been translated into technology transfers and a rise in employment (more than 200 000 new jobs), essentially in manufacturing, mainly in the special economic zones that will operate to 2015-17. Poland is increasingly targeting FDI to technologically advanced sectors or the so-called rising sectors. Although it is too early to assess this policy, trends are encouraging; more than 30 multinational enterprises have recently set up R&D centres in Poland. Strategies to attract FDI face two main challenges: one is that they seem to underestimate the role played by quality sub-contractors in international investors' decisions to locate in specific areas; the second is that better support services at the local level are needed to attract FDI to complement approaches taken by the central government, in particular in eastern regions.

*Rural development – restructuring of agriculture and diversification towards non-agricultural activities – is another essential element of the broad national development strategy*

Rural development is another major priority on Polish political agenda. The strategy for 2007-13 was developed separately from the NSRF, as EU funds for rural development are dissociated from cohesion funds. Poland faces the twofold challenge of focusing on rural development beyond agriculture, given the low labour productivity in agriculture and the decrease of agriculture in the share of rural incomes (20% in 2002, compared to 72% in 1950), while modernising agriculture through a reduction in the number of small farms. The slow restructuring process is due to the ability of the majority of small farms to live on a semi-subsistence basis. Most farmers have secondary activities and receive pensions that are sufficient even for extended households (of several generations). These transfers, along with the support to small farms, constitute rents that work against efforts to transform agriculture and increase productivity as well as against labour mobility from agriculture to more productive rural or urban activities. The current large inflows of EU funds, increases in direct payments to farmers as well as the boost in farmers' incomes due to rising global prices, offer a window of opportunity to change the system of social transfers to farmers. It is important to ensure that CAP funding is better related to modernisation and productivity gains, in particular for small farms in south-eastern Poland.

Co-operation among farmers, export firms, foreign investors and public authorities has positive externalities both for agriculture and other sectors of the rural economy. Rural clusters (food and wood clusters) in the Lubelskie region are good examples of co-operation among public and private actors. Policies to enhance co-operation among local actors, such as LEADER+, should be strongly supported. Opportunities to diversify Poland's rural economy are numerous and so far seem to be under-exploited; they include tourism, forestry, rural services, energy and residential needs. Since 2000 the net outflow of population from urban to rural areas, especially near large cities, offers opportunities for employment in new services activities. The potential for tourism is underexploited partly owing to limited accessibility and weak infrastructure for tourism, but also because cities that could promote nearby natural assets (such as Bialystok, Lublin and Rzeszow) do not enough do so. Poland's eastern regions are among the best preserved in the European Union and contain 38.4% of the EU's natural reserves.

Poland's policy statements clearly show a desire to modernise agriculture and enhance rural diversification, but the main policy directions are less clear. Less than 5% of the budget for rural development for 2007-13 has been allocated to the LEADER programme whereas Spain, Portugal, the Netherlands and Ireland plan to allocate twice that share. Moreover, the rural development strategy is not well articulated with the regional development strategy and lacks a strong territorial dimension; there is one central operational programme for rural development rather than 16 regional ones. Besides, voivodeships do not play any role in the implementation of the rural development strategy, as it is the responsibility of the central agency for restructuring and modernisation of agriculture. As rural challenges vary considerably across Polish regions, the diversity of rural regions' needs has to be addressed effectively by taking an encompassing multi-sectoral place-based approach to co-ordinating the actions of multiple agencies. The fact that the rural and regional development strategies are separated raises governance challenges, at the central and regional levels.

## Overall, the challenge of implementing a place-based rather than a one-size-fits-all policy remains

The broad policy mix for regional development shows that, although inter-ministerial co-ordination has improved, a multi-sectoral strategy tailored to various territorial needs is still to be implemented. So far, there are only a limited number of tools for enhancing the territorial dimension of sectoral policies. Apart from the programme on the development of eastern Poland (3% of total funding); central programmes lack a strong place-based orientation. Although the NSRF gives large cities a driving role, no metropolitan policy has yet been developed, nor are there specific tools to enhance metropolitan co-operation and urban-rural linkages. Appropriate place-based policies require an adequate scale of planning and an appropriate time horizon, but so far planning remains restricted to the administrative boundaries of municipalities and multi-year budgeting has to be developed. The Ministry of Regional Development increasingly needs to encourage differentiated territorial place-based approaches, with appropriate incentives, rather than a one-size-fits-all policy. It should increasingly focus on its strategic functions and play the role of facilitator with local actors. There is also a need to enhance the territorial dimension of the rural development strategy and to improve co-ordination with the regional development strategy, at both central and local levels. So far, there is no inter-ministerial structure for rural development. A number of OECD countries have developed a new integrated governance approach to rural policy that might serve as inspiration for Poland. The Finnish Rural Policy Committee has been a central actor and a force for change in Finland. In Canada, the "rural lens" approach aims to ensure that rural priorities are taken into account in the various sectoral policies of the federal government.

## Better differentiate regional operational programmes according to specific regional needs

The decentralisation of around 34% of EU funding in 2007-13 may help to tailor the policy mix to each region's needs, but this is not guaranteed. Given the recent creation of the regions and the disparities in their management skills, marked differences in regional implementation are to be expected. Regional leadership and local capacity building will be essential to ensure efficient management of funds. Most regions have carefully followed the central government's guidelines and their regional operational programmes clearly target Lisbon-related objectives (competitiveness and employment creation). Regions such as Dolnoslaskie, Wielkopolska and Malpolska have developed promising ROPs focused on metropolitan development, transport connections, innovation and SME networks, and social infrastructure. Yet, most ROPs could have been better adapted to specific regional competitive advantages, assets, opportunities, challenges and needs, as well as socio-demographic and geographic characteristics. For example, it is unclear to what extent the strong financial support currently devoted by the eastern regions' ROPs to innovation transfers can be expected to foster development in regions where SME networks are currently quite weak and which lack an adequate scientific and technical base. In some places a stronger focus on basic education would be warranted.

## To improve effectiveness of regional development policies and enhance its territorial dimension, governance challenges will be determinant

The impact of European cohesion policy on the Polish multi-level governance system goes well beyond financing. The design and implementation of EU operational programmes – not only regional ones – has led to decentralisation and enhanced collaboration with private actors and civil society as regional and local actors become empowered and engaged in a strong learning process. Cohesion policy thus strongly influences the decentralisation process, which is dynamic and ongoing. To further improve the effectiveness of regional development policies and enhance the territorial dimension of various policies requires careful attention to three broad challenges: i) enhancing co-operation across levels of government, local governments and public and private actors; ii) strengthening capacities of sub-national governments, as many municipalities still have little experience with promoting initiatives to increase local competitiveness with private and social participation; iii) supporting accountability, at all levels of government and monitoring the performance/impact of regional as well as sectoral policies. Poland also needs to think about longer-term options for better matching competencies and resources in some areas after 2013, when Polish regions will no longer benefit from the same level of external funding, and for further increasing the strategic role of regions.

## Better co-operation by local and metropolitan authorities is necessary in order to implement effective territorial development strategies

To implement effective territorial development strategies, improving co-operation among local and metropolitan authorities is a key priority. The current lack of co-operation across municipalities (gminas) makes it difficult to reap economies of scale in terms of public service delivery and appropriate place-based competitiveness policies. An integrated spatial planning approach is particularly urgent for the large urban areas that drive Polish growth and face problems relating to housing, public transport and the environment (including water and waste management). In large cities, the lack of a metropolitan perspective also creates problems for absorbing EU funds, as many projects extend beyond specific administrative areas and are more complex to prepare than in small towns. Co-operation by gminas, particularly at the metropolitan level, needs to be promoted through specific incentives and an integrated approach to spatial planning to improve public service delivery and to implement long-term competitiveness strategies. Fiscal incentives could give large urban areas flexible institutional tools for co-operating at the functional scale. Metropolitan policy has been discussed in Poland since the 1990s, but incentives to enhance co-operation have yet to be adopted. Poland could draw inspiration from the French *communautés d'agglomération*, which offer the advantages of enhancing horizontal collaboration across municipalities and improving vertical collaboration with the central government. The *communautés d'agglomération* have constituted valuable tools for promoting territorial development strategies and implementing strategic spatial planning.

## *Enhanced co-operation among regions is important as a learning process and can help better exploit some macro-regional public goods*

Greater co-operation among regions (voivodships) can also contribute to learning and help better exploit some macro-regional public goods. This is particularly true for the five eastern regions, for which the central government has developed a specific macro-regional programme for 2007-13, co-financed with EU funds and with a budget of EUR 2 billion. It targets in particular infrastructure and urban development, the information society, modernisation of the economy and tourism. It is the first "macro-regional" programme developed in the context of cohesion policy. Because the five peripheral eastern regions share the same challenges – in particular accessibility, little economic diversification, an ageing population and out-migration (173 000 inhabitants left these regions between 2000 and 2004) there is a logic to adding a macro-regional dimension to the regional programmes. Although this programme has the right targets, it does not seem to make sufficient use of the potential for co-operation among these regions. The cross-regional dimension of the programme should be enhanced, with a focus on *joint* infrastructure projects, tourism and environmental issues; cross-regional leadership of the programme could also be introduced.

*A key to increasing the effectiveness of regional policy is better co-operation between policy makers and the private sector*

In addition to co-ordination across public institutions, effective regional policy requires improving co-operation between policy makers and the private sector. Poland's experience from 2004 to 2006 indicates that the lack of collaboration between public and private actors was an obstacle to the effective absorption of EU funds, particularly for infrastructure programmes. Poland's absorption of EU funds in early 2008 presents a mixed picture: after a slow start in 2004, it has improved regularly since 2006, with faster progress in 2007, reflecting the experience accumulated by public servants in previous years. There are strong variations in absorption (defined as the share of budgeted resources paid to final beneficiaries) across sectors and regions. Owing to the complexity of administrative procedures, there are clear advantages for firms and municipalities to collaborate on a smaller number of large joint projects rather than present a larger number of smaller individual projects. The surprisingly low absorption rates in large urban areas (such as Mazowieckie, Dolnoslaskie, Slaskie) suggest that co-operation between actors has been difficult to achieve, especially in infrastructure, human capital and entrepreneurship projects, for which the administrative procedures are more complicated than for rural development projects for example.

Regulatory obstacles make public-private co-operation more difficult in Poland than in most OECD countries. Strategic alliances, based on reciprocal understanding and common trust, among public, social and private actors, are crucial for absorption of 2007-13 EU funds but also for regional development more broadly. It is not easy to change a tradition of arm's length relationships between the public administration and the private sector. On the one hand, the former has long cultivated a climate of suspicion *vis-à-vis* the private sector which reinforces a risk-adverse attitude. On the other hand, the latter have shown relatively little interest in closer involvement in local development policies. Three directions might be explored. One is to reduce the administrative barriers relating to public-private collaboration in Poland, as they are high, especially in comparison to other Central and Eastern European countries. The main problems appear to be a constantly changing legal framework, difficulties for access to finance and slow public procurement. Delays in the preparation of state aid plans also make it difficult for firms and private investors to plan investments, and delays in calls for tender have strong repercussions on the local economy. Second is to enhance public-private partnerships (PPPs). Not only can they improve the availability of investment resources (complementing public funds with private resources), but they may also, under certain conditions, increase the efficiency of spending. However, adequate regulation

OECD TERRITORIAL REVIEWS: POLAND – ISBN 978-92-64-04926-0 – © OECD 2008

must be in place to ensure transparency, integrity and adequate rules for risk-sharing between the public sector and private investors. Third is to increase public-private collaboration in planning processes, as these remain very formal and legalistic in Poland.

## *Effective implementation of regional development policy requires lifting local capacities*

While much attention has been devoted to the sub-national level's capacity to absorb EU funding in a given period of time, the magnitude of the tasks to be carried out during the current programming period calls for a broader effort to upgrade regional capabilities beyond absorption capacity. The challenge is mainly to strengthen more systematically the capacities of local public officials by building a more effective public employment system at regional/local levels. The lack of such a system has generated risks of politicization of civil service, which seemed to be held down prior to EU accession but has returned two years afterwards, especially in the local public sector and at the senior management level. Attempts to rationalise public employment since the early 2000s have translated into successive adoptions and abolitions of legislation relating to the civil service. The Polish government has recently stated that new regulations to build a more standardised civil service, at both central and local levels, are a key priority. Further improvements in local capacities could come from: improving recruitment and promotion mechanisms, especially at middle and senior management levels; introducing performance management systems to better monitor individual and team performances; focusing training programmes on practical skills (to facilitate day-to-day work on the planning and operational implementation of development strategies); enhancing staff mobility (both nationally between central and local governments, and internationally between Poland and other EU countries, for instance via temporary stays to obtain new skills); exploiting ICTs and e-government tools to raise the efficiency of public service delivery (the 47% increase in the number of e-public services between 2004 and 2007 is a promising start, and plans to create fully integrated electronic platforms should be pursued).

## *Poland's monitoring and evaluation systems have improved significantly but their impact will depend on their use for policy making*

Poland is one of the most advanced EU member states in planning evaluations for 2007-13, *e.g.* in terms of establishing evaluation units and drafting evaluation plans. As the largest recipient of EU structural funds for 2007-13,

Poland appears to recognise its obligation to demonstrate performance. Although significant progress has been made since 2004 in developing systems to monitor performance, the impact of these systems will largely depend on improved data collection at both regional and central levels and the use of this information in policy making. The introduction of a performance reserve fund (3% of the funding) – to be used to provide incentives for satisfactory performance – may be a positive element even if EU experience with the performance reserve in 2000-06 has been mixed. In any case, its impact depends greatly on making criteria for its use transparent. So far, it is not yet clear whether specific evaluations will be carried out, and no *ex ante* criteria for distributing the reserve have been established. If the cohesion policy has acted as a major incentive to introduce evaluation and monitoring systems, these should be gradually expanded to cover all public policies in Poland, not only those financed under the cohesion policy.

*Poland needs to take a forward-looking perspective to strengthening the multi-level governance system, as most regions will not benefit from the same level of external support after 2013*

To improve the effectiveness of the multi-level governance framework and regional development policy, the following challenges need to be tackled in priority:

- *Enhancing the strategic role of regions* by increasing the political legitimacy of regions and their capacity to arbitrate. It is difficult for voivodships to play a strategic (and arbiter) role in regional development, as they lack sufficient resources, flexibility in budget management, political visibility and enforcement power for spatial planning. The marshal's (head of regional assembly) visibility and legitimacy would be enhanced if he were elected directly.

- *Better exploiting the role of contracts for regional economic development.* Although regional contracts have helped regions to prepare for managing EU funds and boosted their role as partners of the national government, there is a gap between the long-term objectives of regional strategies and the regional contracts, which are short-term (one year) and practical. The focus in contracts has been on investments for major public service needs, essentially health and education, rather than support for economic development. The time frame of contracts could be longer, as in France, to help partners overcome the drawbacks of an annual budget, and contracts should have an important focus on proactive development/competitiveness approaches, negotiated through inter-ministerial collaboration.

OECD TERRITORIAL REVIEWS: POLAND – ISBN 978-92-64-04926-0 – © OECD 2008

- *Increasingly moving towards a multi-year budgeting framework.* There is no multi-year budget in Poland, apart from limited provisions for multi-annual budgeting for EU funds introduced in 2006 (three-year perspective). These multi-year budgeting provisions are not translated at the regional level, so the question of how best to combine the central budgeting system and local governments' budgets remains. Co-ordination of the budget planning process among different levels of government needs to be improved.

- *The distribution of competencies between regions, districts and municipalities requires further clarification*, in particular for education, health and labour market policies, and additional revenues for gminas and regions need to be secured. It could be envisaged to increase the shared taxes that go to regions to enhance fiscal capacity of voivodships and the property tax could be gradually expanded to increase revenues of gminas.

## Summing up…

Poland has made remarkable progress toward multi-level governance in a short time and has moved quickly to orient its regional development policy towards a greater focus on competitiveness through a balanced regional development policy mix that targets human capital and innovation as well as physical infrastructure. The next steps are to enhance the place-based dimension of the national policy mix and to consider ways to strengthen the multi-level governance system, given that external funding may diminish significantly after 2013. In particular, it is important to introduce specific incentives for metropolitan/urban co-operation and to shift strategic planning from the administrative perimeters of municipalities to functional scale. Enhancing the strategic role of regions is important, as is improving local capacities. More effective regional development policy also requires significant progress in public-private co-operation, a reduction in regulatory obstacles to co-operation and better involvement of SMEs and universities in regional development strategies. The effect of cohesion policy on broader public governance and management is as important objective as its more direct impact on regional growth and disparities. Poland has the advantages of high growth and large inflows of EU funds that provide momentum for reforms. This window of opportunity should be exploited to the greatest extent possible.

ISBN 978-92-64-04926-0
OECD Territorial Reviews: Poland
© OECD 2008

# Chapter 1

# Drivers of Growth and Challenges for Regional Development

*Poland is one of the fastest growing countries in the OECD: average annual growth rate in Poland was above 4% between 1995 and 2005. However, the growth of GDP is not distributed evenly throughout the country. Poland has one of the OECD area's greatest territorial disparities in terms of GDP per capita at TL3 level. Moreover, the disparities have increased since 1995, as the growth dynamics have been concentrated in certain locations. Three sets of disparities are visible: i) a persistent gap between eastern and western Poland; ii) a gap between Warsaw and the rest of the country; iii) rising intra-regional disparities, in particular in the regions of Warsaw (Mazowieckie), Poznan (Wielkopolskie) and Cracow (Malopolskie), which are largely due to rising disparities between large urban areas and rural ones. The growth rate in Polish urban areas has been among the OECD leaders for 1998-2003. While some challenges are specific to urban or rural areas, the need to hasten the move to the knowledge economy and to improve the transport infrastructure is common to all regions. This chapter assesses main trends in regional performances and disparities and identifies key challenges for the development of Poland's regions.*

## Introduction

Poland is one of the fastest growing countries in the OECD: average annual growth rates in Poland was above 4% between 1995 and 2005 and GDP growth exceeded 6% in 2006 and 2007, the second-best performance among OECD countries. Among other noteworthy successes, Poland has become one of the most attractive countries for foreign direct investment (FDI) and has significantly enhanced the educational attainment of its population. However, high growth goes hand in hand with persistent and rising territorial disparities, especially between large urban areas and rural ones. In spite of a few signs of renewal in some rural places and medium-size cities, most rural areas face a vicious circle of stagnation while large cities enjoy a virtuous circle of growth, concentrating sources of growth and attracting most FDI. Like many OECD countries, Poland is challenged to achieve an appropriate balance between supporting poles of growth and supporting the development of lagging regions, in particular the eastern peripheral regions, which are among the poorest of the European Union.

Poland is currently one of the best "laboratories" for regional development in the OECD area and in the European Union which it joined in 2004. In addition to significant inflows of private investment, Poland is the first recipient of EU funds for the 2007-13 period (including EUR 67 billion under the cohesion policy). Regional development has become a priority on the political agenda, for both economic/social reasons – territorial disparities in GDP per capita are rising – and political/administrative reasons – the need to enhance the decentralisation process and the functioning of the 16 regions (voivodships) created in 1999.

This chapter assesses main trends in regional performances and disparities and identifies key challenges for the development of Poland's regions. It first analyses the uneven distribution of high growth. It then examines the motors of national growth – mainly large urban areas. The following section focuses on specific challenges for rural areas. The final section diagnoses challenges for building competitive regions, in particular in terms of knowledge and infrastructure.

## 1. A fast growing economy, with rising territorial disparities

### 1.1. One of the most dynamic economies in the OECD area

Poland has had one of the highest growth rates in the OECD area since 1992. GDP per capita has increased remarkably in the past two decades. In 2006, compared to 1989, the value of the Polish economy had increased by two-thirds.[1] The economy grew by an average annual rate of 4% between 1995 and 2005 and accelerated throughout 2006 to 6.2% in the second half. Growth at the national level has been mainly driven by domestic demand, productivity gains, FDI, exports and more recently, EU funds. Domestic demand is expected to remain the main driving force in the next few years. Investment growth is anticipated to remain strong, while private consumption should remain robust (EIU, 2006).

However, GDP per capita remains low compared to the OECD average. In 2006, it stood at 44% of the OECD average and 53.4% of the EU average. Among OECD countries, only Mexico and Turkey have a lower level. It is estimated that achieving the average EU level of GDP per capita will require about 20 years if the growth rate in Poland is around 5% a year (and in the EU around 1.9%) (Ministry of Regional Development, 2008).

## Key assets

A qualified workforce and young population, combined with an increasingly diversified industrial mix and a strategic position in Eastern Europe, are Poland's main assets and explain its attractiveness. Poland is not only a large country in terms of surface (the sixth largest in the EU), it is also the sixth most populated in the EU with 38.2 million inhabitants (in 2004).[2] Poland has the largest labour force among new EU member states. In addition, the Polish population is relatively young: half are under 37 and more than one-third are under 25. Both availability and age in the labour force contrast with the situation in most European countries. Although Poland faces major challenges in terms of education, it has upgraded human capital significantly in the past two decades by increasing educational attainment and improving the quality of education. Progress is particularly evident in secondary schooling. Moreover, the number of students in higher education is also nearly five times what it was in 1991 (OECD, 2006d). In addition, the OECD 2006 PISA study indicates that performance in education is slightly above the OECD average in all the subject areas tested (OECD, 2006c).[3]

As for the sectoral mix, Poland stands out as a relatively successful example of a transition from a partially state-directed economy to a primarily privately owned market economy, with above 75% of total output now produced in the private sector (OECD, 2006b). As in other OECD countries, industrial and agricultural sectors have seen their shares of GDP shrink (even though the agriculture sector remains one of the largest in the OECD, with 17% of the labour force),[4] in contrast, the services sector has grown rapidly (EIU, 2006). These shifts are evident in all indicators of economic structure – GDP, employment and exports. Entrepreneurship is well developed and Poland has a large proportion of small and medium-sized enterprises (SMEs) (which account for 99% of the total number of businesses in Poland,[5] and 45.9% of total employment).[6] Among SMEs 95% are micro-enterprises (fewer than ten employees). Such a high degree of entrepreneurship can be a valuable spur to innovation if the other necessary conditions are met, such as the capability to absorb knowledge and technologies, proper links between R&D centres and universities and SMEs, as well as financial support for innovation.

In a rather short period of time, Poland has diversified its economy towards services (in particular business services) and to more labour-intensive manufacturing activities. It has retained its position as a world leader in manufacturing (see Figure 1.1) and has specialised in fast-growing sectors – such as pharmaceuticals and electronic components. Market services and industry are expected to make the largest contribution to growth in 2008, while the rate of increase in value added in construction will be markedly lower.

Figure 1.1. **Specialisation changes and employment in Poland (manufacturing)**

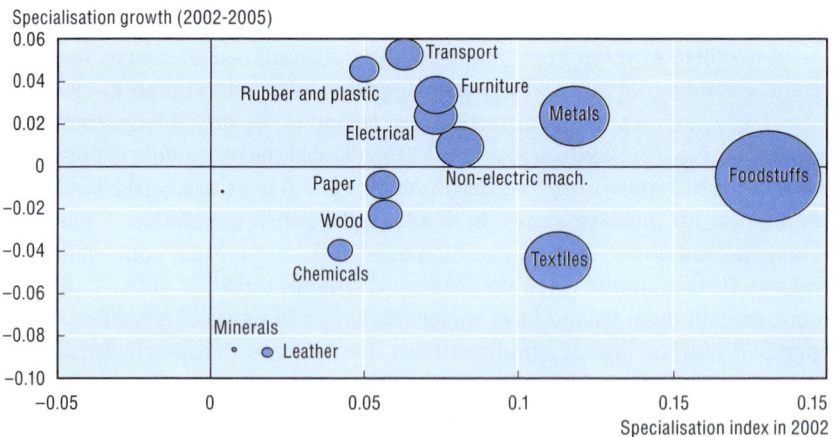

Note: Specialisation Indexes are built using relative industry-specific employment figures in Poland with respect to total manufacturing employment. Growth in specialisation refers to average annual growth rates in specialisation indexes between 2002 and 2005. Bubble shows size of the industry in terms of employment.

Source: Based on CSO (2008).

Three types of agglomeration of firms can be defined in Poland, all of them characterised by the concentration of enterprises in the same sector (vertical links), the diversity of the supply chain (horizontal links) and high exports. The first group involves new and innovative networks in electronics, pharmaceuticals and cosmetics and information technologies; the second involves the traditional sectors of furniture, chemicals, plastics, construction, leather and textiles, which are widely disseminated (the Aviation Valley in southeast Poland around Rzeszow, the Construction Materials Cluster in southern Poland around Kielce, and the Plastic Valley in Tarnow); and the third group involves agro-transformation and food processing, in particular in the Lubelskie region.

Owing to its geographical position – it is at the heart of the European continent and surrounded by seven countries (Belarus, Czech Republic, Germany, Lithuania, Russia, the Slovak Republic, Ukraine) – Poland has a strong potential to play a strategic role between western and eastern Europe, with Russia and Asia and within the Baltic Sea Region. A qualified workforce and diversified industrial mix, combined with lower labour costs, are the main reasons for Poland's attractiveness. Labour costs in Poland remain lower than in the EU15; they are 4.5 times higher in Germany.[7]

In nominal terms Poland has been the main recipient of FDI among the recent EU entrants; flows to Poland were around twice as large as to the Czech Republic or Hungary. The EU15 is the major investor in Poland (over 80% of FDI inflows; Germany,[8] the Netherlands and France top the list with almost 61% of the cumulative inflow. However, Asian countries are increasing their investments (in particular China, Japan and Korea). Manufacturing still dominates in total FDI (27.6% in 2006). FDI increased from EUR 8.2 billion in 2005 to a record-breaking EUR 15 billion in 2006 (NBP, 2007), and 12 billion for 2007. As a proportion of GDP, FDI in Poland jumped from 2.9% to 4.1% between 1996 and 2006, for cumulative growth of 41%. Although this growth is lower than the OECD average (140%), FDI represents almost twice as much for Poland as for the OECD average country. Poland is one of the top ten OECD countries in terms of FDI flows as a proportion of GDP.

Polish growth is also led by exports which doubled between 2000 and 2005.[9] More than 77% of exports are directed towards EU countries (Germany is the main economic partner), but exports are also rising with Asian countries, especially China. Poland has retained its traditional role as an exporter of raw materials and semi-processed products. Food exports rose sharply after Poland's entry into the EU in May 2004, increasing by nearly 60% between 2003 and 2005. However, in some regions, such as Slaskie or Wielkopolskie, there is a trend towards increased specialisation in more capital-intensive activities.

## Public investment

In addition to large inflows of private investment, Poland is receiving large amounts of public funds, mainly EU funds. Among recent new members of the European Union, Poland is the main beneficiary of these funds. The entire Polish population lives in convergence regions.[10] For 2007-13, Poland will receive EUR 67.3 billion under the cohesion policy, out of a total of EUR 348 billion in Community cohesion policy funds (i.e. 20% of the total). These amounts should be added to the EUR 16.6 billion that the country will receive as part of the European Agricultural Rural Development Fund. In total, together with co-financing, Poland will have a total of EUR 108 billion for 2007-13 for its national development strategy, 85% of which are EU funds. An analysis of the first financial period (2004-06) using the HERMIN model has shown that EU funds are likely to have a significant impact on Polish growth and the reduction of unemployment (Box 1.1).

## Box 1.1. **Impact of EU funds on the Polish economy**

EU funds have provided the Polish economy with extra spending capacity which has had an impact on the economy. The HERMIN model was used to establish a link between the three aggregate elements of the structural funds, namely physical infrastructure, human resources and direct aid to the productive sector, and economic performance. Using Keynesian multipliers for each of the three aggregate elements and looking at supply- and demand-side effects, the HERMIN model was used to forecast the impact of EU funds on the Polish economy. The model incorporated the fact that EU funds fostered the implementation of Poland's National Development Programme (NDP) 2004-06, but assumes that the programme continues from 2006 until 2013. The model also assumes that Poland will grow at the EU average economic growth rate and that public spending will grow at 2.5% annually. Both assumptions are conservative and therefore the results should be taken as a minimum.

The results show that in terms of economic growth, the combined impact of NDP and EU funds will be to increase economic growth progressively to more than 9% in 2015. Similarly, unemployment rates will be reduced between 2 and 3% between 2006 and 2015, a reduction that would not have been achieved without the programme (Bradley *et al.*, 2003). However, the HERMIN results do not shed any light on whether these impacts will have any effect on internal regional disparities.

### Impact of Polish NDP and EU funds on the Polish economy

Impacts on economic growth and unemployment rates

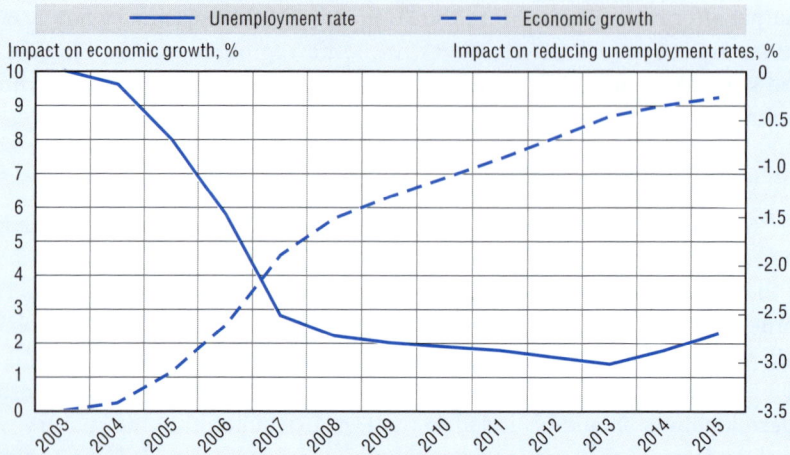

*Source:* Bradley *et al.* (2003).

Associated with strong assets – human capital in particular – the current levels of private and public investment (among the highest in the OECD area) provide a major window of opportunity to accelerate the country's socio-economic development. To optimise the management of such large inflows of funds, Poland will have to manage the risk of inflationary pressures, as annual consumer price inflation (CPI) increased in January 2008 to 4% (National Bank of Poland, February 2008). Fast-rising wages in non-tradables sectors reinforce these pressures. These challenges have to be considered in the context of the preparation of the economy to meet the strict economic criteria for entry into the European single currency. The date of entry into the euro zone has not yet been decided by the Polish government; but it is expected to occur after 2011.

## 1.2. Main macro-economic challenges

To sustain its high growth rates, Poland faces important challenges, in particular low labour market participation rates, weak infrastructure development, and limited innovation and R&D; which have a strong territorial dimension. This will be explored in more detail in the rest of the chapter.

Labour market challenges are huge; they are mostly due to low participation rates and high out-migration, which have led to staff shortages in key sectors. Poland has one of lowest labour participation in the OECD area (54.5%). Those under 24 year of age and those over 45 year of age are the most affected by unemployment and inactivity, in particular long-term unemployment. However, although unemployment remains high, it has decreased rapidly in the past five years (from 19.6% in 2003 to 8.5% at the end of 2007). This decrease can mainly be attributed to two factors, which are hard to disentangle: i) job creation (850 000 new jobs were created from 2004 to 2006); ii) out-migration. Estimates vary widely, but between 1 and 2 million of Poles have left Poland since 2004 mainly to go to the United Kingdom and Ireland, which have opened their labour markets. Poland is now facing skill shortages in key areas (in particular health and construction) and losing qualified workers. It is one of the few OECD countries with negative migration rates (see Figure 1.2).

In addition to labour market problems, there are huge challenges in terms of infrastructure development and knowledge transfers and innovation. Poland's weak infrastructure development is a barrier to realising the full potential of economic growth. This concerns above all transport infrastructure (roads, rail, air) but also telecommunications. Besides, progress towards the knowledge economy is slow; Poland has one of the weakest levels of innovation and R&D in the OECD area. In 2004 Poland spent 0.58% of GDP on R&D, below the levels of the Czech Republic (1.27%) and Hungary (0.89%).

Figure 1.2. **Net migration rate per 1 000 population**

Annual average 2000-2006 or latest available period

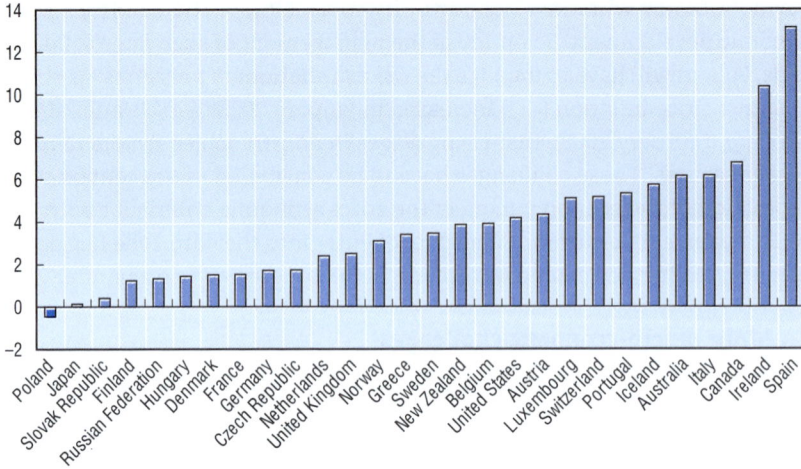

*Source:* OECD Factbook 2008 (OECD 2008c).

## 1.3. Various dimensions of territorial inequality in Poland

Poland's high GDP growth is not distributed evenly throughout the territory. This situation is not specific to Poland, as many OECD countries that are catching up or have high growth rates also face increasing territorial disparities (Figure 1.3). The following section focuses on the various dimensions of territorial inequality in Poland. These are of three types. One is the persistent gap between eastern and western Poland. The second is the gap between the Warsaw region (Mazowieckie) and other regions. The third is rising intra-regional disparities (within voivodships); these are among the highest in the OECD area and are largely due to the increasing gap between large urban areas and rural ones.

### The east-west divide

Poland is clearly divided between the relatively more developed west and the lagging east. With the exception of the Warsaw region, located in the centre-east of the country and the richest sub-region in Poland, the most developed areas are in central and western Poland (Poznań, Kraków, Gdańsk-Gdynia-Sopot, Legnicki, Wrocław, Łódź, Bielsko-Bialski). Historical legacies are an important factor in explaining Poland's structural territorial disparities (see Box 1.2). The east-west divide, often referred to as Poland A and Poland B, has proven quite resistant over the past decades. Long-term inherited trends in sectoral specialisations, institutional development, educational attainment and social capital building still affect Poland's development patterns (Gorzelak, 2006; Piasecki, 2006).

Figure 1.3. **Annual growth rates (1992-2005) and GINI index of regional disparities (TL3) in OECD countries**

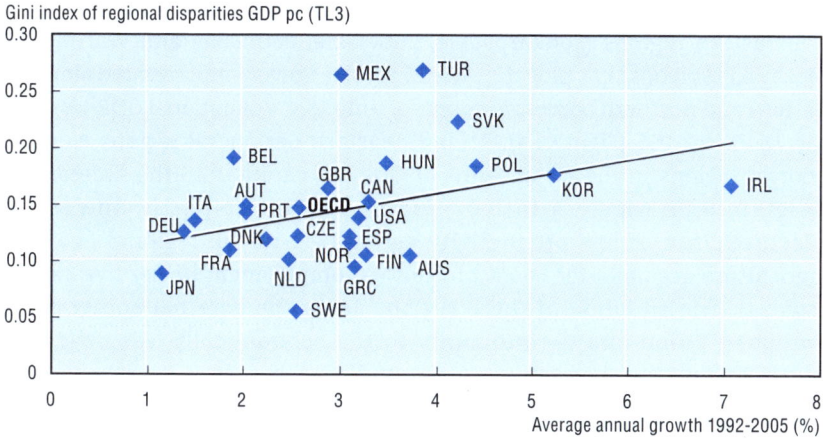

Gini index of regional disparities GDP pc (TL3)

Average annual growth 1992-2005 (%)

*Source: OECD, Regional Database, 2007.*

---

### Box 1.2. **Long-term factors and historical legacies: the persistent east-west divide**

Analysis of regional development patterns in Poland needs to take into account long-term factors and historical legacies. In the 18th century, Poland was divided between Prussia (northwest), Austria (southeast) and Russia (central-east). Trends in institutional development, educational attainment and social capital building clearly show that this old partition still has an impact; in particular, eastern Poland lags behind in terms of institutional development and educational attainment.

This legacy is known as Poland A (for western Poland) and Poland B (for Poland east of the Vistula river). After the Second World War, Poland's borders were shifted 200 kilometres to the west. This has not alleviated the east-west divide.

Another legacy is the national economic planning of the post-war communist period. This involved the concentration of industrial and agricultural resources in certain areas (such as the development of state farms in northern Poland), the focus on medium-sized cities for economic development, and east-west linkages rather than north-south linkages.

The east-west divide has also not been alleviated by the transition to the market economy since the early 1990s. Market competition has revealed the strong components of regional economies – mainly large cities where the activities of private investors are concentrated – and also exposed the weakest regions (Piasecki, 2006). Today, the gap between eastern and western Poland remains an important feature of the country's territorial development.

The greatest part of the GDP is produced in the central and western regions. Five out of 16 regions (Mazowieckie, Slaskie, Wielkopolskie, Dolnoslaskie and Malopolskie) account for 59.2% of the total GDP in 2005. The five eastern regions (Podkarpackie, Lubelskie, Podlaskie and Warmińsko-Mazurskie voivodships, plus the Świętokrzyskie voivodship) situated along the eastern and northern borders account for only 15.4% of national GDP, less than the 16.9% in 1995 (Figure 1.4). Poland's eastern peripheral regions were the poorest regions in the EU in terms of GDP per capita until the accession of Bulgaria and Romania in 2007 (Map 1.1). This is partly due to the predominance of low-productivity agriculture in the regional economy (agriculture accounts for 30.2% of the total employment of the five eastern regions). The situation of these regions along the external border of the European Union and the proximity to the economically less developed countries limit the opportunities for fruitful cross-border co-operation.

Figure 1.4. **Share of regions (TL2) in GDP, 2005**

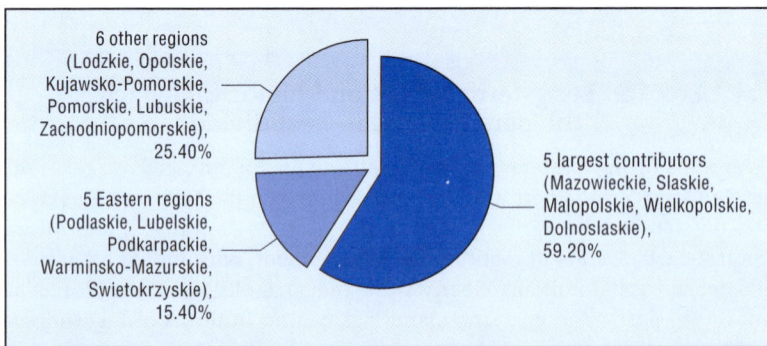

6 other regions (Lodzkie, Opolskie, Kujawsko-Pomorskie, Pomorskie, Lubuskie, Zachodniopomorskie), 25.40%

5 Eastern regions (Podlaskie, Lubelskie, Podkarpackie, Warminsko-Mazurskie, Swietokrzyskie), 15.40%

5 largest contributors (Mazowieckie, Slaskie, Malopolskie, Wielkopolskie, Dolnoslaskie), 59.20%

*Source:* Central Statistical Office, 2005.

The divide between eastern peripheral regions and the rest of the country, in particular urban areas, has been widening over the last decade in terms of GDP per capita and contribution to GDP. Richer regions have had the highest GDP per capita growth rates since 1995 (Map 1.2). In contrast, the poorest areas of the southeast are also the poorest performers in terms of GDP growth. The peripheral regions, with their poorer infrastructure and greater distance from western markets, continue to suffer from lower GDP per capita and limited development. However, growth in some regions bordering Germany (such as the region of Szczecin) has also been slower than the national average. Several reasons can explain this: they started from a higher point, have experienced important out-migration, the break-up of state-farms, a slowdown in industrial areas (in Gorzów Wielkopolski) and crises in small cities bordering the Oder (Gubin), as well as rising competition with Berlin and German ports.

## Map 1.1. **Regions' GDP per capita (2006)**

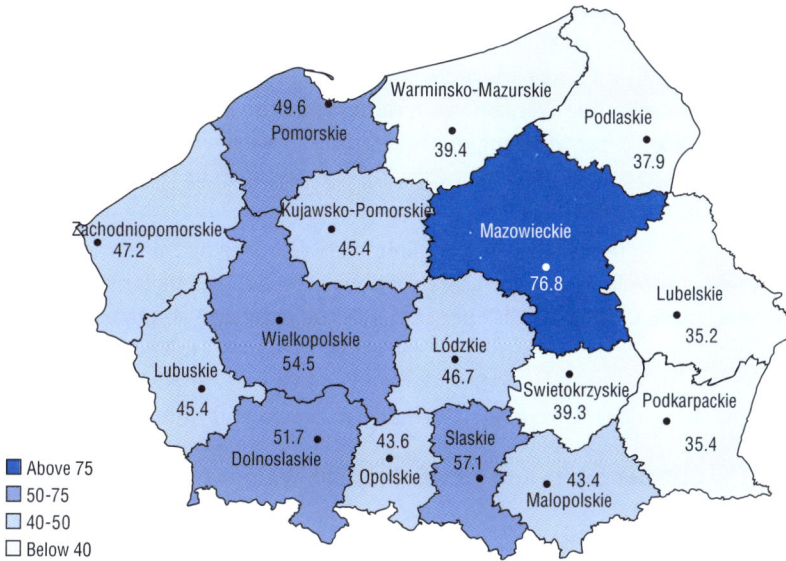

Warminsko-Mazurskie

49.6
Pomorskie

39.4

Podlaskie

37.9

Zachodniopomorskie
47.2

Kujawsko-Pomorskie
45.4

Mazowieckie

76.8

Lubelskie

35.2

Wielkopolskie
54.5

Lódzkie
46.7

Lubuskie
45.4

Swietokrzyskie
39.3

Podkarpackie

35.4

51.7
Dolnoslaskie

43.6
Opolskie

Slaskie
57.1

43.4
Malopolskie

■ Above 75
■ 50-75
□ 40-50
□ Below 40

*Source:* OECD, Regional Database, 2008.

## Map 1.2. **GDP growth 1995-2005, TL3, constant prices**

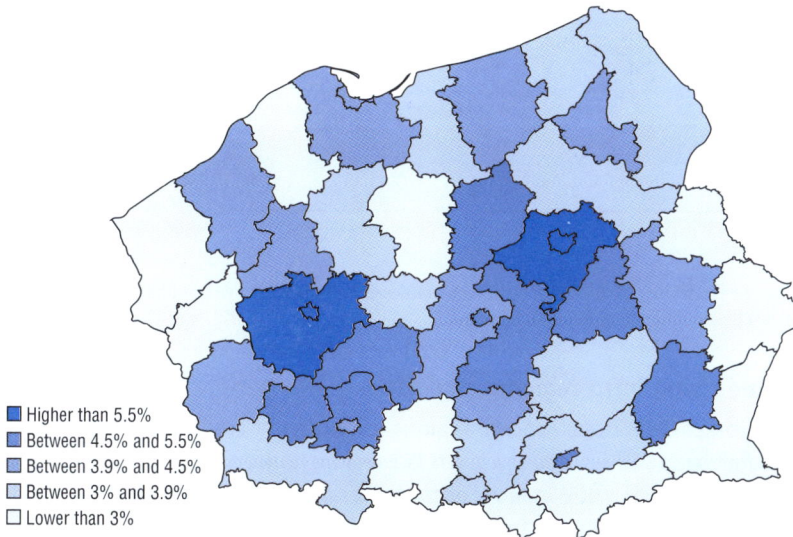

■ Higher than 5.5%
■ Between 4.5% and 5.5%
■ Between 3.9% and 4.5%
□ Between 3% and 3.9%
□ Lower than 3%

*Source:* OECD, Regional Database, 2008.

## Fast-growing Warsaw region

Since 1995, the gap has increased between Mazowieckie and the rest of the country. Mazowieckie was by far the fastest-growing region in the 1995-2004 period (Figure 1.5) and has played a significant role in widening regional disparities. However, it is Warsaw itself, rather than the region as a whole, that plays the leading role; as intra-regional disparities in Mazowieckie are very high. In addition, the gap with other fast-growing regions, such as Dolnoslaskie and Wielkopolskie, is narrowing.

Although differences in GDP per capita between Mazowieckie and the five eastern regions are large (Figure 1.5), variations across the 16 regions (TL2 level) are not exceptional. In 2005, GDP per capita in the richest region (Mazowieckie) was 2.32 times higher than in the poorest (Lubelskie). However, this ratio exceeded 3 in Belgium, France, Slovakia and the United Kingdom, and it was even higher in the Czech Republic, Germany, Romania and Hungary.

Figure 1.5. **GDP per capita and growth in Polish regions (voivodships – TL2)**

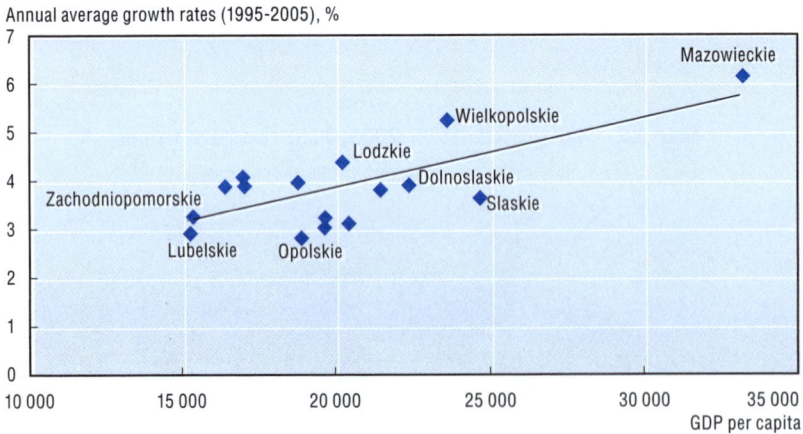

Note: For the readability of the chart, only a few names of voivodships have been indicated.
Source: Based on OECD (2008) Regional Database.

## High and rising intra-regional disparities

Although disparities *between* regions are not very great, disparities *within* regions (between TL3 regions of a given TL2 region) rank among the highest in the OECD area. The region of Warsaw[11] accounts for the second largest income gap in the OECD area (Figure 1.6). In total, three out of the ten widest intra-regional gaps in GDP per capita in the OECD are in Poland: in addition to Mazowieckie, these are Wielkopolskie (region of Poznan) and Malopolskie (region of Cracow). Moreover, if σ-convergence coefficients[12] are used, five Polish regions are among the most unequal, notably Mazowieckie which ranks third (Figure 1.7).

Figure 1.6. **Intra-regional disparities in the OECD area (GDP per capita), 2005**

Widest gaps for TL3 regions within their TL2

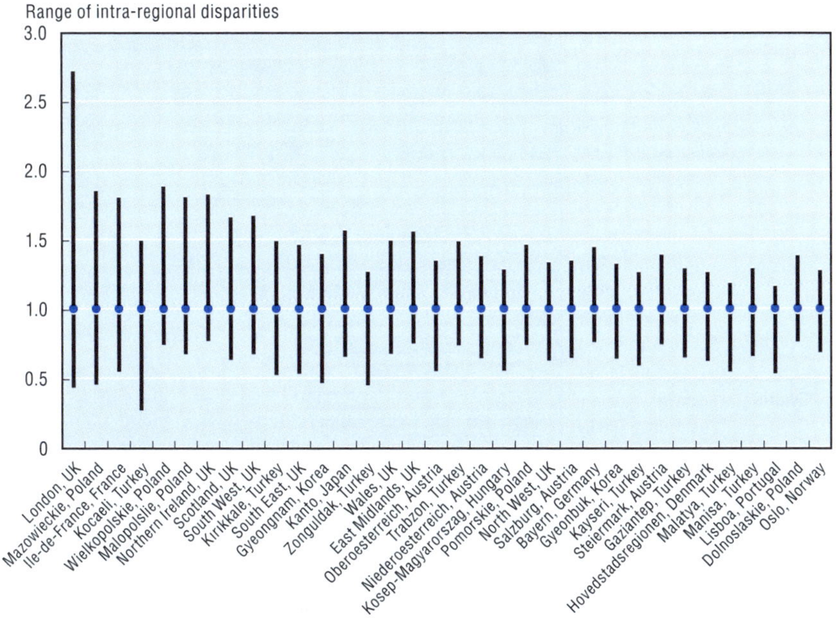

Source: Based on OECD (2007) *Regional Database* (the analysis excludes North American regions).

Thus, in spite of the increase in GDP per capita over the past 15 years, Poland's territorial disparities at the sub-regional level (TL3) are the sixth highest in the OECD area (Figure 1.8) and they have persisted over time. Turkey and Mexico, as well as three EU countries have larger disparities (at TL3 level): Belgium, the Slovak Republic and Hungary.

Most importantly, territorial disparities have *increased* since 1995 at both TL2 and TL3 levels, signalling an accumulation of growth dynamics in specific places. The increase in disparities can best be seen using σ-convergence coefficients (rather than Gini coefficients) (Figure 1.9). Disparities have grown particularly since 1999, especially at TL3 level. This confirms that some sub-regions – the wealthiest – benefit the most from current growth trends, and, by growing, they help to expand the inequality gap.

Rising disparities at the *sub-regional level* are mainly explained by the increasing economic gap between urban areas (large cities) and predominantly rural and intermediate areas (which include medium-sized cities). In large urban areas the role of services in their economies has increased significantly since the mid-1990s, and they have the most employment opportunities, knowledge workers and FDI. Predominantly rural areas are lagging behind in

Figure 1.7. **Intra-regional disparities in GDP per capita in the OECD area (standard deviation), 2005**

σ-convergence coefficients

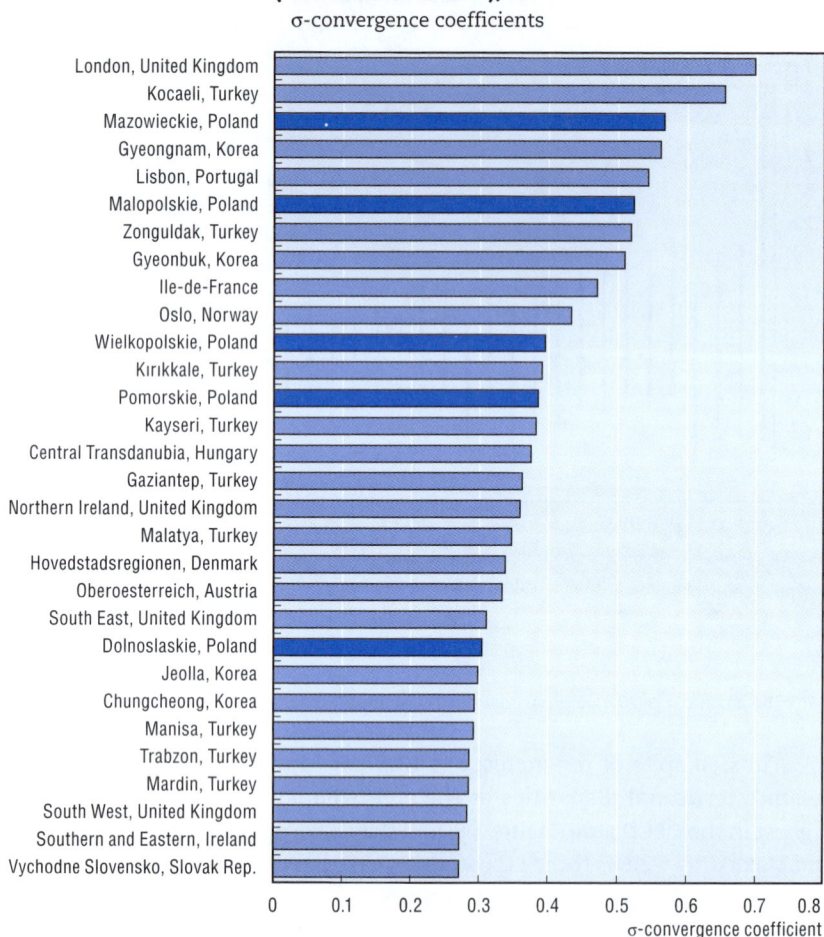

*Source:* Based on OECD (2007) *Regional Database.*

terms of attractiveness and diversification into non-agricultural activities. In addition, the decline of traditional industry branches has caused serious problems to certain small and medium-sized cities which have lost their traditional economic base. After 1990, medium-size cities (Starachowice, Ostrowiec, Radom) have suffered crises because of high levels of structural unemployment due to industrial restructuring, important out-migration and the loss of their former administrative powers.[13] The following section looks at the widening gap between large urban areas and the rest of the country.

Figure 1.8. **Regional disparities in the OECD (GINI Coefficient)**

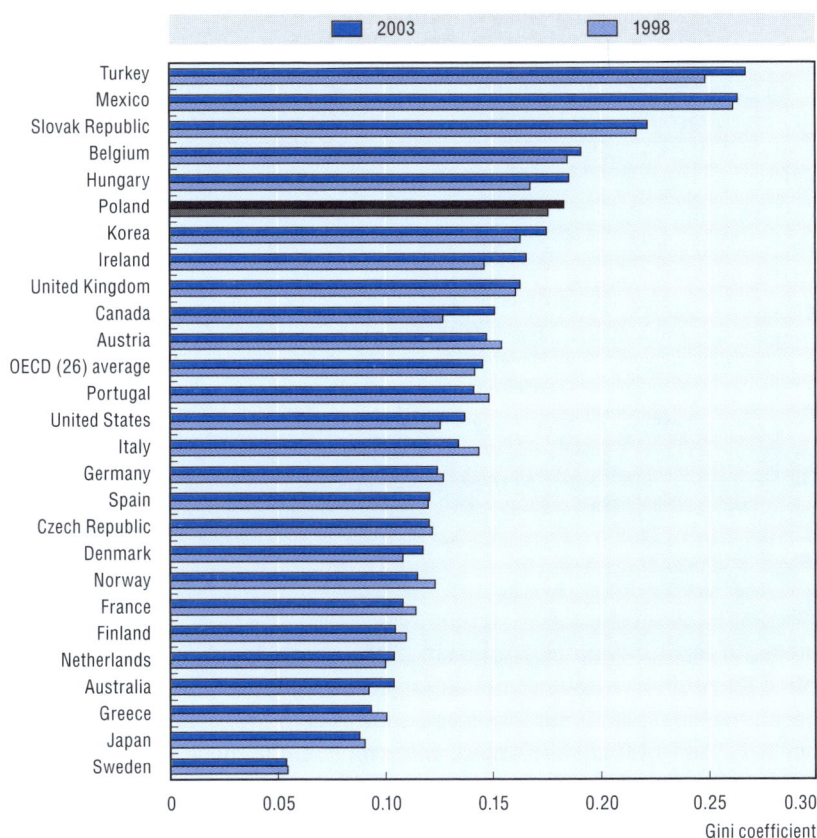

Source: OECD (2007f).

## Unemployment disparities

Unemployment rates reflect the widening east-west divide analysed above. While western regions have managed to reduce their unemployment rates significantly relative to the national average, eastern – and particularly border regions in the east – have experienced substantial rises. Within voivodships, disparities are also important. For instance in Mazowieckie, unemployment rates vary from 3% in Warsaw to 20% in Radomsky, which is only about 80 kilometres south of the capital. Unemployment rates are related to the intra-regional disparities discussed above.

Improved labour-market conditions have not sufficed to trim regional inequalities in unemployment. One reason for the limited impact may be a lack of labour mobility, which is lower in Poland than in most OECD countries, including those with similar characteristics in terms of population density or

Figure 1.9. **Regional convergence analysis for Poland (GDP per capita) 1995-2004**

σ-convergence

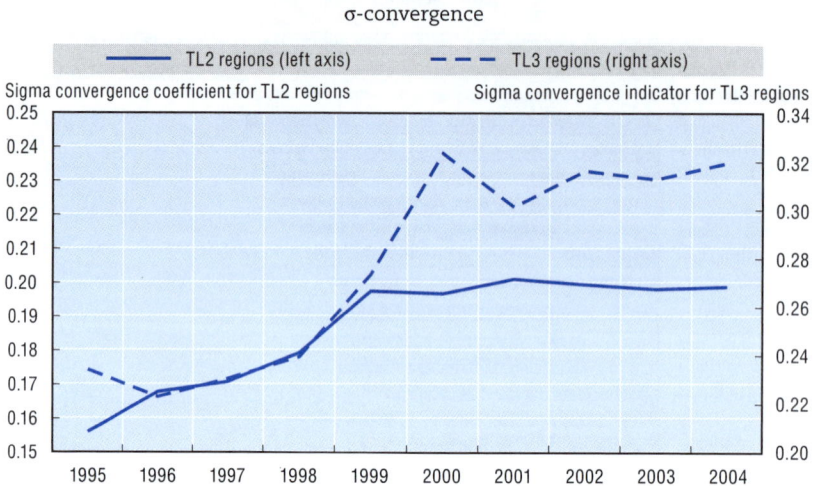

Note: The results are similar when the same analysis is carried out using GDP per worker – by place of residence or by place of work-.

Source: Based on OECD (2008) *Regional Database*.

number of territorial units. For instance, the Czech Republic, France and the United Kingdom have labour mobility rates seven times those of Poland.[14] As a result, regional labour surpluses and shortages in particular sectors are not matched. The fact that Poles appear more reluctant to move within their own country indicates the presence of specific barriers. In part, restrictions to internal labour mobility relate to housing and commuting constraints. These two factors are extensively discussed in Chapter 2.

Labour shortages not compensated by regional mobility are exacerbated by out-migration. The annual flow of Poles going abroad for periods longer than the typical length of a seasonal job is estimated to have increased by between 40 and 80% shortly after EU accession. High out-migration flows have contributed both to the rapid decline in unemployment and to the recent emergence of widespread labour shortages in sectors such as health, financial services and construction. Yet, Poland's experience in this regard is by no means exceptional among the transition economies that have recently joined the European Union. For instance, the outward migration rate reported above is comparable to those observed in Estonia and Slovakia, and still well below those in Latvia and Lithuania (OECD, 2008a).

## 2. Large cities: drivers of growth

Increasing disparities across sub-regions (TL3) are mainly due to the rising gap between urban and rural areas. The following discussion uses OECD criteria to define predominantly urban areas to ensure comparability with other OECD countries. The OECD definition classifies as predominantly urban TL3 areas with less than 15% of the population living in rural communities (see methodological note in Appendix 1). On this basis, Poland has eight urban areas: Centralny Slaski (Katowice-functional area); Cracow, Gdansk-Gdynia-Sopot, Lodz, Poznan, Rybnicko-Jastrzębski, Warsaw and Wroclaw. Together, these eight urban areas represent 22.8% of the total Polish population and 37.4% of total GDP.

## 2.1. A polycentric urban framework: potential strength for territorial development

Poland has a polycentric urban framework, composed of large and medium-sized cities, well distributed over the territory, except in eastern Poland (see Maps 1.3 and 1.4 and Box 1.3). This polycentric settlement creates

---

### Box 1.3. **Distribution of the urban population and "metropolitan areas"**

The distribution of Poland's population is relatively well balanced between urban and rural areas. At 61.78% (CSO, 2005), the urban population has remained almost unchanged since 1990. The distribution is more balanced than that of OECD countries such as Canada, Mexico or Korea. The population is concentrated in Mazowieckie (13.5%), Slaskie (12.3%), Wielkopolskie (8.8%) and Małopolskie (8.6%), while the eastern rural Polish regions are the most sparsely populated. Western regions are characterised by higher urban densities than eastern ones, owing to Poland's historical urbanisation from the west to the east (Centre for European Regional and Local Studies, 2005).

The 2005 amendment to the National Spatial Development Policy Scheme (which does not have legal status) has identified nine so-called metropolitan areas, *i.e.* large cities which, along with the surrounding gminas, have in aggregate a population of more than 500 000. These are Bydgoszcz-Torun (724 700), Cracow (1 227 200), Lodz (1 061 600), Poznan (1 227 200), so-called "Silesia" (including Katowice and Rybnik-Jastrzebie, (3 239 200), Szczecin (683 900), Gdańsk/Gdynia/Sopot, Warsaw (2 680 600), and Wroclaw (1 136 900).

Eastern regions are characterised by a sparse network of medium-sized towns. As none of eastern Poland cities meets the population-related requirement for this category, it is assumed that there are at least two urban centres, sometimes referred to as potential metropolitan areas: Lublin (465 900) and Bialystok (365 700).

Small towns (with a population of up to 20 000) play a decisive role in the urbanisation process. They represent 75% of the total number of cities and towns in Poland. A vast majority have fewer than 5 000 inhabitants.

*Source:* Gorzelak *et al.*, 2006; and Ministry of Regional Development, 2007.

---

Map 1.3. **Cities in Poland**

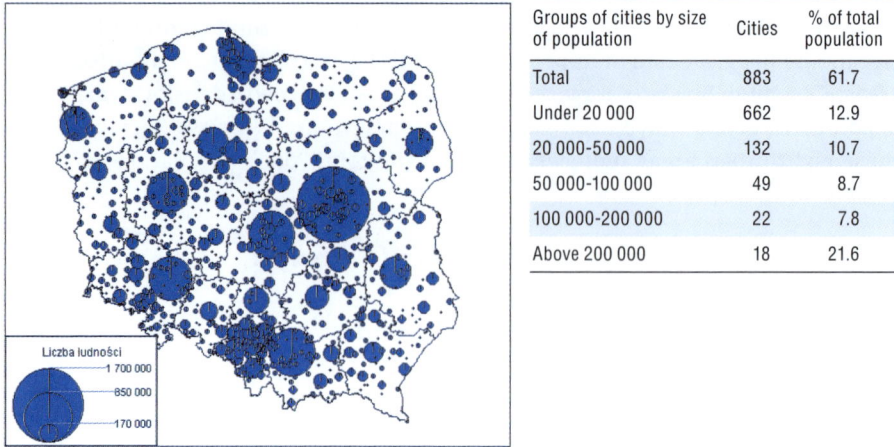

| Groups of cities by size of population | Cities | % of total population |
|---|---|---|
| Total | 883 | 61.7 |
| Under 20 000 | 662 | 12.9 |
| 20 000-50 000 | 132 | 10.7 |
| 50 000-100 000 | 49 | 8.7 |
| 100 000-200 000 | 22 | 7.8 |
| Above 200 000 | 18 | 21.6 |

Source: Centre for European Regional and Local Studies, 2005, based on GUS data.

Map 1.4. **Typology of cities and towns in Poland developed for the purposes of Urban Audit**

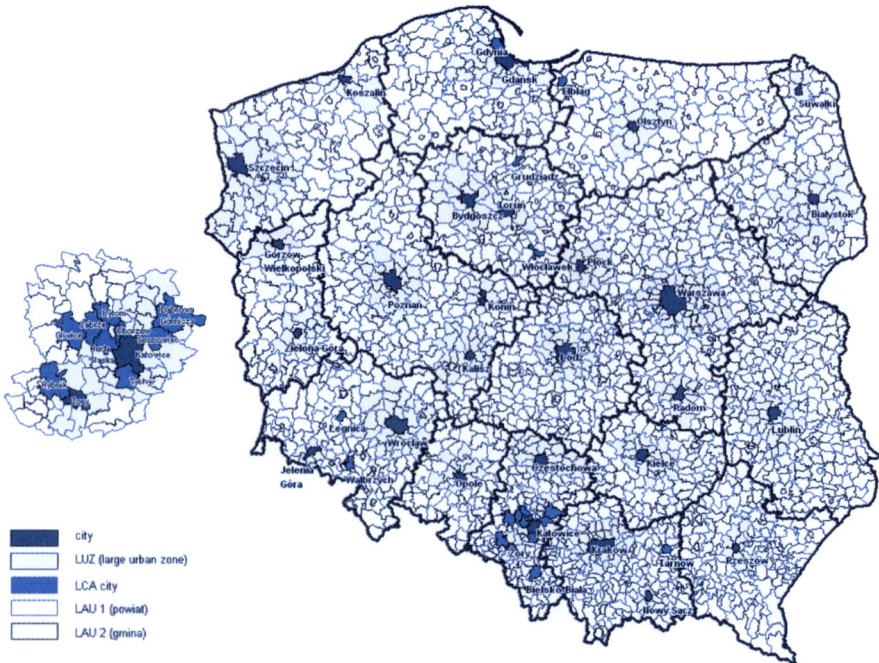

Source: Centre of Urban Statistics in Poznan.

a potential for more balanced development as contributions to national GDP are not concentrated in one or two dominant cities. There is no major imbalance between Warsaw and the rest of the country in terms of population and contribution to national growth. Warsaw has only 7% of the national population and accounts for 16% of GDP. Although this is significantly higher than other Polish cities, it contrasts with OECD countries such as Korea, the Netherlands or Denmark, where the capital city region represents almost half of the national GDP.

## 2.2. Higher growth and productivity

Although growth rates vary quite significantly among large urban areas (between Katowice and Warsaw for instance), large cities have grown faster on average than intermediate and rural areas in the past two decades. The group of rich and dynamic sub-regions only includes large urban areas (Figure 1.10). The urban areas' share of national GDP has increased constantly since 1995, while that of rural and intermediate areas has decreased (Figure 1.11). The growth rate of Polish urban areas has been among the highest in the OECD area for

Figure 1.10. **Economic growth and GDP per capita in Polish sub-regions (TL3), 1995-2004**

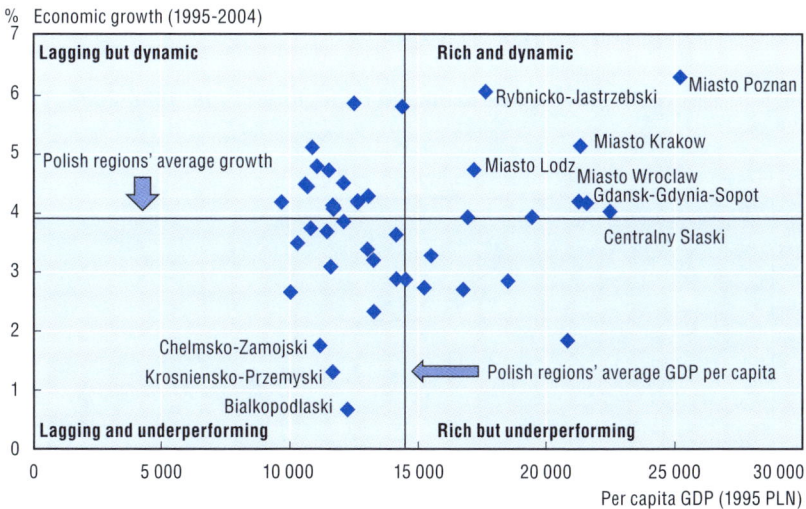

Notes:
1. Warsaw is excluded because the differential in GDP per capita is too large compared to other TL3.
2. Economic growth rates are annual average rates using real GDP per capita figures for 1995 and 2004. However, data for Warszawski, Czestochowski, Bielsko-Bialski, Centralny slaski and Rybnicko-jastrzebski were only available for 2000-04 so that the average annual growth rates for these TL3 regions are for that period.
3. The word "Miasto" means city. Some urban TL3 are classified with this term in the OECD database (see table of the classification of the Polish TL2 and TL3 in the methodological note).

Source: Based on OECD(2008) Regional Database.

Figure 1.11. **Share of GDP by type of region, 2004**

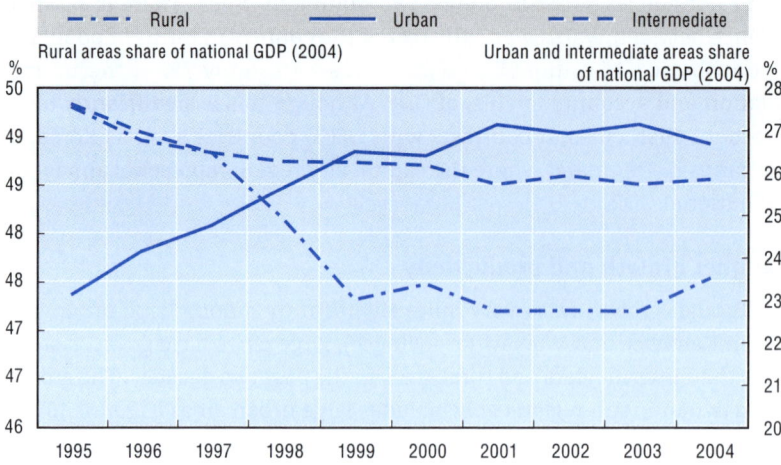

Note: Urban areas refer to the OECD typology: Centralny Slaski, Cracow, Gdansk-Gdynia-Sopot, Lodz, Poznan, Rybnik-Jastrzebie, Warsaw and Wroclaw.

Source: Based on OECD (2008) Regional Database.

the 1998-2003 period, behind only Ireland, Korea and Hungary (Figure 1.12). In addition, urban areas show per capita GDP that is more than double the average level in predominantly rural areas (Figure 1.13).

Figure 1.12. **GDP growth rate averaged by regional type, 1998-2003 (TL3)**

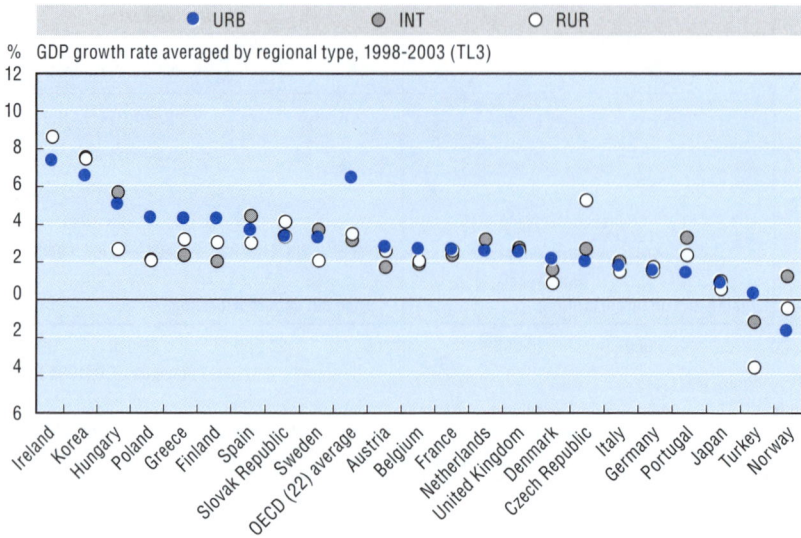

Source: OECD (2007f), Regions at a Glance.

Figure 1.13. **GDP per capita by type of region in Poland (2005)**

Real per capita GDP in Polish zloty (2005)

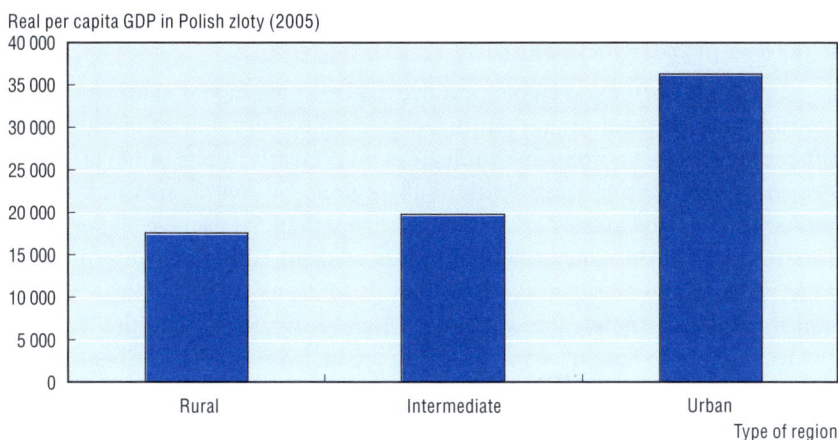

*Source:* Based on OECD (2008) *Regional Database.*

The growth differential between large cities and the national average is mainly due to higher employment and productivity rates (Figure 1.14). Most employment opportunities are in urban areas, and unemployment and high inactivity rates remain key variables in explaining economic difficulties in some

Figure 1.14. **Explanatory factors for growth differential compared to the national average**

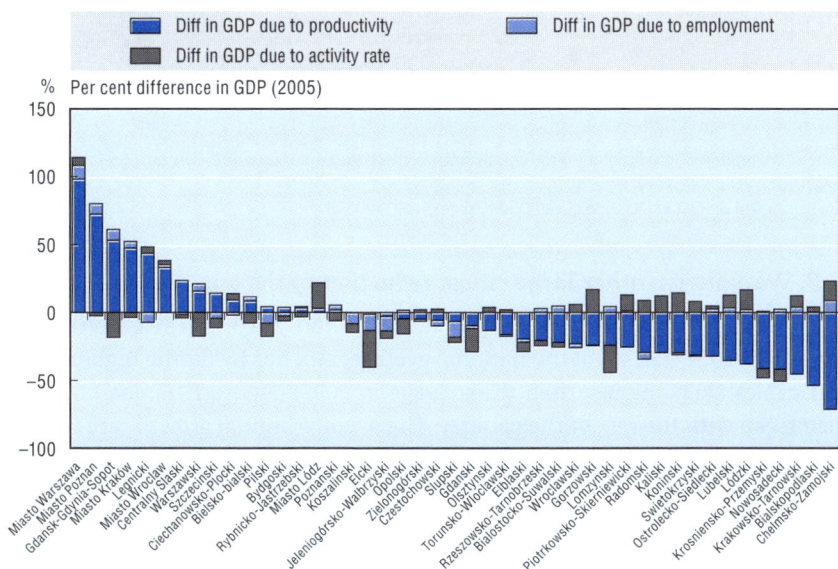

*Note:* "Miasto" means city (see note in Figure 1.10).
*Source:* OECD, 2008, own calculations based on OECD (2008) *Regional Database.*

intermediate/rural areas. Higher productivity also plays a significant role; Poland displayed the largest regional variation in productivity rate in the OECD at TL3 level in 2003 (OECD, 2007f).

Both multi-factor and labour productivity levels are higher in urban than in intermediate or rural areas. Multi-factor productivity shows productivity differentials between urban and rural areas most clearly. While urban areas are 20% more productive than Polish sub-regions on average, multi-factor productivity in rural areas is more than 5% lower than the average (Figure 1.15). In terms of labour productivity (man-hours worked), urban and intermediate areas outperform the average whereas rural areas underperform.[15] The concentration of knowledge workers, FDI and innovative activities in large urban centres is the main reason for rising productivity growth in cities.

Figure 1.15. **Labour and multi-factor productivity compared**

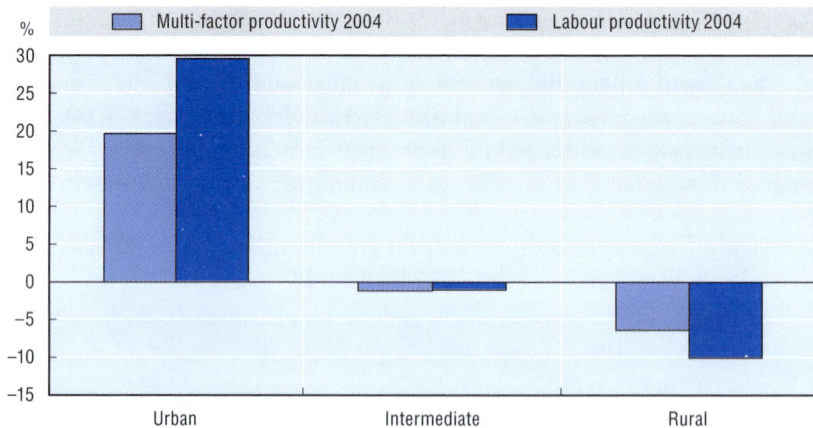

Note: Bars represent productivity differentials with respect to the average of Polish regions (depicted as 0%).
Source: Based on OECD (2008) Regional Database and CSO (2008).

### 2.3. Warsaw vs. other large cities: reduction of the gap

Among the largest cities, Warsaw has had the highest growth rate over 1995-2004 (151.4% of the national average) and has by far the highest GDP per capita (263% higher than the average in 2005) (Figure 1.16), leading to a rising gap with the rest of the country. The average annual growth rate in GDP per capita stood at 7.3% for 2000-04. Warsaw had one of the highest growth rates among OECD metropolitan regions between 1998 and 2003 (Figure 1.17). Growth in Warsaw is largely due to the rise in employment in services, from 49.2% in 1995 to 63.2% in 2005 (CSO, 2005), mainly in trade, telecommunications, financial services, insurance and IT. Out of Poland's 100 largest companies, 43 are based in Warsaw. In addition, Warsaw has become one of the largest

Figure 1.16. **GDP per capita in Polish urban areas in 2005**[1]

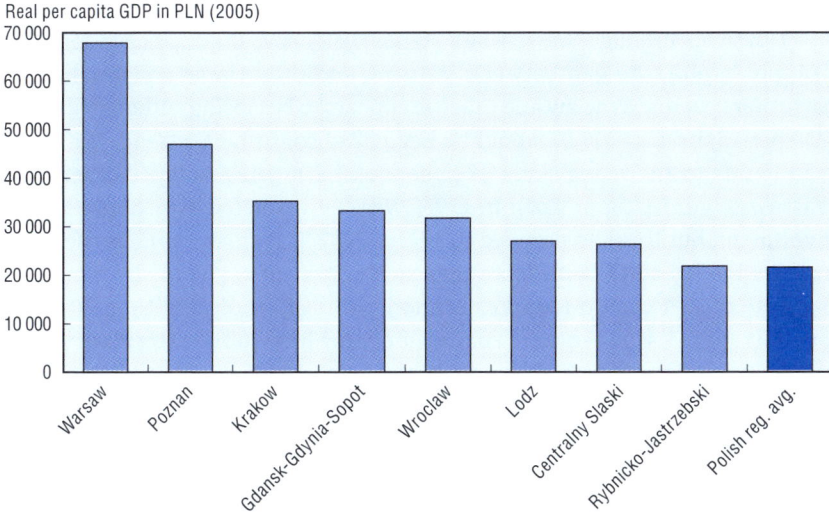

Real per capita GDP in PLN (2005)

1. The figure shows only the eight predominantly urban areas in Poland according to the OECD Regional Database definition.

*Source:* Based on OECD (2008) *Regional Database.*

Figure 1.17. **Average annual growth rates in GDP per capita, 1995-2002**[1]

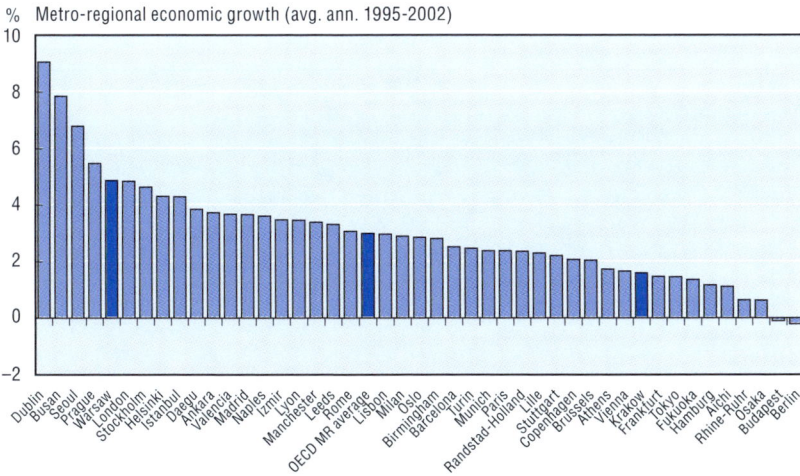

% Metro-regional economic growth (avg. ann. 1995-2002)

1. Although the latest data for Polish metro-regions (Warsaw and Cracow) refer to 2005, to allow for comparability with the rest of the OECD and given data restrictions for other metro-regions, the latest comparable data are for 2002.

*Source:* Based on OECD (2006) *Metropolitan Database.*

investment sites in central Europe after Berlin and has attracted the highest share of greenfield FDI to Poland since 1995.[16]

However, although Warsaw still stands well above other cities in terms of GDP per capita, the gap between Warsaw and other large Polish cities, in particular Poznan, Wroclaw and Cracow, appears to be closing, although data on GDP per capita for 2006-07 would be needed to confirm this trend. It may be mainly due to the rising share of (greenfield) FDI going to cities other than Warsaw (Figure 1.18, at TL2). In 1996, Warsaw attracted 40% of greenfield investment, but this had dropped to 17% in 2001. If Warsaw remains the main location for FDI stock, with more than half of the total, a study by the Polish Institute of Research on Market Economy (IBnGR) indicates that Wroclaw (see Box 1.5), Katowice and Poznan became the most attractive cities in 2005-06 in terms of FDI inflows, for both high technology and services (IBnGR, 2007). Slaskie, which includes Katowice and Rybnik-Jastrzbie, is the most attractive region for FDI linked to industrial activities, while Jelenia-Góra-Waębrzych (Dolnoslaskie) ranks third. Lodz has also experienced a strong increase in FDI (Box 1.4). According to the Polish Agency for Foreign Investment (PAIZ), the main criteria privileged by foreign investors when choosing an investment location are the availability of a qualified workforce and the quality of infrastructure (accessibility) (PAIZ, 2006). The correlation between human capital and FDI attraction is clear (Figure 1.19).

Figure 1.18. **Growing disparities in FDI attraction**
FDI growth and initial levels[1]

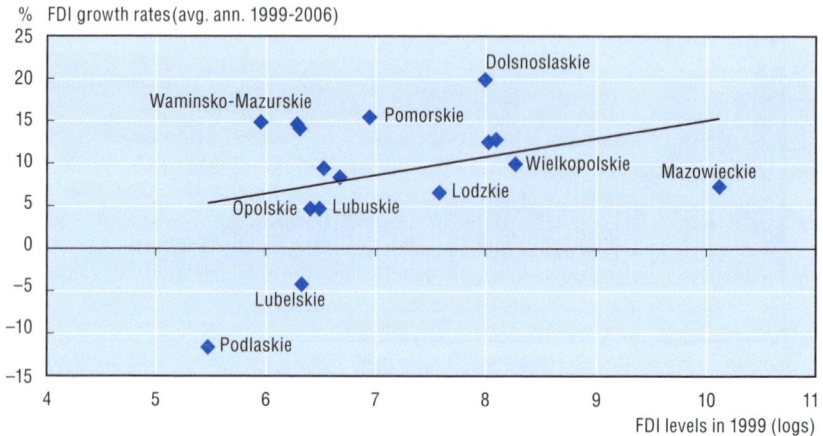

1. Data are not available at TL3 level.
*Source:* Based on OECD (2008) *Regional Database.*

Box 1.4. **Growth trends in Katowice and Lodz**

*Katowice* (Centralny Slaski), the capital of Silesia, has had a slower growth, largely owing to industry restructuring. However, unemployment has decreased rapidly in the past few years (4.7% in 2007, compared to the national average of 13%) owing to increased diversification to services and an increase in FDI. Mining, metal milling, energy and other branches of industry remain crucial for Katowice's economy as they account for 25% of total employment. In spite of significant progress in industrial restructuring, Katowice remains heavily dependent on variations in general economic conditions, particularly fluctuations of the demand for coal and steel.

*Lodz* faces huge restructuring, similar to that of Katowice despite significant differences between them because of their initial economic structure: Lodz was the capital of light industry (textile), while Katowice was the capital of heavy industry (coal mining and steel). Paradoxically, Lodz may have suffered from its proximity to Warsaw; Katowice is more distant and has been able to elaborate its own development strategy. However, in the next few years, proximity to Warsaw could be a strength, with the new fast train between the two cities, and the opportunities for development in Lodz (see Chapter 3).

Figure 1.19. **FDI and human capital in Polish regions (2006)**

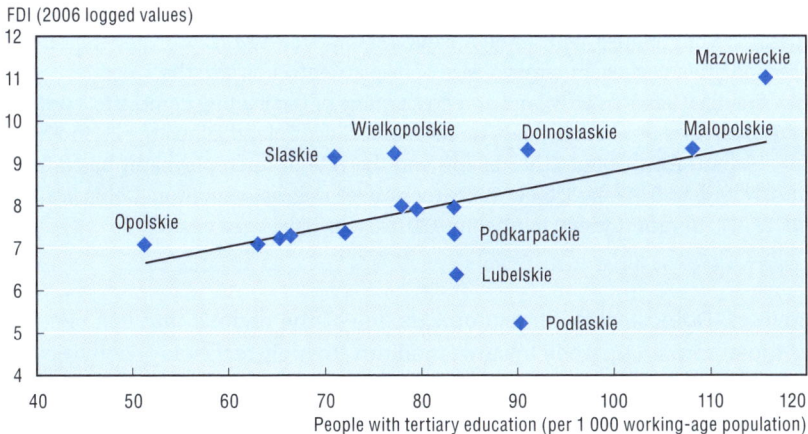

*Source:* Based on OECD (2008) *Regional Database* and CSO (2008).

## Industrial specialisations

The urban areas that have grown faster are those that have diversified their economy the most to services, mainly in financial and business services (consulting, marketing, legal, accounting firms). In addition, faster-growing regions have moved quickly to more capital-intensive manufacturing

---

### Box 1.5. **Wroclaw: The development of knowledge**

Wroclaw is one of Poland's most dynamic cities. It has a multicultural history and a tradition of openness. It has about 630 000 inhabitants (with over 1.1 million in the agglomeration). It is the capital of Dolnoslaskie, a rapidly growing region in the southwest of Poland. In 2005, Dolnoslaskie's GDP per capita was 53% of the EU25 average, slightly above Poland's average (103.3%), and it was in fourth place among the 16 Polish regions. The region's economic activity is based on industry (32.8% of employment) and increasingly on services (57% of employment). The agricultural sector is relatively weak compared to other Polish regions (10.2% of employment).

Within Lower Silesia, which has the country's densest transport infrastructure and good cross-border co-operation with its German and Czech neighbours, Wroclaw is an important transport hub at the intersection of three international routes with two major railway stations, two river ports and an international airport. The city has the largest number of bridges in the world after Venice, Amsterdam and St. Petersburg. It is nearly equidistant from Berlin, Prague and Warsaw.

Thanks to its favourable geographical position at a commercial crossroad as well as to a recent wave of foreign investment (especially in the IT sector), Wroclaw has become a frontrunner of economic development. Its location on the A4 motorway which links Wroclaw with Germany and two other major Polish metropolitan areas (Katowice and Cracow) has been crucial. Wroclaw has attracted a number of leading multinational companies (Volvo, LG, Toyota, Wabco, Whirpool, Electrolux, etc.), and some have decided to establish R&D or services facilities (Siemens, Capgemini, Hewlett-Packard, Macopharma). Around 27% of the 92 954 registered firms in Wroclaw (2006 data) are companies with foreign capital. Moreover, Wroclaw's agglomeration ranks second after Warsaw in terms of size of investments. It is also the second largest centre of financial services in Poland and hosts many of the leading domestic IT firms, which further raises its attractiveness for investors. Since Poland joined the EU in 2004, Wroclaw has attracted about EUR 5 billion and the rate of unemployment has fallen from nearly 14% to 5.1% in October 2007 (the rate of unemployment in Dolnoslaskie exceeds 11.7%). In recent years, more than 120 000 jobs have been created.

---

activities. Dolnoslaskie, for example, is one of the regions that has benefited the most from an upgrade towards medium- to high-technology activities and more intensive use of capital and technology (Figure 1.20). There has been a slight reduction of specialisation in traditional sectors such as textiles, and enhanced specialisation in transport (automotive), metals and non-electric machinery. Globalisation forces are clearly playing a role. This is also the case in Wielkopolskie, and to a lesser extent Slaskie and Malopolskie (see Annex 1.A2 and the charts for the different regions).

Although cluster development remains at a very preliminary stage in Poland (see Chapter 2), some co-ordination between firms and knowledge institutes in some areas has developed in the largest cities, especially in high-

Figure 1.20. **Changes in specialisation and employment in Dolnoslaskie**

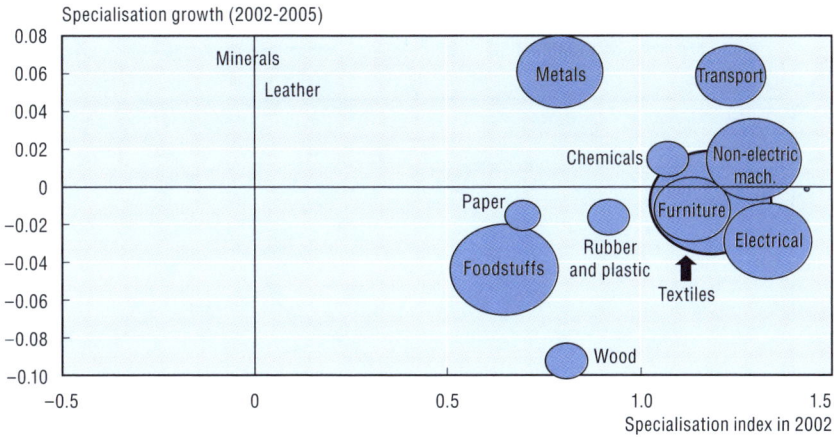

Specialisation growth (2002-2005)

Specialisation index in 2002

Note: Specialisation Indexes are built using relative employment industry-specific figures in Poland with respect to total manufacturing employment. Growth in specialisation refers to average annual growth rates in specialisation indexes between 2002 and 2005. Bubbles show size of the industry in terms of employment.
Source: Based on CSO (2008).

technology sectors (electronics in Warsaw and Crakow), in pharmaceuticals and cosmetics (Crakow and Lodz) and in more traditional sectors such as the automotive industry in Katowice and in Dolnoslaskie (Walbrzych and Wroclaw) and industrial automatics in Gdańsk (shipyards and mechanics).

## 2.4. Challenges for large cities

Large cities are the motors of national growth. This has clear implications for the need to strengthen agglomeration economies in a sustainable way in order to enhance productivity growth and transfers of knowledge. There are critical challenges for making better use of the knowledge economy: little private R&D, under-developed Internet and broadband, mismatch between university supply and labour market needs (see Section 1.4).

Most importantly, large urban areas have to face the challenge of managing the adverse consequences of very high growth rates, in particular urban sprawl. This is strongly linked to the rise in housing prices, especially since 2004. While residential property prices in Poland[17] have been rising steadily since 2003 at a yearly pace of 10-20%, increases have been even greater in Warsaw, Poznan, Lodz, Cracow, Gdynia, Gdansk and Wroclaw (Figure 1.21). Prices in Warsaw are among the highest in Central and Eastern Europe and even equal to those in some western European countries. This is leading to a new type of migration, a move towards close rural areas and medium-sized cities surrounding large cities and commuting to work on a daily basis. Although there are signs that a

Figure 1.21. **Residential property price inflation in the largest cities**[1]
In nominal terms, year-on-year changes

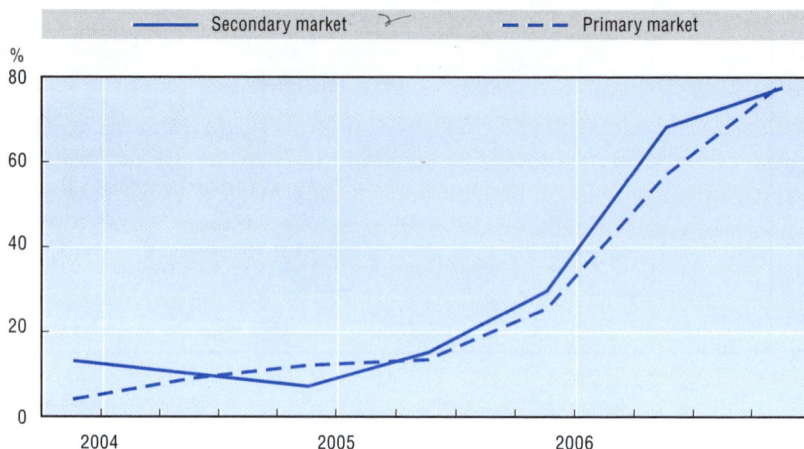

1. Average of prices in Warsaw, Poznan, Lodz, Cracow, Gdynia, Gdansk and Wroclaw.
Source: National Bank of Poland (2007) in OECD (2008a).

turn-around may be under way, with prices starting to decline in several major cities – linked in part to the recent global financial turmoil – Poland's central statistical office expects that migration to nearby rural areas will continue to increase until 2025 (CSO, 2005).

Urban sprawl and increased commuting flows around large cities call for specific attention to urban-rural linkages in terms of transport and housing. This makes development and modernisation of urban public transport and development of metropolitan roads essential. Traffic congestion, road accidents and parking difficulties are now listed among the most critical problems for cities (Brzezinski, 2003). The absence of ring roads around large cities leads to negative externalities (pollution, danger), in particular for freight transport. Besides, as Polish cities – in particular Warsaw and Katowice – are very polluted (in particular for water pollution), this can diminish their attractiveness.

Policy support to medium-sized cities and rural areas is also crucial, for cohesion reasons but also given Poland's new migration patterns. New population inflows are an opportunity for medium-sized cities and rural areas to develop. An increasing number of companies are establishing their businesses outside Warsaw and large cities, where operational costs are lower. Quality of life becomes more important, especially for the younger generation, and, perhaps surprisingly, young adults are becoming more mobile and more ready to relocate to smaller towns for business opportunities (AmCham, 2006). In addition to improved transport connections with large cities, priorities should include the development of telecommunications – in particular broadband – and education. These challenges are all the more pressing in rural areas, where development has lagged behind for many reasons. The rural question is the focus of the next section.

## 3. Trends and challenges for rural development

The urban-rural[18] gap has widened in terms of GDP and productivity growth. Many rural areas have been caught in a vicious circle, with little diversification towards non-agricultural activities, low level of attractiveness, and low educational attainment. The rural economy is dominated by agriculture. In eastern Poland, urban networks are weakest and there are no metropolitan areas. At the same time, there are a few positive trends. First, migration to rural areas has increased since 1999 (Figure 1.22). Second, agricultural development is regionally differentiated, and some areas (the dairy sector for example) have become competitive. Third, rural areas have much under-utilised potential, such as tourism in the northeast, which is one of the best preserved natural environments in the European Union. This section first analyses the key features of agricultural development, then the challenges for overall rural development with a focus on education and infrastructure.

Figure 1.22. **Population living in rural areas (thousands)**

Population (thousands)

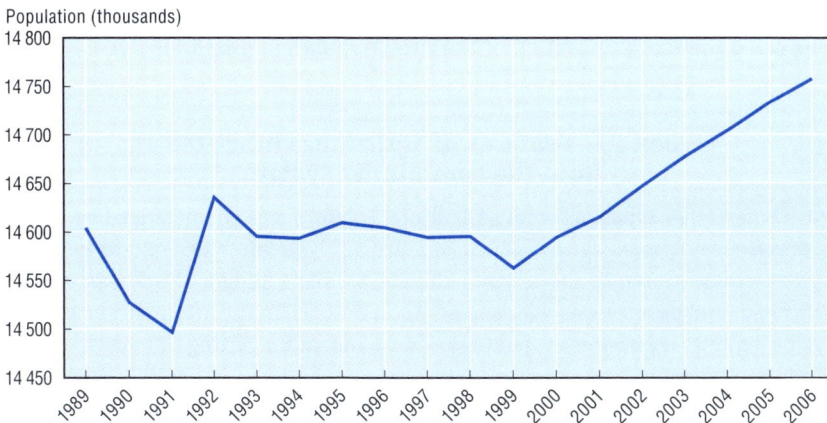

*Source:* CSO, 2006.

### 3.1. A large and enduring agriculture sector

The economy in rural areas is still mainly oriented towards agriculture. A large part of the labour force (around 17%) still works in the agriculture sector (although this figure is much debated (Box 1.6), it is much higher than the OECD average). Agriculture occupies more than 2 million people, and 50.8% of the land (forests account for 28.2%) (GUS, 2005). Although the proportion of the

> ### Box 1.6. **Statistical debates on employment in agriculture in Poland**
>
> There is some uncertainty surrounding the figures concerning agriculture now being produced and used in Poland, owing to high hidden unemployment. Overall estimates vary from 15% to more than 20% of the labour force. It seems impossible to obtain statistics on which everyone can agree, whether they concern farm size, income derived from agricultural activity or the different types of activity. Professor Jerzy Wilkin has no hesitation in writing that "the most difficult thing is to determine the exact number of peasant farmers". Until 2002-03, the statistics showed that 27% of the population was employed in the farm sector. There was then a change in the statistics in 2003 to make CSO methodology closer to the Eurostats one, when subsistence farming was removed from the official figures, which had the effect of reducing employment in the farm sector by 10 points.

population working in agriculture has decreased since the early 1990s, as in most OECD countries, agriculture has remained more resistant to structural change than industry. Historically, agriculture has played a key role in Poland's identity.[19] Some aspects (such as the small size of farms) have been present for centuries, while others are inherited from the communist period and have reinforced the marginalisation of the rural population (Box 1.7).

> ### Box 1.7. **Features of agriculture inherited from the communist system**
>
> Unlike other types of soviet agriculture, Poland's was characterised by the prevalence of small farms, which remained private after 1956. State farms were concentrated in the north. Public investment in agriculture was very limited, and poverty was widespread in rural areas. in the aftermath of 1990 this led to three important features; i) no problem for getting property back, contrary to many ex-communist countries; ii) strong mistrust of the state, low levels of education and high rural poverty (marginalisation); iii) lack of collective action and significant social assistance.

Labour productivity is low in the agriculture sector: the 17% of the population working in agriculture contributes 4.6% of GDP (National Accounts, OECD 2005). There is a broad consensus that current levels of agricultural employment are not sustainable. Encouraging labour mobility to other sectors, enhancing education in rural areas, diversifying the rural economy to non-agricultural sectors and reinforcing labour productivity through technological investments and human capital development will be crucial to achieving a sustainable balance.

The structure of agriculture in Poland is highly fragmented, with mainly small and very small farms. The average size of farms in 2006 was 8.4 hectares, half of the EU average. More than 60% of Polish farms have fewer than five hectares, and 34% have less than one (CSO, 2005). Most farms (90%) are too small to provide satisfactory income (Ministry of Agriculture, 2007). An east-west divide is noticeable, as the eastern regions are primarily characterised by a myriad of small, semi-subsistence farms, while the largest farms are in the centre and the west. The 20% of farms of over 15 hectares (mostly located in the west) contribute more than 80% of agricultural output (*The Economist*, 2001, in Crescenzi, 2004). Besides, a north-south divide is also noticeable, the largest farms being in the north.

Since the early 1990s, there has been a reduction in the number of farms, especially state farms in the north and the west (which were very large farms of around 7 000 hectares), and the average size of farms has increased. However, the closure of state farms has not necessarily led to the reduction in the number of farms, as many State farms were divided into smaller more manageable units, of over 15 hectares. Besides, the number of farms between five and 20 hectares has decreased slightly since the early 1990s. A possible explanation is that a certain economic scale and specialisation is essential and these farms were too small to compete with very large farms, but too large to develop a secondary activity, as very small farms did.

Some segments of Polish agriculture are competitive on a European or even global scale. Poland is currently the largest producer of potatoes and rye in Europe and is one of the world's largest producers of sugar beet. The dairy sector is one of the most successful. The most important crops are grains, with the highest yields from rye, wheat, barley and oats. Other major crops are potatoes, sugar beets, fodder crops, flax, hops, tobacco and fruits. In most areas, soil and climatic conditions favour a mixed type of farming. The agro-food sector, which was strongly affected by the crisis in the 1990s, has expanded rapidly in the 2000s, in particular for cereals, fruits and vegetables. About half of Poland's agricultural exports go to EU countries.

### Regional variations in agriculture development

Three main macro-regions can be distinguished for agriculture development.[20] Two-thirds of competitive farms are located in the west, in particular in Wielkopolskie and Kujawsko-pomorskie (Bydgoszcz), where levels of productivity are higher. Wielkopolskie takes top position in Polish agriculture in terms of productivity, owing to long-standing traditions of high standards of farming (Map 1.5). The north has lost employment owing to the closure of state

Map 1.5. **Gross agricultural output in 2006 (constant prices in 2005)**

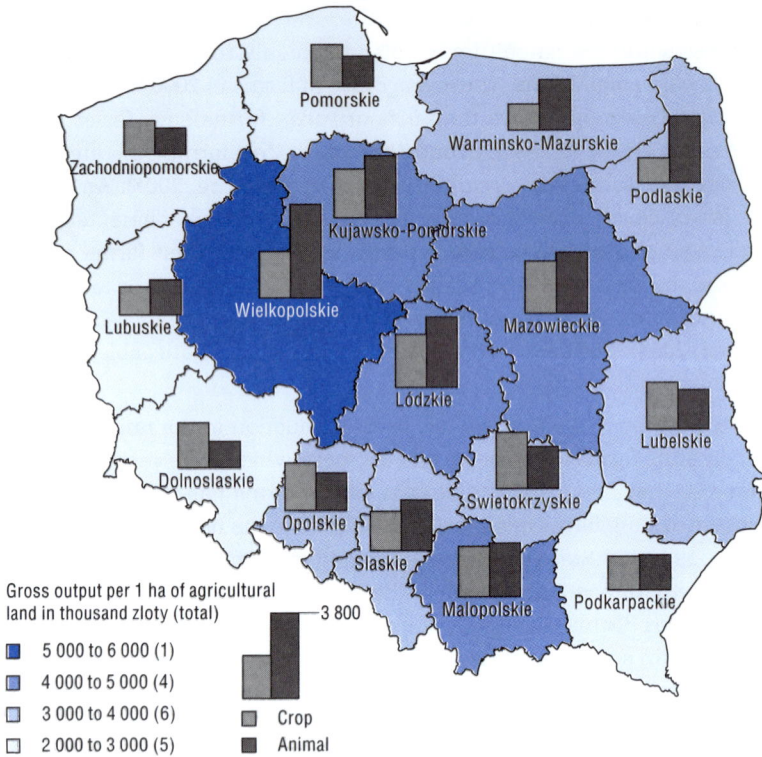

Source: Regions of Poland, CSO, 2007.

farms. Structural problems are mostly concentrated in the five regions of eastern Poland, where hidden unemployment is high, small uneconomic farms dominate and labour productivity is very low. Poland's largest fertile areas (Dolnoslaskie, Malopolskie, Kujawsko-Pomorskie, Pomorskie, and Lubelskie) are not necessarily the most productive, which suggests structural imbalances in the use of labour force, size of holdings and technological developments.

Northern Poland is one of the area most affected by the restructuring process in the 1990s, because the vast majority of the region had been state farms (*panstwowe gospodarstwa rolne* – PGR) and, to a lesser extent, co-operatives. After 1989, the government closed state-owned farms, which led to widespread poverty and high unemployment. People previously employed on state farms have no qualifications and no roots in the peasantry. This population is strongly concentrated in some villages (PGR villages). In many powiats previously dominated by state-owned farms, the unemployment rate is currently above 30%.

## Eastern Poland and high hidden unemployment

The large weight of agriculture in eastern Poland[21] – 30.2% of total employment in the five regions – is one reason for the regions' economic difficulties. Agricultural productivity is only 69% of the national average. Large enterprises dominate in the northern part, while small, uneconomic family farms prevail in the southern part. Most farming households produce only for their own needs with little commercial activity. Many people have two jobs. A large share of the rural population is older than the national average, and there is an outflow of young people from the poorest areas: 173 000 inhabitants left the five Eastern regions between 2000 and 2004 (CSO, 2005).

Unemployment is high in eastern Poland – especially long-term unemployment, although the official statistics indicate a lower rate than in western regions (for example 15.5% in Podlaskie in the East compared to 25.6% in Zachodniopomorskie in 2005). However, hidden unemployment[22] is very high in eastern Poland, especially in the agricultural sector – estimated at 1 million persons (Wilkin, 2004). Inter-family solidarity plays a key role in eastern Poland, where several generations tend to live in the same place, with one primary source of revenue in the form of a pension.

The informal economy has developed since 1990 and now plays a significant role, especially because the population on the other side of the border (Russia, Belarus and Ukraine) is poorer. It is particularly prevalent in the south-east, especially with Ukrainians, where very small plots require labour-intensive agriculture. However, the Schengen rules, which apply in Poland since January 2008, make the crossing of the border more difficult.

However, there are a few positive exceptions. Some small farms – such as those specialised in fruit in the southeast – have performed well over the past few years and are likely to remain important in Polish agriculture. The dairy sector is also successful in that part of the country. However, most farms dedicated to agriculture for self-consumption find it difficult to move towards more profitable activities such as dairy or horticulture.

## Limited diversification of the rural economy

In about half of all municipalities (*gminas*), agriculture is the main economic activity (Bański and Stola, 2002). In only 20% of rural municipalities is the leading role played by non-agricultural functions, mainly forestry or tourism, or is mixed (Bański, 2003). The lowest level of diversification is along the eastern border, in the regions of Podkarpackie, Lubelskie and Podlaskie. The greatest concentration of farms engaged in an activity other than agriculture is in the hinterlands of large cities, as well as in tourism areas. Among these activities, services play the most important role, followed by trade and small-scale manufacturing (Banski, 2006). The most important "second" activities are industry (19.5%), construction (17.8%), and transport (5.1%) (CSO, 2004). Among the farmers with other sources of revenue, 73% have less than 5 hectares. Diversification of the rural economy is positively correlated with higher income in predominantly rural regions in OECD countries (Figure 1.23).

Figure 1.23. **GDP per capita in rural areas and diversification of the rural economy to secondary and tertiary sectors**

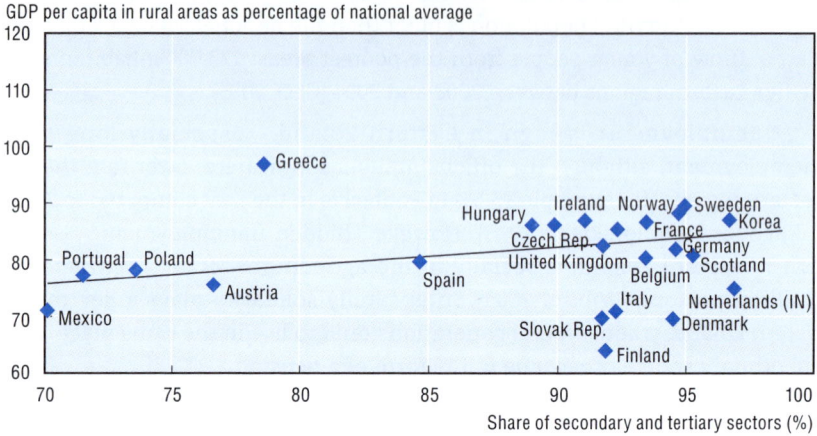

GDP per capita in rural areas as percentage of national average

*Source:* OECD *Territorial Database,* 2007.

### 3.2. Obstacles to mobility and rural diversification

Four major challenges need to be addressed to enhance labour mobility out of agriculture and diversify the rural economy: i) enhance educational attainment in rural areas; ii) enhance access to capital; iii) Improve the role of financial transfers in serving rural people and iv) improve infrastructure development.

### Enhance educational attainment

Education is the most important challenge. Lower educational levels of rural populations contribute to limit labour mobility and to inadequate rural diversification. Only 5.4% of the rural population has higher education, compared to 17.5% in urban areas (CSO, 2004).[23] In some rural municipalities, the percentage with no more than elementary education exceeds 40% (CSO, 2004). In 2001, Poland, along with Mexico, had the largest regional disparities in tertiary attainments in the OECD area. Although the situation has improved since 2001, major problems remain:

● Access to pre-school remains very limited. Only 18% of 3-to-5-year-olds went to kindergarten in the school year 2004-05 in rural areas, compared to 55% in urban areas (CSO, 2005). In poor, remote areas with high unemployment and social problems, small *gminas* often have no kindergartens and participation rates are close to zero (Herbst, 2004). The overall rural-urban gap in pre-school access in Poland may have a negative impact on women's work, participation in the labour market and the overall educational attainment of rural children in view of the link between attendance at pre-school and overall tertiary attainments in education (OECD, 2006b),

- Rural populations have increasing difficulty for financing tertiary education. Even in public universities, where tuition is free, some poorer students who could attend the most prestigious institutions do not do so because they cannot finance their living expenses (OECD, 2006b). Despite the strong increase in the supply of higher education institutions since the late 1990s, the urban-rural gap in educational attainment has not been significantly reduced.

## Enhance access to capital

Important obstacles to mobility are the lack of private capital and the rising cost of housing in cities. As explained in Section 1.2, housing prices in Polish cities have boomed over the past few years, making it very difficult for some categories of the rural population to move. Added to farmers' limited access to capital – owing to limitations on loans (particularly long-term loans), mobility towards urban areas is increasingly difficult. In addition to education and finance, labour mobility is also limited by mentalities and cultural factors.

## Improve the role of financial transfers in serving rural people

In Poland, as in most OECD countries, the rural population does not obtain their revenue from agriculture alone. The structure of wages has changed drastically in the last 50 years (Figure 1.24). If in 1950, agriculture represented the

Figure 1.24. **Sources of income of rural populations in Poland, 1950, 1988 and 2002**

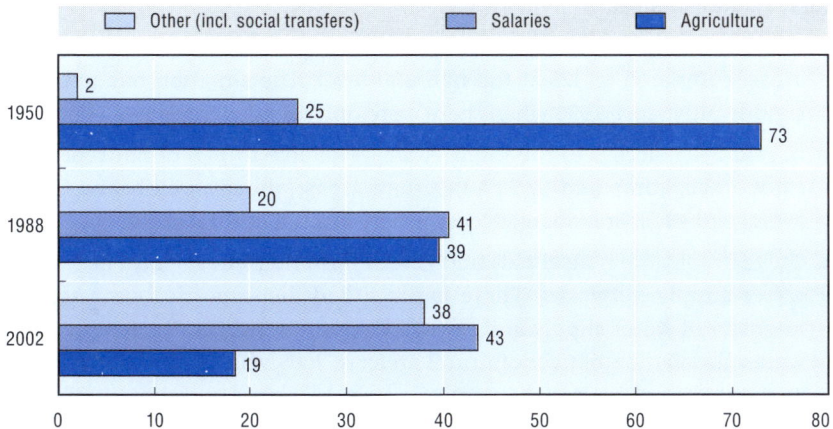

*Source:* Ministry of Agriculture, 2006.

largest part of the incomes of the rural population, this proportion was less than 20% in 2002 (Ministry of Agriculture). A peasant budget includes an increasingly large part of non-agricultural revenue, in particular social transfers (pensions).

The high level of support to the rural world and agriculture in particular – while important to ensure smooth restructuring and maintain social cohesion [2] – has a negative economic cost when it contributes to helping small uneconomic farms to survive despite very low productivity and offers no incentive for mobility. The agriculture sector is strongly supported by several policy instruments:

- **High spending on social protection** helps to maintain high employment. The special farmers' pension and disability system (KRUS) is the main source of revenue for farmers in eastern Poland. Many people who do not engage in agriculture use this system to obtain social security.

- **Fiscal advantages.** Farmers are exempted from income tax, as well as most property taxes. This leaves some rural municipalities with little fiscal resources (see Chapter 3).

- **The Common Agricultural Policy.** Poland's accession to the EU has clearly increased the level of support for agriculture and rural areas. Between 2003 and 2005, public expenditure on agriculture, rural areas and agricultural markets tripled, domestic funds increased by 59%, and resources from the EU grew by eleven times.

### Improve infrastructure development

Other major infrastructure needs in rural areas are related to the provision of gas supply (much lower than in urban areas), sewage networks, telephone and Internet access. Although there have been significant improvements since the early 1990s in all these fields, there are still considerable imbalances between rural and urban areas:

- There are only 196.7 telephones (fixed lines) per 1 000 population in rural areas, compared to 329 at the national level. The situation has improved significantly since 1990 when there were only 26 telephones per 1 000.

- In mid-2005, access to the Internet was available to 11% of households in rural areas, compared to 29% in urban areas (already well below the EU average of 43%). Broadband access is very limited in rural areas.

- Only 60% of rural households and 72% of farm households have access to a water supply networks. There is a marked disproportion between the intensity of water supply and sewage disposal networks: the length of the water distribution network in rural areas in 2005 was 65.5 km per 100 km$^2$, whereas that of sewage disposal was only 12.6 km. Development of water supply networks is much higher in the hierarchy of needs of the rural population; sewage treatment projects are perceived as an additional financial burden.

### Conclusion

Challenges for rural areas are national ones, as better diversification of the rural economy and improved mobility out of the agriculture sector would have a significant impact on national output. Agricultural production alone is not sufficient to stimulate development of the wider rural community. Education seems to be the main long-term lever of change, although infrastructure development is also crucial. Specialisations in competitive agricultural products and wider rural development have to be implemented hand in hand, with a focus on territories rather than farmers. Chapter 2 explores the main policy recommendations for rural development. It seems that there is currently a large window of opportunity to reform rural/agriculture policy, in the global context of higher prices for agricultural products, injections of large amounts of funds for rural development and reform of the Common Agricultural Policy.

## 4. Common challenges to build competitive regions

While some challenges are specific to urban or rural areas, the need to hasten the move to the knowledge economy (in particular innovation) and improve transport infrastructure are shared by all regions. An econometric model was developed to identify challenges for building competitive regions (described in Annex 1.A1). It indicates that the growth of Polish regions is driven by human capital development and proximity/access to large markets. It also shows that there is too little innovation to have a significant impact on regional performances.

The econometric model seeks to identify some factors of growth and challenges for regions. Based on earlier theoretical and empirical literature, the model focuses on variables for which data are available (at TL2 level), such as human capital, patenting and distances to markets. Although the model has to be interpreted with caution as an analysis at TL3 level would be more appropriate; the model is helpful in that it confirms a process of regional divergence (analysed in Section 1.1), fuelled mainly by differences in human capital endowments. The model indicates that regional growth is more determined by workers with secondary education than by those with university degrees. This may reflect the fact that most regions host activities with medium-level technology. It may also reveal anomalies in regional labour markets (graduates' skills may not match industrial demand). Finally, it shows that the level of patenting does not have a significant impact on regional performance, which may be linked to the fact that patenting remains low and that knowledge transfers are not well developed. The model also suggests that distances to relevant markets are determinant for regional performance. This has clear implications in terms of transport infrastructure development.

## 4.1. Human capital and innovation

### Education

Poland scores well on secondary education, but less well on tertiary education. Although Poland's tertiary education attainment has improved considerably (those with tertiary attainment increased by 140% between 1994 and 2004 in the 25-34 age group, the highest increase in the OECD area), tertiary attainment for this age group (23.2%) remains below the OECD average (31%) (Figure 1.25). For Poland as a whole, the percentage of the population with tertiary level attainment is still low: 15.6% in 2004 compared to an OECD average of 25.2% (26.4% for Spain), slightly less than Hungary (16.7%) and a bit better than the Czech Republic and Slovak Republic.

Figure 1.25. **Tertiary attainment for age group 25-34 as a percentage of the population of that age group, 2005 or latest available year**

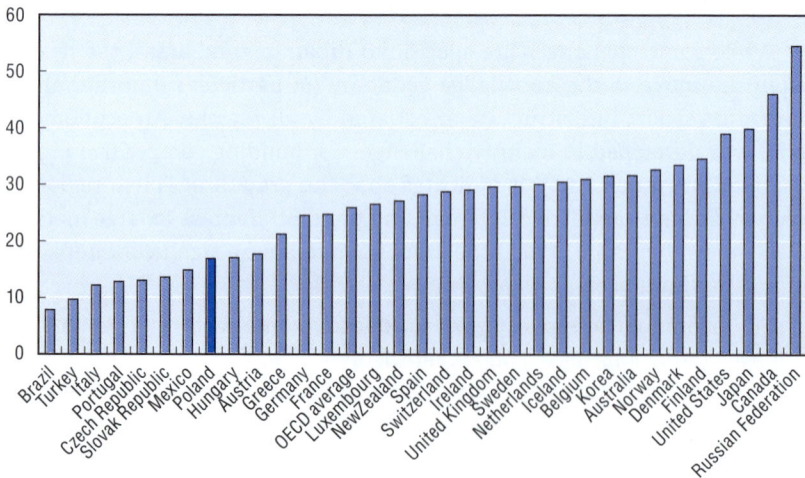

*Source:* OECD Factbook 2007.

Although regional disparities in educational attainment do not appear clearly at TL2 level (except for Mazowieckie, which stands above the other regions); it is the rural-urban gap that matters in educational attainment. As noted above, only 5.4% of the rural population has tertiary education, compared to 17.5% for the urban population (CSO, 2004). While there has been considerable progress since the late 1990s, the challenges remain huge.

Figure 1.26. **Tertiary education in Polish regions**

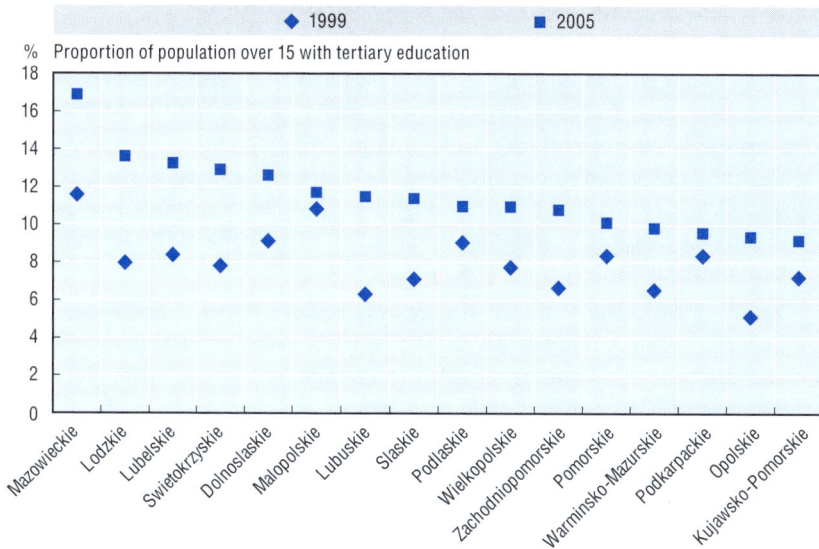

Source: Based on OECD (2008) *Regional Database.*

## Out-migration

Poland's human capital potential has been affected by out-migration since the 1990s, in particular following accession to the EU in 2004. Various estimates indicate that between 1 and 2 million Poles have left the country since 2004, mainly to go to the United Kingdom and Ireland (Box 1.8).[24] Out-migration is hard to assess as only registered migration is compiled (353 000 between 1990 and 2005). Polish migrants are generally younger and relatively better educated than the average population. The share of young people (under 35 years) among migrants grew from 51% in 2000 to 61% in 2004, and 93% of Poles entering the United Kingdom are less than 34 years old. Migrants are often overqualified for jobs they take abroad.

Due to data limitations, regional variations in out-migration are difficult to assess. However, looking back to the early 2000s, official data indicate that the regions of Slaskie and Opolskie experienced the largest flows of out-migration from 1999 to 2005. This may be linked to the high unemployment in these regions in the early 2000s. However, all Polish regions have been confronted with out-migration, and the problem is more a national than a regional challenge, as the most dynamic cities, such as Poznan, Warsaw and Wroclaw, have also lost qualified workers, leading to important shortages of staff. The latest information seems to indicate anyway a slowdown in the scale of the out-migration phenomenon. For example, the number of Poles

> ## Box 1.8. **Poland and out-migration**
>
> Emigration is not a new phenomenon in Poland. Since the 18th century, the Polish population has been quite mobile, especially to western Europe and the United States (10% of all post-war emigrants went to the United States, where the largest community of Poles is in Chicago). Under communism, Polish citizens could not easily leave the country because of restrictive passport and exit visa policies. Through the 1990s, out-migration was high and increased with entry into the European Union in 2004 and the opening of labour markets. Some estimates consider it was multiplied by ten.
>
> Analysts from the Ministry of Economy believe that the estimates by European Citizen Action Service (ECAS), an NGO, based on official statistical tables compiled by countries receiving the migrants, give the truest picture. According to ECAS, Polish economic emigrants represented some 3% of the Polish population (close to the emigration rate from Italy to other EU states). Of the 1.1 million emigrants (including recipients of seasonal work permits), the breakdown of Polish emigration by country of destination was as follows: 535 000 to Germany, 264 000 to the United Kingdom, 100 000 to Ireland; 90 000 to France, and 72 000 to Italy. Altogether, 95% of all migrants from Poland undertook work in the above five EU states, while the remaining 5% took jobs in other EU countries.
>
> Source: Ministry of Economy (2007), "Wpływ emigracji zarobkowej na gospodarkę Polski" (The Impact of Economic Emigration on the Polish Economy), February.

entering the United Kingdom in the third quarter of 2007 decreased by 18% compared to the previous year,[25] probably linked to the strong Polish zloty and the economic growth in Poland.

While out-migration has negative effects on regional economies, it may also have some positive ones. The negative effects are mainly linked to "brain waste", when the loss of qualified workers and talents leads to critical shortages (in the health and construction sectors for instance). On the other hand, there can also be "brain drain" linked to seasonal out-migration (high in Poland) and to acquisition of competencies and new networks. In addition, cash inflows (remittances) can also help to increase incomes and help develop local firms. In sum, there is a mixture of effects linked to out-migration which is complex to assess.

### R&D and innovation

Innovation is not yet a driver of regional growth. In part, this may be related to the fact that patenting is not a sufficient indicator of innovation, which is related to new processes and/or products in the market. It may also be that the links between higher education institutions (HEIs) and research centres and the entrepreneurial environment are weak, resulting in few patents for improved processes or new products. Poland lags far behind other EU and OECD countries in terms of R&D as a share of GDP. It also ranks unfavourably when compared with other countries that joined the EU in 2004. In 2004, the business sector financed only 22.6% of gross expenditure on R&D, government financing accounted for 61.7% and 5.2% was financed from abroad. Low business spending on R&D is also reflected in the structure of exports; low- and medium-technology products account for more than half of total manufacturing exports. The majority of expenditure on innovation activities in 2004 went to machinery and technical equipment (59.8%), 23.2% to building and structures, only 7.5% to R&D activities, and about 3% to the purchase of patents, licences and know-how.

According to the European Innovation Scoreboard, Poland ranks 21st among EU members for innovation (EIS, 2006). The EU index of innovation has ranked 246 regions (excluding Romania and Bulgaria). The highest ranked Polish region is Mazowieckie, which is in 155th place.[26] Other Polish regions rank well below Mazowieckie in terms of patenting (Figure 1.27) and score lower in the EU ranking.

Conditions for knowledge creation are worsening, particularly owing to a decline in business research and development, from 0.28% of GDP in 1998 to 0.15% in 2003. There is insufficient co-operation between R&D centres and business, and higher education R&D expenditures financed by the private sector diminished from 9% in 1998 to 6% in 2004, indicating that firms have not outsourced research to make up for declining R&D expenditures. There is little will to co-operate between businesses (SMEs) and research institutions,

Figure 1.27. **Patenting activity and human capital by voivodship**

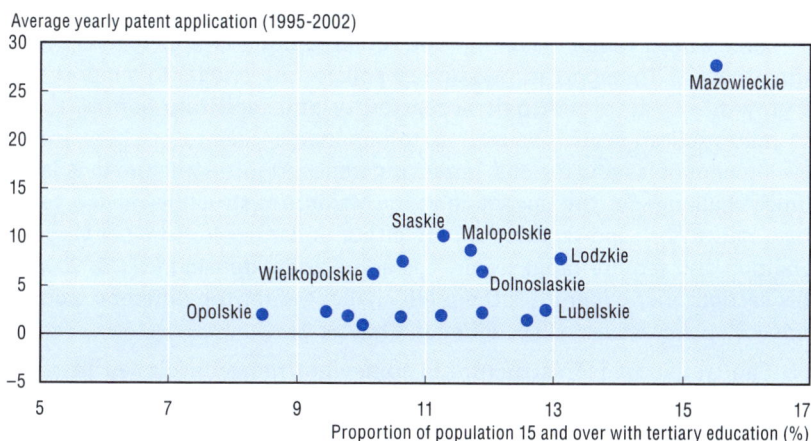

*Source:* Based on OECD (2008) *Regional Database.*

owing in part to entrepreneurs' concerns about the risk involved in investing scarce resources in research.

Although the number Polish institutions supporting innovation has grown since 2000 by 91%,[27] 55% of these offer predominantly training, advisory and information services. Only one in ten is capable of supporting innovation activities of enterprises in terms of technology transfer. Thus, the impact of these organisations remains limited. In addition, 50% of districts (powiats) and 75% of municipalities (gminas) do not have any institution supporting innovation (Ministry of Regional Development, 2007).

### Limited use of ICTs

The transition to the knowledge economy is also affected by the limited development of information and communication technologies. Although ICT expenditures are 14% above the EU average (EIS, 2006), Poland as a whole remains one of the most weakly developed EU members in terms of the use of new technologies. Even if Poland's communications infrastructure has improved greatly since 1989, progress has been uneven, with use of cellular telephones rising rapidly but the development of the land-line network progressing only slowly, especially in the countryside. For computer equipment in households, Poland remains at the bottom of the list. Only 40% have access to a home computer, behind Hungary and the Slovak Republic. In 2005, Internet access was available to 23% of Polish households (29% of urban households, 11% in rural areas) compared with 43% on average in the EU (CSO, 2005). In 2004, only 4% of individuals (the lowest figure in the EU) use the Internet for learning in the education system (schools, universities). This is five times less than in the countries where this means of acquiring education is most common: Estonia (21%), Lithuania and Finland (20% each).

### 4.2. Transport infrastructure

The second major challenge for Polish regions is linked to transport infrastructure. Transport infrastructure policies are crucial to support poles of growth – to improve their accessibility and facilitate commuting at the metropolitan scale – as well as to enhance access to markets and the development of lagging regions. Improving transport infrastructure in Poland is a huge challenge for the upcoming years. Major infrastructure-related sectors (road, railways, seaports, aviation) are either underdeveloped or in very poor condition and require rapid repair, upgrading and extension (OECD, 2008a).[28] This section briefly identifies the main challenges for the different modes of transport; policy issues will be found in Chapter 2.

The transport infrastructure is somewhat more developed in south-western Poland and relatively less so in the northern and eastern regions, in particular in the eastern part of the Lubelskie voivodship and Warminsko-Mazurskie. The network of cross-border roads is dense along the border with

Germany and the Czech Republic and sparse in areas bordering Ukraine and the Slovak Republic. The eastern border is still crossed by a number of roads at which there are no border crossings (Ministry of Regional Development, 2007).

## Roads

The poor state of the road network is one of the weakest aspects of Poland's infrastructure and a major handicap for business and economic development (Figure 1.28.). There are 99.4 km of road network per 10 000 inhabitants in Poland (the EU25 average is 145 km). In 2005, the density of Poland's road network was 1.19 km per $km^2$ of land, less than Hungary (1.73 $km/km^2$) and the Czech Republic (1.62 $km/km^2$), and far below the EU

Figure 1.28. **The road network in kilometers per million inhabitants (2004)**

Kilometres, 2004 or latest available year

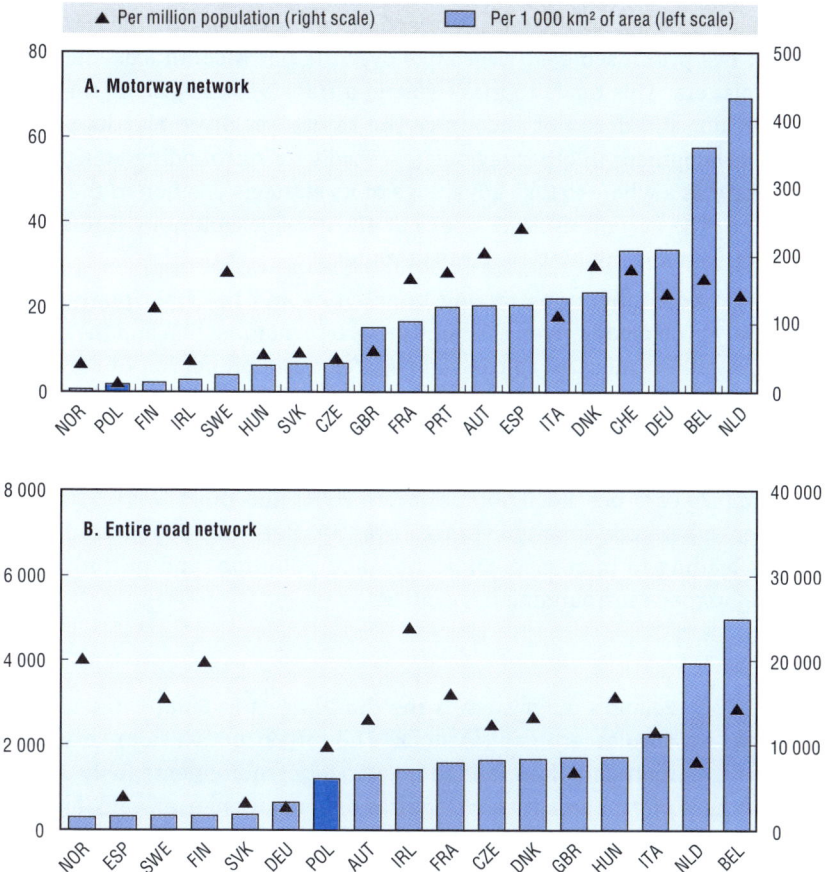

*Source:* European Commission (2007), *Panorama of Transport* and *New Chronos database* (in OECD, 2008a).

average. With 663 km of motorway, Poland has the most limited motorway network in Europe. It has only 297 km of expressways. The length of the actual network is insufficient and it lacks secondary roads.

The quality of the road network is also very problematic. Only 3% of Polish roads currently meet EU standards in terms of security and freight transport. Most roads have a load capacity of only 8 or 10 tonnes per axle, whereas 11.5 tonnes per axle is the standard that complies with EU regulations (OECD, 2008a). Traffic in the form of heavy international lorries leads to rapid deterioration of the main transit routes. Poland's situation as regards road safety is particularly alarming, as the number of people killed per 1 000 inhabitants is one of the highest in the OECD.[29]

Three major shortcomings are: i) the lack of development of roads at the functional scale of large cities (lack of ring roads, bad connections with surrounding municipalities); ii) connections between large cities (capital regions) are poor; iii) north-south connections are poor because the transport network has prioritised east-west links over the north-south axis since the communist era. This tends to make Poland a transit country along the east-west corridor and does not encourage the capital region to play its part in driving development in other regions (especially its surrounding areas) or in the country as a whole to take advantage of its strategic position in the Baltic Sea region. The current network does not allow traffic continuity throughout the country on any international transit route.

Poor road connections among large cities and their peripheries are particularly problematic given the rapid growth of motorisation and the modal shift from public transport to cars. In the 1990s, the proportion of car users rose from 40 to 72% while rail users declined from 30 to 10%. The number of cars per 1 000 population increased from 138 in 1990 to around 313 by 2004. Further growth is likely, since car density remains below the level in the Czech Republic (374 cars per 1 000 population in 2004) and most west European countries (where car density averages over 500 per 1 000 population). This trend is leading to increased congestion and pollution, and putting more pressure on roads surrounding large cities.

## Rail

Although Poland's rail system is the third largest in Europe, the railway sector has an obsolescent capital stock. The infrastructure is in very poor technical condition and often fails to meet safety requirements (only 30% of the network is of good quality and requires only maintenance work), and the bulk of the rolling stock is out-dated and/or worn out (OECD, 2008a). This leads to important speed limits as the maximum speed on 40% of the operating network is less than 80 km/h. There has been little investment in track, signalling systems and stations since the fall of communism (EIU, 2006). The lack of investment and thus the insufficient quality of service provision as well as falling demand for coal and smelting products have led to a constant decline in rail passenger and freight traffic since the beginning of the 1990s.

## Ports

Polish ports play a crucial role for the national and regional economies. Four ports are crucial for Poland's economy, in particular in the northern regions: Gdansk, Gdynia, Szczecin and Świnoujscie. The role of Szczecin, the seaport nearest to the Berlin agglomeration, has been increasing. Traffic in ferry terminals in Swinoujscie (ferries to Malmö, Ystad, Copenhagen and seasonally to Bornholm), Gdansk (to Oxelosund) and Gdynia (to Karlskrona) has been growing. Polish ports offer the advantages of better connections with landlocked central Europe (Lepesant, 2005). However, competition from German ports and eastern neighbours is rising (Table 1.1). All ports are plagued with a number of problems that severely undermine their competitiveness on the Baltic Sea. In particular, the ratio of obsolete capital stock in ports is very high, ranging from 40 to 70% (OECD, 2008a). The Scandinavian ports (Gothenburg in Sweden, Copenhagen/Malmö and Aarhus in Denmark. and Kotka in Finland) benefited from massive investment in the 1990s and ship owners from these countries acquired interests in the Baltic ports.

With the worldwide recovery of sea transport, the activity and profitability of the sector has increased since 2000 (with a decrease in 2005). Among the largest ports, some have recorded growth in transhipment volumes. The largest transhipment volumes are recorded in Gdańsk. The ports of Szczecin-Swinoujscie and Gdynia have seized new market opportunities, catering, for example, to oil tankers from the Middle East. Addressing the issue of ports' competitiveness is crucial for regional policy, in particular the question of improved connection with the hinterland and neighbouring urban areas. Although the situation is improving, three main "internal" problems affect the competitiveness of Polish ports: i) their poor connection with the neighbouring hinterland, in particular urban areas; ii) the underdevelopment of modern port services; and iii) the under-capitalisation and weak financial positions (OECD, 2008a).

## Airports

In 2005, Poland occupied 49th place worldwide in air transport although its growth was the highest in Europe. Poland has a central airport located in Warsaw and 11 regional airports. Air transport has been growing very rapidly in recent years as a consequence of sustained demand spurred by market liberalisation due to Poland's EU accession and the entry of low-cost companies (OECD, 2008a). In addition to Warsaw, fast growth was also noted in Cracow (50%

Table 1.1. **Assessment of seaports' competitiveness**

| Competitive factors of seaports | Germany | | Poland | | | Russia | Lithuania | Weight |
|---|---|---|---|---|---|---|---|---|
| | Lübeck | Rostock | Szczecin-Swinoujscie | Gdynia | Gdansk | Kaliningrad | Klaipeda | |
| Port location | | | | | | | | |
| Area | 1 | 4 | 4 | 2 | 4 | 2 | 3 | 0.07 |
| Length of piers | 3 | 1 | 4 | 4 | 3 | 1 | 4 | 0.07 |
| Acceptable vessel parameters | 2 | 3 | 3 | 3 | 5 | 2 | 3 | 0.11 |
| Increase in share in reloading activity of south Baltic seaports in 2001-06 | 3 | 3 | 1 | 4 | 4 | 5 | 4 | 0.05 |
| Development of modern reloading facilities | | | | | | | | |
| Container reloading | 2 | 0 | 1 | 5 | 2 | 2 | 3 | 0.08 |
| Ferry and ro-ro cargo reloading | 5 | 5 | 5 | 4 | 2 | 2 | 5 | 0.08 |
| Cruise ship service | 3 | 5 | 1 | 4 | 3 | 1 | 3 | 0.05 |
| Port connections to sea and land transport | | | | | | | | |
| Line navigation | 5 | 4 | 2 | 5 | 5 | 4 | 5 | 0.10 |
| Ferry navigation | 5 | 5 | 4 | 3 | 2 | 2 | 3 | 0.10 |
| International connections | 5 | 5 | 2 | 4 | 1 | 2 | 2 | 0.10 |
| Port access infrastructure | | | | | | | | |
| Road infrastructure | 5 | 4 | 3 | 3 | 3 | 2 | 2 | 0.11 |
| Inland navigation | 3 | 0 | 4 | 0 | 2 | 0 | 0 | 0.08 |
| **Average grade** | **3.65** | **3.32** | **2.92** | **3.40** | **3.00** | **2.07** | **3.03** | $\Sigma = 1$ |

Notes: 0 = nil competitive position. 5 = high competitive position.
Source: Ministry of Maritime Economy (2007), *Seaports Development Strategy until 2015*.

increase in 2006 compared to 2005), Katowice (by 33%), Gdansk (by 87%), and Poznan (by 63%). There is considerable scope for further development of the air transport industry as the number of travellers using Polish airports is expected to grow by three and a half times by 2020 (Ministry of Transport, 2007). The key priorities in terms of regional development are to support the expansion of selected regional airports and to develop quick and efficient road and railway connections between airports and nearby urban centres and national road and railway networks, as most of them are of poor quality (OECD, 2008a).

## Conclusion

The development of transport infrastructure is a priority for regional development and competitiveness. However, what counts most is not how many kilometres are built but where these are built and how strategic they are in terms of linking investments to local opportunities and needs. This requires careful evaluations of rural-urban linkages and robust calculations on migrations trends and service delivery targets. The main challenges for public policy are discussed in Chapter 2.

## Notes

1. However, 1989 is an atypical year, as it was the year of a change in the political regime. It was also the lowest point of a decade-long crisis during the 1980s. Therefore, comparing a particularly low point in the Polish economy and a particularly high performance in 2006 might appear misleading. Nevertheless, the Polish economy grew significantly over the last 15 years.

2. Poland is the most populated country to have entered the European Union in 2004.

3. More than a third of Polish children scored higher than the average mathematics score for Switzerland, the highest ranked country (OECD, 2006c).

4. 17% according to the 2006 OECD Economic Survey of Poland; 15.8% according to the latest official statistical data in Poland (for 2006). See Section 1.4.

5. Structural Changes of Groups of Businesses in Poland, 2006, GUS, Warsaw, 2007.

6. For enterprises with less than 49 employees (CSO, 2008).

7. Although labour costs have risen (from 17% of the EU average in 1997 to 28.4% in 2005), it will take time before they are aligned on western EU countries.

8. If small projects (less than EUR 1 million) are taken into account, Germany is the largest investor in Poland, especially on the western Polish border. In this area, many clothing or mechanical products undergo "passive transformation". Raw materials are exported from Germany to Polish workshops, where they are finished and re-exported to Germany where they are sold.

9. Exports growth doubled from EUR 34.4 billion in 2000 to EUR 71.4 billion in 2005. In 2005, EU nations accounted for 77.2% of Polish exports and 65.6% of the total value of imports. Apart from Germany, other major trade partners are: Russia, Czech Republic, United Kingdom, Ukraine, France, China and Belgium.

10. Although Mazowieckie stands now above the GDP per capita threshold of less than 75% of the EU average.

11. The eastern and northern parts of Mazowieckie are mainly rural, with low economic growth (except for Ostroleka). In the southern part of the region, Radom suffers from industrial restructuring and lost large firms in various sectors in the 1990s.

12. Based on the standard deviation of logged values of per capita GDP.

13. In its Regional Development and Urban Revitalization Project. A Feasibility Study, the Centre for European Regional and Local Studies (2005) has identified five crisis areas, insisting on the fact that those that have suffered the most have fewer than 30 000 inhabitants: the southern part of Lower Silesia (with Walbrzych); the central part of Western Pomerania; the eastern part of Mazowieckie (with Siedlce); the area bordering the Lodz region and Great Poland; and the northern part of the Swietokrzyskie region (with Starachowice).

14. OECD (2008a), *Economic Survey of Poland*.

15. These data are given at TL2 as data at TL3 levels on man-hours worked is not available.

16. Companies that have invested in the region include France Telecom, Citigroup, Gazprom, Vivendi, UniCredito Italiano and Nestlé.

17. The increase in housing prices in Poland is part of a wider phenomenon, which affects many OECD countries and all transition economies in central and Eastern Europe (CEE).

18. 35% of the population lives in predominantly rural areas, according to the OECD definition based on a population density of up to 150 people per km$^2$. Rural areas occupy more than 93.2% of the Polish territory (CSO 2005). According to the CSO definition, 38% of the Polish population lives in rural areas; according to the EU definition (population density of up to 100 people per km$^2$), 32.8% of the population lives in rural areas.

19. Polish agriculture's marked resistance to change has deep historical roots, as the peasant has been the traditional representative of resistance against the occupant. Agriculture is an essential component of the national perception of historical continuity, with Catholicism.

20. The influence of the partition of Poland in the 19th century is still felt to some extent.

21. Eastern Poland is defined as the five voivodships in the eastern part of the country: Podkarpackie, Lubelskie, Podlaskie and Warminsko-Mazurskie Voivodships plus the Swiętokrzyskie Voivodship which is also classified in this group.

22. Hidden unemployment is the unemployment of potential workers that is not reflected in official unemployment statistics, owing to the way the statistics are collected. In many countries only those who have no work but are actively seeking work (and/or qualifying for social security benefits) are counted as unemployed. Those who have given up looking for work (and sometimes those who are on government "retraining" programmes) are not officially counted among the unemployed, even though they are not employed. The same applies to those who took early retirement to avoid being laid off, but would prefer to be working.

23. In this section, rural areas refer to the CSO definition of "rural", unless stated explicitly.

24. From 1 May 2004, Polish nationals were allowed to work without restrictions in the new member states (with the exception of Malta), while only the United Kingdom, Ireland and Sweden in the EU15 opened their labour markets to Poles. The following additional countries abolished labour market restrictions for Polish nationals on 1 May 2006: Spain, Portugal, Greece and Finland; Italy followed in July 2006, and the Netherlands in May 2007. The labour market restrictions for Germany and Austria should be lifted in 2011 at the latest.

25. More UK-based Poles are returning to Poland than are entering Britain (The Times, February 2008). *www.timesonline.co.uk/tol/news/uk/article3378877.ece*.

26. London and Stockholm take first and second place.

27. In 2005 44 centres of technology transfer, 7 technology incubators, 18 academic business incubators and 8 science parks *i.e.* 77 innovation centres were operating and 86 were under construction.

28. For more detail on transport infrastructure, see *OECD Economic Survey of Poland* (2008).

29. 138 road fatalities for one million inhabitants, compared to 49 in Sweden (OECD, 2008c).

APPENDIX 1

# Methodological Note: Poland in the OECD Regional Database

## Regional grids

- The OECD has classified regions within each member country. The classifications are based on two Territorial Levels (TL). The higher level (Territorial Level 2) consists of 335 macro-regions while the lower level (Territorial Level 3) is composed of 1 679 micro-regions.

### MAP OF TL2 and TL3 IN POLAND

**Territorial level 2: 16 voivodships**
**Territorial level 3: 45 sub-regions**

| | | | |
|---|---|---|---|
| **PL11** | **LODZKIE** | **PL41** | **WIELKOPOLSKIE** |
| PL111 | Lódzki | PL411 | Pilski |
| PL112 | Piotrkowsko-Skierniewicki | PL412 | Poznanski |
| PL113 | Miasto Lódz | PL413 | Kaliski |
| **PL12** | **MAZOWIECKIE** | PL414 | Koninski |
| PL121 | Ciechanowsko-Plocki | PL415 | Miasto Poznan |
| PL122 | Ostrolecko-Siedlecki | **PL42** | **ZACHODNIOPOMORSKIE** |
| PL124 | Radomski | PL421 | Szczecinski |
| PL126 | Warszawski | PL422 | Koszalinski |
| PL127 | Miasto Warszawa | **PL43** | **LUBUSKIE** |
| **PL21** | **MALOPOLSKIE** | PL431 | Gorzowski |
| PL211 | Krakowsko-Tarnowski | PL432 | Zielonogórski |
| PL212 | Nowosadecki | **PL51** | **DOLNOSLASKIE** |
| PL213 | Miasto Kraków | PL511 | Jeleniogórsko-Walbrzyski |
| **PL22** | **SLASKIE** | PL512 | Legnicki |
| PL224 | Czestochowski | PL513 | Wroclawski |
| PL225 | Bielsko-Bialski | PL514 | Miasto Wroclaw |
| PL226 | Centralny slaski | **PL52** | **OPOLSKIE** |
| PL227 | Rybnicko-Jastrzebski | PL520 | Opolski |
| **PL31** | **LUBELSKIE** | **PL61** | **KUJAWSKO-POMORSKIE** |
| PL311 | Bialskopodlaski | PL611 | Bydgoski |
| PL312 | Chelmsko-Zamojski | PL612 | Torunsko-Wloclawski |
| PL313 | Lubelski | **PL62** | **WARMINSKO-MAZURSKIE** |
| **PL32** | **PODKARPACKIE** | PL621 | Elblaski |
| PL321 | Rzeszowsko-tTarnobrzeski | PL622 | Olsztynski |
| PL322 | Krosniensko-Przemyski | PL623 | Elcki |
| **PL33** | **SWIETOKRZYSKIE** | **PL63** | **POMORSKIE** |
| PL330 | Swietokrzyski | PL631 | Slupski |
| **PL34** | **PODLASKIE** | PL632 | Gdanski |
| PL341 | Bialostocko-Suwalski | PL633 | Gdansk-Gdynia-Sopot |
| PL342 | Lomzynski | | |

- This classification – which, for European countries, is largely consistent with the Eurostat classification – facilitates greater comparability of regions at the same territorial level. Indeed, these two levels, which are officially established and relatively stable in all member countries, are used by many as a framework for implementing regional policies.

- TL2 and TL3 levels in Poland correspond to NUTS 2 and NUTS 3 (Eurostat classification)

- There are 16 TL2 levels in Poland, corresponding to the administrative perimeters of regions (voivodships) and 45 TL3 (sub-regions), which are different classification from the counties (powiats).

## OECD regional typology

- A second important issue for the analysis of regional economies concerns the different "geography" of each region. The OECD has established a regional typology according to which TL3 regions have been classified as predominantly urban, predominantly rural and intermediate. This typology, based on the percentage of regional population living in rural or urban communities, enables meaningful comparisons between regions belonging to the same type and level.

- The OECD Regional Typology classifies regions into three categories: predominantly rural (more than 50% of the population living in rural communities), intermediate (between 15-50%) or predominantly urban (less than 15%). A rural community is a community with a population density below 150 inhabitants/km$^2$.

- The OECD Regional Database classifies Poland into:
  - ❖ 8 predominantly urban sub-regions;
  - ❖ 15 intermediate sub-regions;
  - ❖ 22 predominantly-rural sub-regions.

  Following this classification, the population of Poland is divided into:
- 22% living in predominantly urban regions;
- 39% living in intermediate regions;
- 39% living in predominantly rural regions.

**MAP OECD REGIONAL TYPOLOGY**

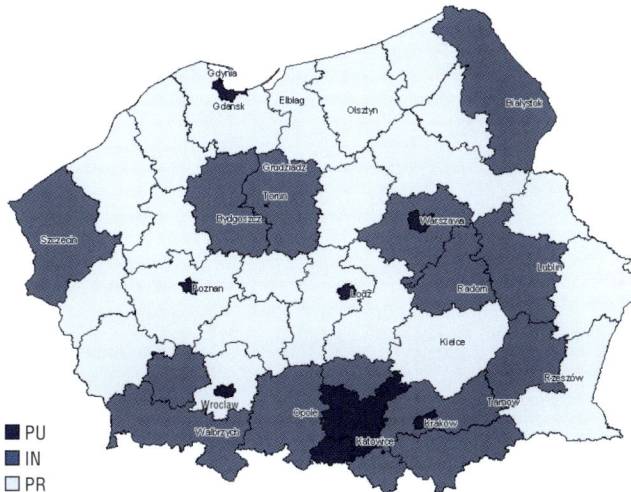

## Urban areas in Poland

Eight predominantly urban areas are identified: Poznan, Cracow, Lodz, Warsaw, Wroclaw, Gdansk-Gdynia-Sopot, Centralny Slaski (Katowice-functional area) and Rybnicko-Jastrzêbski. The other cities fit into the category: "Intermediate areas."

OECD TERRITORIAL REVIEWS: POLAND – ISBN 978-92-64-04926-0 – © OECD 2008

ANNEX 1.A1

# Econometric Model to Measure Regional Economic Growth

An econometric model to measure regional economic growth was developed using the following equation:

$Y_t = f(y_{t0}, K_0, H_{t0}, m, \text{innov}_{t0}, \text{disGER}, \text{disWSW}, G_0)$

Where:

$Y_t$ = real GDP per capita growth

$y_{t0}$ = real per capita GDP at the beginning of the period

$K_0$ = logged values of total (private and public) investment at the beginning of the period

$H_{t0}$ = school attainment (log of number of students in particular schooling levels)

m = international out-migration rates

$\text{innov}_{t0}$ = Logged values of number of patents in each region at the beginning of the period.

disGER = logged values of the distance in kms from each *voiovodship* capital to the nearest border town with Germany.

disWSW = logged values of the distance in kms from each *voiovodship* capital to Warsaw

$G_0$ = logged values of public expenditure at the beginning of the period

The above model addresses both absolute and conditional convergence. Whereas the first type only explores the direction and speed of convergence/ divergence, the latter also explores the reasons for such convergence, so that the process is conditional on the factors included in the model. As in any absolute convergence model, the variable that measures convergence is the initial GDP per capita level ($Y_t$). Therefore, a positive sign in the coefficient would signal that richer regions are growing faster and hence, a process of divergence is in motion. Alternatively, a negative sign in the coefficient would evince a process of convergence whereby poorer regions are growing faster.

The model, in line with both neo-classical and endogenous growth theories, also tries to explore whether capital and/or human capital spur growth. Different variables were tested for different levels of schooling; thus, $H_{t0}$ was in the model tested with the variables *prim*, *sec* and *tert* that were included as logged values of students in primary, secondary and tertiary education respectively. Another crucial element of endogenous growth theories, namely innovation ($innov_{t0}$) is also included in the model by using patents as a proxy for innovation.

In order to test whether migration has been having an impact on the performance of regions, different migration rates were included in the model among which: total international out-migrants as a proportion of population (*m*), as well as those with primary (*mp*), secondary (*ms*) and tertiary (*mt*) education. Both, schooling and migration variables were included to identify what type of skills have been driving economic growth in Polish regions, as well as to clarify what type of out-migrants are having the greatest impact on regional economies.

One of the salient features of the New Economic Geography is that proximity to the relevant market matters. As Poland had recently joined the EU, the model is also useful to measure the extent to which there has been a shift in the relevant market from the dominant market of Warsaw to the EU. In order to test these ideas, the model includes also variables that incorporate distances to Warsaw (*disWSW*) and the border to Germany (*disGER*) as a proxy for the EU.

Finally, public expenditure is also considered as a variable to explain regional economic growth. The variable (*G*) is introduced as the initial level of public resources spent in each *voivodship* at the beginning of the period. The variable will capture the extent to which some policies might be shaping regional economic growth.

The reader should be aware of some caveats of the model. While the best effort was made to include all available variables, some of them are missing in the model and could bear importantly in the power of our tests as they may imply a misspecification error. In addition, due to the lack of data at TL3 level, the model focuses on TL2 level data, which gives a less precise picture of factors of growth.

The results show that there is little evidence of convergence or divergence as the tests are not statistically significant in the vast majority of the models using the full sample. The economic performance of Warsaw has led its region, Mazowieckie to be an outlier for this exercise. Therefore, a second exercise was carried out using a sample excluding Mazowieckie albeit its impact on the already small sample and the degrees of freedom on the residuals.

In addition, the high levels of model fit (by the results in the adjusted $R^2$) and lack of significance in virtually any of the coefficients, as well as the high levels in some of the variables of the VIF indicator signal the model has clearly a problem of severe multi-colinearity. The table of correlations also showed strong influence of the initial capital variable over those of human capital and to a lesser extent on initial income. However, little can be done to address the violation of the OLS assumption of no significant relationship among independent variables. Although in the models that exclude Mazowieckie from the sample, initial capital will still be considered, will later be removed from the model if found to remain an offending variable as some of its effect should be captured by initial income, so as to avoid model misspecification problems.

The models using the reduced sample (excluding Warsaw) show that the process of divergence is statistically significant but only if such models include tertiary education and either migration of unskilled or skilled workers (primary or tertiary education but not secondary). Regional performance in Poland seem to be mainly explained by schooling at secondary level; whereas tertiary education may render better regional performances in the future, with the right adjustments in regional labour markets – by matching skills and industrial demands for instance. It is also important to note that innovation is not yet a driver of regional growth in none of the models tested. In part, the result might be related to the fact that patenting does not mean innovation which is related to new processes and/or products in the market. It might also be that the links between Higher Education Institutes (HEI) and research centres with the entrepreneurial environment are weak resulting in few patents producing processes improvements or new products in the market.

Another important condition for regional economic growth is the level of international out-migrants. The lack of performance in poorer regions may be partly associated by the fact that these regions are losing relatively less skilled workers to other countries in the EU, which may push wages in the region upwards along with firms overall cost structures. However, the fact that lost population may arithmetically help the GDP per capita indicator should not be ignored.

Finally, the model suggests that distances to the relevant market may explain around 40% of the model fitness. Although the variable that portrays distance to EU markets was not found to shed meaningful figures, the one for Warsaw improves the model significantly. That is not only explained by sheer access to final consumers, but also additional costs for firms that need to be closer to buyers and suppliers along a value chain (backward and forward linkages). Transport and infrastructure policies are therefore crucial in changing territorial imbalances in Poland.

## Table 1.A1.1. OLS regression results (full sample)

Results for the 1995-2004 period

| | (1) | (2) | (3) | (4) | (5) | (6) | (7) | (8) | (9) | (10) | (11) | (12) | (13) | (14) | (15) |
|---|---|---|---|---|---|---|---|---|---|---|---|---|---|---|---|
| $\beta_0$ | -0.158 (-1.188) | 0.040 (0.323) | 0.186 (1.546) | 0.610 (2.655)[1] | 0.592 (2.467)[1] | 0.265 (1.843) | 0.132 (0.918) | 0.128 (0.857) | 0.157 (1.201) | 0.168 (1.019) | 0.145 (1.025) | 0.177 (1.015) | 0.295 (1.487) | 0.415 (1.371) | 0.137 (1.692) |
| $Y_0$ | 0.021 (1.482) | 0.000 (-0.021) | -0.023 (-1.585) | -0.052 (-2.75)[1] | -0.052 (-2.58)[1] | -0.029 (-1.85) | -0.016 (-0.910) | -0.015 (-0.848) | -0.019 (-1.176) | -0.020 (-1.015) | -0.016 (-0.875) | -0.022 (-1.101) | -0.032 (-1.598) | -0.028 (-1.018) | – |
| WSW | – | 0.025 (3.039)[2] | 0.016 (2.006) | 0.003 (0.319) | 0.001 (0.066) | 0.014 (1.795) | 0.015 (1.873) | 0.015 (1.862) | 0.015 (1.93) | 0.015 (1.745) | -0.047 (-0.448) | 0.015 (1.834) | 0.021 (1.918) | -0.138 (-1.274) | -0.016 (-0.99) |
| $K_0$ | – | – | 0.008 (2.476)[1] | 0.029 (2.754)[1] | 0.03 (2.497)[1] | 0.015 (1.95) | 0.007 (1.855) | 0.007 (1.79) | 0.007 (1.938) | 0.007 (1.936) | 0.007 (2.219)[1] | 0.008 (2.109) | 0.014 (1.493) | 0.03 (2.382)[1] | 0.018 (1.962) |
| prim | – | – | – | -0.025 (-2.082) | – | – | – | – | – | – | – | – | – | – | – |
| sec | – | – | – | – | -0.026 (-1.9) | – | – | – | – | – | – | – | – | -0.027 (-1.822) | -0.032 (-2.01) |
| tert | – | – | – | – | – | -0.007 (-1.00) | – | – | – | – | – | – | – | – | – |
| m | – | – | – | – | – | – | -1.309 (-0.718) | – | – | – | – | – | – | – | – |
| mp | – | – | – | – | – | – | – | -5.043 (-0.694) | – | – | – | – | – | – | – |
| ms | – | – | – | – | – | – | – | – | -9.511 (-0.669) | – | – | – | – | -15.952 (-1.068) | -30.025 (-2.15) |
| mt | – | – | – | – | – | – | – | – | – | -53.6 (-0.165) | – | – | – | – | – |
| disWSW | – | – | – | – | – | – | – | – | – | – | -0.003 (-0.599) | – | – | -0.007 (-1.279) | – |

Table 1.A1.1. **OLS regression results (full sample)** (cont.)

Results for the 1995-2004 period

| | (1) | (2) | (3) | (4) | (5) | (6) | (7) | (8) | (9) | (10) | (11) | (12) | (13) | (14) | (15) |
|---|---|---|---|---|---|---|---|---|---|---|---|---|---|---|---|
| ***disGER*** | – | – | – | – | – | – | – | – | – | – | – | 0.000 (0.077) | – | – | .004 (2.133) |
| ***G*** | – | – | – | – | – | – | – | – | – | – | – | – | -0.009 (-0.7) | – | 0.015 (1.399) |
| ***innov95*** | – | – | – | – | – | – | – | – | – | – | – | – | – | 0.000 (-0.822) | – |
| **Adj R²** | 0.074 | 0.417 | 0.582 | 0.673 | 0.657 | 0.582 | 0.564 | 0.563 | 0.562 | 0.545 | 0.558 | 0.544 | 0.563 | 0.639 | 0.628 |
| **F** | 2.196 | 6.362[1] | 7.96[2] | 8.713[2] | 8.170[2] | 6.226[2] | 5.858[2] | 5.832[2] | 5.807[2] | 5.493[1] | 5.74[2] | 5.477[1] | 5.839[2] | 4.795[1] | 5.22[1] |
| ***df*** | 14 | 13 | 12 | 11 | 11 | 11 | 11 | 11 | 11 | 11 | 11 | 11 | 11 | 8 | 10 |
| ***d*** | 1.388 | 1.885 | 1.447[3] | 1.935 | 1.972[3] | 1.214[3] | 1.695[3] | 1.699[3] | 1.734[3] | 1.483[3] | 1.36[3] | 1.42[3] | 1.598[3] | 2.118[3] | 2.102 |
| **Collinearity** | – | No | Borderline | Yes | Yes | Yes | Yes | Yes | Yes | Yes | Yes | Yes | Yes | Yes | Yes |

1. Significant at the 95% level.
2. Significant at the 99% level.
3. Some evidence of autocorrelation (indecision zone).

*Source:* Own calculations.

Col-linearity in the models that show the best performance is no longer a problem when removing initial capital. Although there might be some evidence of autocorrelation as many of the models lay in the indecision zone using the Durbin-Watson indicator, there is no definite proof of it being a problem. However, running a plot to test heteroskedasticity using standardised residuals of the linear regression and the level of initial income in 2000, shows that variances are not distributed homogeneously.

In order to fix heteroskedasticity, a Weighted Least Squares (WLS) Model was used. If the full sample is included no significant variables are found and the model fit is rather poor. However, excluding the region of Warsaw yields the same results as in OLS only the results are statistically significant for all variables that were found to be associated in OLS. Once again, innovation is not associated to regional growth perhaps due to poor links between research and entrepreneurial activity or simply due to the fact that patenting does not mean innovation in the market.

The WLS model was based on weights using initial income in 2000 as the weighting variable. The only significant differences are that using WLS instead of OLS all types of international out-migrants are associated to performance, not only secondary-education workers. It is also notable that secondary education is behind growth trends whereas tertiary education is not; a feature that reinforces the argument about regional labour markets not working properly to seize skills in graduates. Similarly the links between research and entrepreneurial environment should be addressed as perhaps that could be the way to unleash the potential impact of innovation on growth. The importance of Warsaw is still confirmed by the results in WLS.

Table 1.A1.2. **WLS regression results**

For the 2000-2004 period

| | (1) | (2) | (3) | (4) | (5) | (6) | (7) | (8) | (9) | (10) |
|---|---|---|---|---|---|---|---|---|---|---|
| $\beta_0$ | 0.072 | −0.078 | −0.228 | 0.149 | 0.121 | 0.066 | 0.053 | 0.004 | −0.076 | 0.004 |
| | (0.624) | (−0.775) | (−1.893) | (1.077) | (1.019) | (0.464) | (0.463) | (0.036) | (−0.689) | (0.034) |
| $Y_0$ | −0.014 | 0.013 | 0.023 | −0.024 | −0.02 | −0.004 | −0.004 | 0.002 | 0.013 | 0.002 |
| | (−1.042) | (0.96) | (1.593) | (−1.338) | (−1.417) | (−0.236) | (−0.246) | (0.163) | (0.904) | (0.124) |
| prim | − | − | − | − | − | − | − | − | − | − |
| sec | 0.008 | 0.005 | −0.001 | 0.009 | 0.009 | − | 0.007 | 0.005 | 0.005 | 0.006 |
| | (1.565) | (1.291) | (−0.243) | (1.516) | (1.758) | | (1.592) | (1.287) | (1.146) | (0.602) |
| tert | − | − | − | − | − | 0.0002 | − | − | − | − |
| | | | | | | (0.004) | | | | |
| m | − | − | − | − | − | − | − | 4.181 | − | 4.177 |
| | | | | | | | | (2.622)[1] | | (2.486)[1] |
| mp | − | − | − | − | 15.104 | − | − | − | − | − |
| | | | | | (2.062) | | | | | |
| ms | 30.186 | 39.734 | 20.451 | − | − | − | − | − | 39.661 | |
| | (1.923) | (3.23)[2] | (1.76) | | | | | | (3.049)[1] | |
| mt | − | − | − | 489.68 | − | − | 766.96 | − | − | − |
| | | | | (1.323) | | | (2.483)[1] | | | |
| disWSW | 0.000 | −0.015 | − | − | − | − | −0.015 | −0.012 | −0.015 | −0.012 |
| | (−0.795) | (−3.1)[1] | | | | | (−2.766)[1] | (−2.402)[1] | (−2.9)[1] | (−2.09) |
| disGER | − | − | 0.007 | − | − | − | − | − | − | − |
| | | | (3.409)[2] | | | | | | | |
| $innov_{00}$ | − | − | − | − | − | − | − | − | 0.0003 | − |
| | | | | | | | | | (0.071) | |
| G | − | − | − | − | − | − | − | − | − | −0.001 |
| | | | | | | | | | | −0.107 |
| Adj $R^2$ | 0.069 | 0.498 | 0.545 | −0.018 | 0.149 | −0.159 | 0.366 | 0.392 | 0.443 | 0.326 |
| F | 1.278 | 4.473[1] | 5.187[1] | 0.917 | 1.816 | 0.041 | 3.017 | 3.26 | 3.224 | 2.352 |
| df | 10 | 10 | 10 | 11 | 11 | 12 | 10 | 10 | 9 | 9 |
| d | 2.666[3] | 3.06[3] | 2.155[3] | 2.914[3] | 2.922[3] | 2.526[3] | 3.046[3] | 3.252[3] | 3.046[3] | 3.258[3] |
| N | 16 | 15 | 15 | 15 | 15 | 15 | 15 | 15 | 15 | 15 |
| Collinearity | No | No | No | No | No | No | No | No | No | No |

1. Significant at the 95% level.
2. Significant at the 99% level.
3. Some evidence of autocorrelation (indecision zone).
*Source:* Own calculations.

ANNEX 1.A2

# Industrial Specialisations
# of Polish Regions

Figure 1.A2.1. **Specialisation changes and employment in Wielkopolskie**

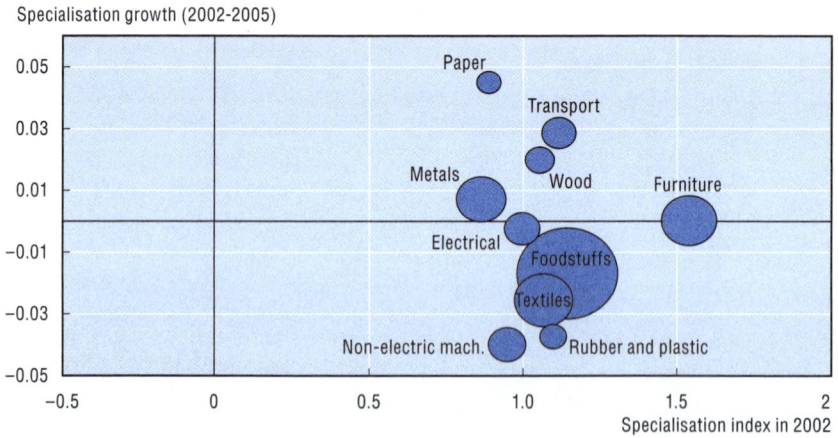

Specialisation growth (2002-2005)

*Note:* Specialisation Indexes are built using relative employment industry-specific figures in Poland with respect to total manufacturing employment. Growth in specialisation refers to average annual growth rates in specialisation indexes between 2002 and 2005. Bubble shows size of the industry in terms of employment

*Source:* Based on CSO (2008).

Figure 1.A2.2. **Specialisation changes and employment in Slaskie**

Specialisation growth (2002-2005)

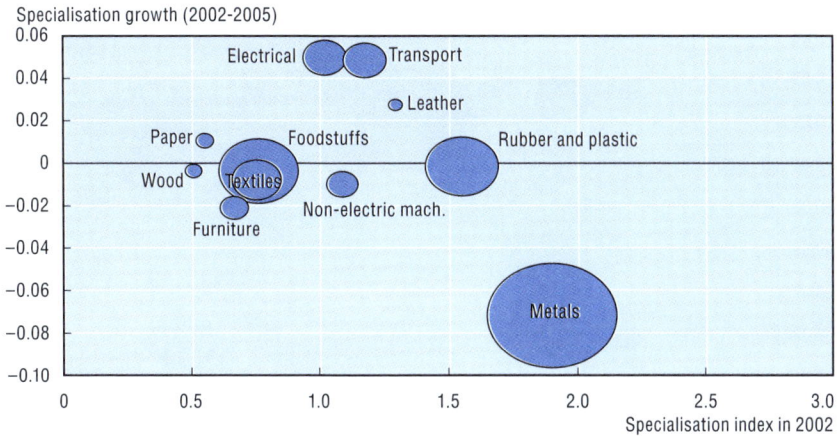

Note: Specialisation Indexes are built using relative employment industry-specific figures in Poland with respect to total manufacturing employment. Growth in specialisation refers to average annual growth rates in specialisation indexes between 2002 and 2005. Bubble shows size of the industry in terms of employment.

Source: Based on CSO (2008).

Figure 1.A2.3. **Specialisation changes and employment in Mazowieckie**

Specialisation growth (2002-2005)

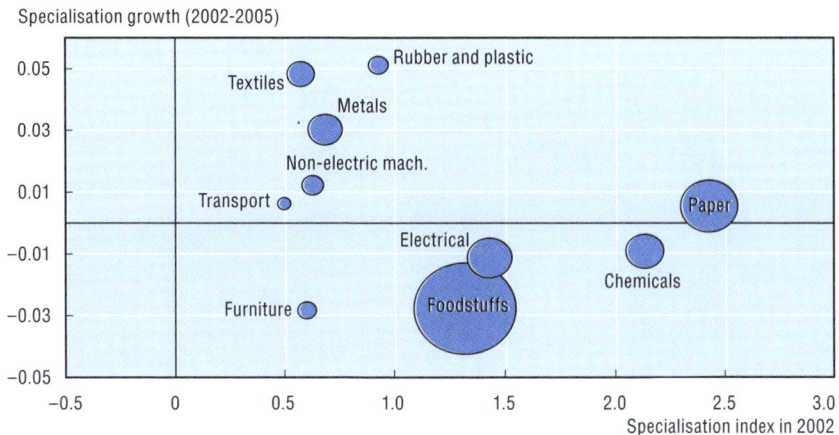

Note: Specialisation Indexes are built using relative employment industry-specific figures in Poland with respect to total manufacturing employment. Growth in specialisation refers to average annual growth rates in specialisation indexes between 2002 and 2005. Bubble shows size of the industry in terms of employment.

Source: Based on CSO (2008).

Figure 1.A2.4. **Specialisation changes and employment in Malopolskie**

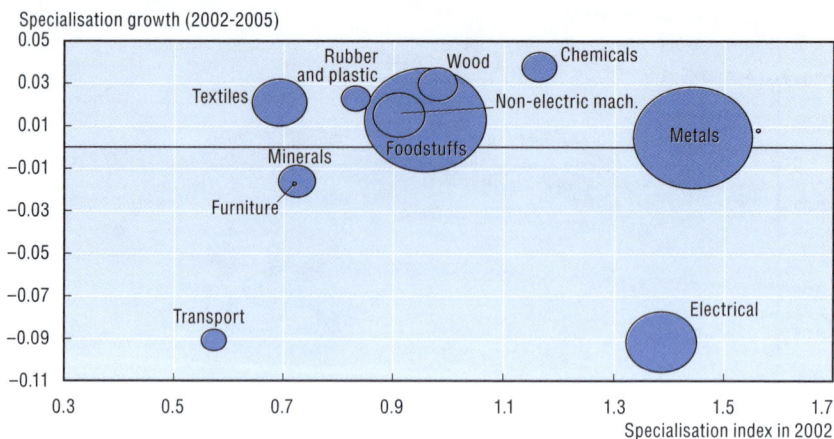

Specialisation growth (2002-2005)

Specialisation index in 2002

*Note:* Specialisation Indexes are built using relative employment industry-specific figures in Poland with respect to total manufacturing employment. Growth in specialisation refers to average annual growth rates in specialisation indexes between 2002 and 2005. Bubble shows size of the industry in terms of employment.

*Source:* Based on CSO (2008).

ISBN 978-92-64-04926-0
OECD Territorial Reviews: Poland
© OECD 2008

# Chapter 2

# Assessing Policies for Regional Development

High growth, foreign capital attractiveness as well as support from EU funds (EUR 67 billion from the cohesion policy) give Poland a unique opportunity to tackle the regional development challenge, and focus on the untapped potential of poles of growth and lagging regions. The broad policy-mix for regional development that Poland has developed since 2004 is well balanced – toward infrastructure investment and competitiveness objectives – and targets Lisbon objectives (i.e. growth objectives) as a key priority for 2007-13 (with more than 64% of the EU funding). As in many other OECD countries, regional policy in Poland has increasingly shifted towards boosting regions' competitiveness by focusing on intangible assets such as human capital. The learning process in Poland has been rapid, as regional policy has mainly developed after the creation of regions in 1999 and the accession to the EU in 2004. Although regional policy in Poland targets the right challenges and has made substantial progress in terms of institutional co-ordination, progress is yet to be made to tailor the policy mix to each region's specific needs, both at the central and regional levels. Besides, challenges related to prioritisation of public investment, short timeframe to absorb the funds and multi-level governance will be determinant to best implement the policy-mix. Chapter 2 analyses the policy-mix for regional development introduced in Poland and the challenges that remain. Four main policy issues are analysed: i) infrastructure policy, in particular transport policy and spatial planning; ii) human capital and innovation; iii) rural development policy; iv) Eastern Poland development and cross-border policies.

## Introduction

High growth, foreign capital attractiveness as well as support from EU funds (EUR 85 billion for 2007-13, including EUR 67 billion from the cohesion policy) give Poland a unique opportunity to tackle the regional development challenge, and focus on the untapped potential of poles of growth and lagging regions. Given the wide variety of development paths across Polish regions, one-fits all sectoral policies are not the best options to better exploit comparative advantages in all parts of the national territory.

As in many other OECD countries, regional policy in Poland has increasingly shifted towards boosting regions' competitiveness by focusing on intangible assets such as human capital and tapping into unexploited resources and assets. This approach, characterised as a "paradigm shift" by the OECD, is also reflected in the new EU regional policy (2007-13) based on the Lisbon agenda, which focuses on growth-oriented activities (notably employment, education, innovation, R&D). In Poland, 64% of expenditures for the 2007-13 programming period have been earmarked for Lisbon-related objectives. However, Lisbon objectives are general and can potentially apply to many different types of policy options, so the policy impact will mainly depend on how the strategy is implemented in practice, in collaboration with local actors and based on partnerships with the private sector. Although regional policy in Poland targets the right challenges and has made substantial progress in terms of institutional co-ordination, progress is yet to be made to tailor the policy mix to each region's specific needs, both at the central and regional levels.

This chapter focuses on the broad policy mix for regional development: it analyses the ambitious regional development policy introduced by the central government, the way it has been tailored to various territorial needs, and the challenges that remain. Section 1 discusses the new trends in Polish regional development policy. Then, the outline of the chapter follows the main challenges for regional development which were identified in Chapter 1. Section 2 analyses the infrastructure dimension – the main priority in terms of funds allocation – and the needs for improved spatial planning, Section 3 focuses on human capital and innovation. Section 4 explores the strategy for rural development and the need to enhance its territorial dimension. Finally, Section 5 discusses the programme for Eastern Poland development and cross-border policies.

## 1. Large window of opportunity to enhance regional development

The learning process as regards regional policy has been rapid. Poland has had to develop its regional policy very quickly, owing to the time constraints on the absorption of EU funds. Given this, the overall framework for regional policy can be assessed as being well designed and balanced. However, the challenge of implementing a multi-sectoral strategy tailored to various territorial needs remains.

### 1.1. From traditional territorial policy to a more dynamic regional policy

#### From a focus on lagging regions...

Before 1999, Poland's territorial policy consisted of specific efforts to support lagging regions, in particular industrial regions in the process of restructuring (OECD, 1993). The central government was in charge of territorial policy (regions as such did not exist administratively at the time). An important step in territorial development policy was the creation in 1994 of special economic zones (SEZ) in areas with structural unemployment and undergoing industrial restructuring. These zones still exist, and are mainly located in the vicinity of major cities (Box 2.1). They have proven quite effective in attracting foreign direct investment (FDI), enhancing technology transfers and, to a lesser extent, creating employment (mainly in the SEZ of Katowice and Walbrzych). However, they have drawbacks, as they mainly rely on costly tax exemptions. In any case, the SEZ are not a viable long-term strategy, as the EU has asked Poland to end special tax exemptions in 2017. Another dimension of early territorial policy involved support (with specific grants) to certain industrial regions with critically high unemployment, particularly small and medium cities like Ostrowiec Swiętokrzyski, Starachowice, and Inowrocław.

#### ... To a more dynamic regional approach

A more dynamic regional policy has emerged in the 2000s from two closely linked institutional processes: first, the creation of the 16 Polish regions (voivodships) in 1999 (with responsibilities, among others, for economic strategy, water management, health and higher education); second, accession to the European Union in 2004 and support from EU funds (both pre-accession aid and structural funds). Regional development has become, partly under the influence of the EU, a key objective on Poland's political agenda. The development of European regional policy has helped to provide a new context for regional policies, as regions have become building blocks of a competitive Europe and are now seen as the appropriate level for building partnerships between local elected representatives, the state and the European authorities. The Ministry of Regional Development was created in 2005 to co-ordinate policies and funding. Given Poland's tradition of strong sectoral policies, this is

---

### Box 2.1. **Poland's special economic zones**

Fourteen areas are designated as special economic zones (SEZ), each consisting of several sub-zones. For instance, the economic zone of Katowice includes Katowice, Bielsko Biala, Tychy, Siemianowice and Sosnowiec/Dabrowa. Preferential conditions for conducting business operations within the SEZ include: tax exemptions; lots developed for investment at a competitive price; assistance free of charge in handling formalities related to investment; and property tax exemptions (in some gminas). The amount of the tax exemption is affected by the size of the investment, the location, the size of the workforce and the industry involved.

SEZ are established through regulations of the Council of Ministers upon request of the minister of the economy in agreement with the minister for regional development. A zone may be established to accelerate economic growth over part of the country's territory, in particular through: i) development of specific areas of economic activity; ii) development of new technical and technological solutions for use in the national economy; iii) enhanced exports; iv) enhanced competitiveness of the products manufactured and services provided; v) management of existing industrial property and economic infrastructure; vi) job creation; and vii) utilisation of unused natural resources, observing the principles of ecological balance.

In practice, zones may be established as: i) a tool for restructuring old industrial districts (Katowicka, Legnicka, Lódzka, Mielecka, Starachowicka, Wałbrzyska zones); ii) an instrument for reviving regions with low levels of economic growth (Słupska, Suwalska, Warminsko-Mazurska); iii) a tool for reducing a high structural unemployment rate (Częstochowska, Kamiennogorska, Tczewska); iv) a way to use scientific and research facilities (Krakowski Technology Park); and v) a means of using a cross-border location (Kostrzynsko-Słubicka, in part also Suwalska).

The regulations concerning the zones have been amended during the past few years to comply with EU state aid rules. The current Polish regulations are similar to those of the European Union with the amount of exemption dependent on investment costs. Regional aid is provided to investors as a percentage of the qualifying cost, including investment outlays (aid for initial investment) and two years of labour costs for newly employed workers (aid for job creation). This aid cannot exceed the admissible amount of state aid[1] (which varies according to the regions from 40 to 50%).[2]

1. Poland, the largest of the new EU member states, is also the biggest spender on state aid. For Poland, negotiations on state aid ended with some transitional arrangements, especially as regards fiscal aid schemes to attract foreign investment and measures to restructure the ailing steel industry, *www.euractiv.com/en/enlargement/state-aid-new-member-states/article-129629*.
2. For the Mazowieckie voivodship, the maximum intensity will be reduced to 30% after 1 January 2011. For small firms, the limit is increased by 20% and for medium-sized firms by an additional 10 percentage points.

*Source:* Ministry of Regional Development, 2007 and *www.kpmg.pl/detail.thtml/en/services/EUAccession/Solutions_new/Tax/*.

Map 2.1. **Special economic zones in Poland (2007)**

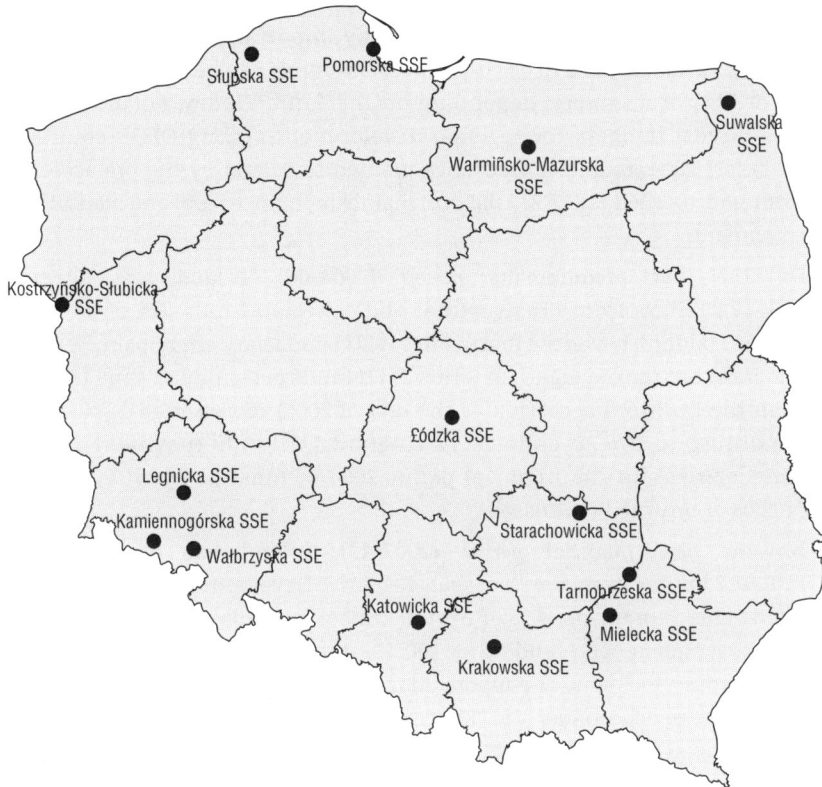

*Source:* Ministry of Regional Development, 2008.

quite a remarkable change. Territorial policy has shifted from a dominant focus on territories in a state of crisis to the development of all regions. Several new tools, such as regional contracts co-financed by the central government and regions to undertake investments in transport, education, tourism and health care, have helped voivodships become new strategic partners for Poland's economic development (see Chapter 3). Even if a significant redistribution component remains, regional development policy today increasingly targets economic development and provides support for projects conducted by the subnational authorities.

A major challenge for Poland is the trade-off between the opportunity of massive external aid (EU funds) and the risk of following aid-driven approaches rather than endogenous development approaches based on the most strategic needs over the long term. Since 2004, the budget for regional development has increased significantly, as all Polish regions were identified as "objective 1 regions", *i.e.* regions considered by the EU to be in convergence and a priority for support from cohesion policy funds (with GDP per capita below 75% of EU average). Although EU funds represent the bulk of the budget for regional policy, they are complemented by important sources of national funding, as projects have to be co-financed. EU funds can be used to finance up to 75 or 85% of a project, depending on the fund.[1] Today, Poland has one of the largest budgets for regional development among OECD countries. Even before 2004, financial assistance granted to Poland by the pre-accession instruments totalled EUR 7 213 billion,[2] mainly to finance rural and institutional development.

- *For the first programming period (2004-06)*, Poland was allocated EUR 12.8 billion from EU structural and cohesion funds (6% of a total of EUR 213 billion). It was the fourth largest EU beneficiary after Spain, Germany and Italy; but ranked eighth in terms of EU funds per capita. Overall transfers from the EU (from accession to the end of 2005) represented 1.7% of GDP. According to the so-called N+2 rule, all EU funds (payment to final beneficiaries) for the financial period 2004-06 must be spent by the end of 2008 or returned to Brussels.

- *For the new financial period (2007-13),* Poland has been allocated EUR 67.3 billion from the European Regional Development Fund/Cohesion Fund. This represents 20% of overall cohesion funds, making Poland the leading recipient of EU funding for 2007-13 (see Figure 2.1) and indeed the all-time leading recipient of support under the Cohesion Policy. All regions in Poland are eligible under the "convergence" objective.[3] Poland will have to manage an average of EUR 9.33 billion a year until 2015 (the funding increases gradually and peaks in 2013). These amounts add to the 16.5 billion euro that Poland will receive under the European Agricultural Rural Development Fund. In all, Poland is to receive EUR 85.6 billion from EU resources. EU aid to Poland will reach almost 4% of GDP between 2007 and 2013.

### 1.2. A balanced policy-mix for regional development

There is a clear continuity between the programmes for 2004-06 and 2007-13 under the National Strategic Reference Framework (NSRF), although the new programmes are slightly more oriented towards infrastructure development. If the allocation of resources broadly fits the main regional development needs, the challenge to increase the place-based dimension remains.

### 2004-06

Poland adopted a multi-sectoral policy mix for regional development for 2004-06, with funds channelled towards competitiveness, development of human resources, infrastructure, and rural and regional development. The management of EU funding has been centralised: the Ministry of Regional Development has acted as the "managing authority" for all programmes under

Figure 2.1. **Structural and cohesion funds, 2007-13, planned allocations**
EUR billions, current prices

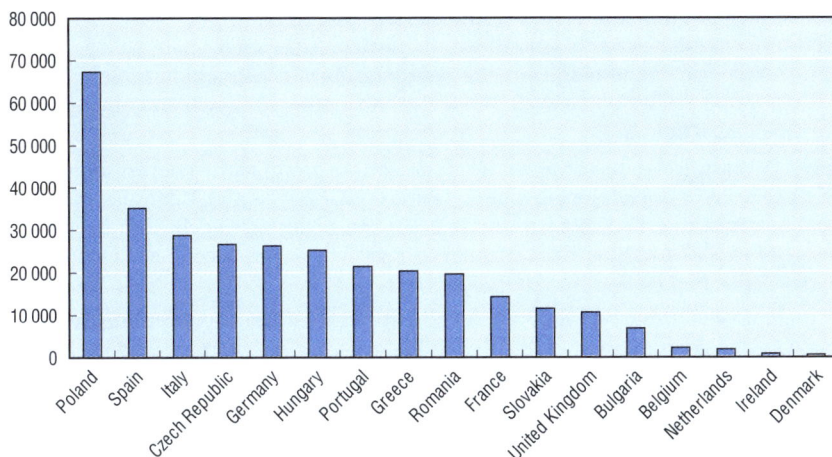

Source: DG Regio, 2007, http://ec.europa.eu/regional_policy/atlas2007/fiche/nsrf.pdf.

the national development plan 2004-06 (except for the Restructuring and Modernisation of Food Sector and Rural Development programme and the Fisheries and Fish Processing programme). Besides, one single Integrated Operational Program (IROP) for regional development co-financed with EU Funds was developed and was managed by the Ministry of regional Development. Regions were little involved in the design of the IROP. Although transport development was the main focus of the strategy, with over one quarter of the funds; the strategy focused to a large extent on the support to enterprises and human capital development. In the years 2004-06, the main portion of the Structural Funds as well as the entire Cohesion Fund were utilised under sectoral programmes which cover the whole territory of Poland, but have been earmarked, in the first place, to carry out projects located in Western and Central Poland (Background Report, 2007). On the other hand, the rural development programme, developed by the Ministry of Agriculture, focused extensively on the support to farms in lagging rural areas.

Poland has benefited from the experience of other EU countries and has not focused exclusively on infrastructure investments, as other EU countries did in the early stage of the cohesion policy. Indeed, for the 1975-1988 period, 80% of committed funds went to infrastructure investments (Nijkamp and Blass, 1995). On the other hand, a predominant focus on the development of human resources and intangible assets – Ireland's strategy of the 1990s – would have been difficult in the early stage of Polish regional policy. Ireland has developed in the 1990s a policy-mix strongly oriented towards human capital development, which has proven very successful to enhance the competitiveness of the country (Box 2.2).

Box 2.2. **Ireland's use of EU funds**

Multiple factors have contributed to the success of Ireland in the 1990s-2000s in addition to favourable external conditions; in particular an appropriate policy-mix targeting human capital development, the restructuring of telecommunications, and the low corporate profit tax rates; all of which contributing to significantly increase foreign direct investment.

In only 15 years, Ireland has moved from the bottom group of the poorest four EU countries to become one of the top four (in terms of GDP per capita). Unemployment fell from 17 per cent in 1987 to 4 per cent in 2003, and government debt shrank from 112 per cent of GDP to 33 per cent. Annual GDP growth in the decade of the 1990s averaged 6.9 per cent (Hill, Hoffmann, 2005).

EU funds played a role to support the competitiveness strategy. EU funds were relatively most important in the 1980s and the early 1990s, but their importance has declined sharply since then. As a share of GDP, they peaked at 6.2 per cent in 1991, with a decline thereafter, falling below 2 per cent beginning in 1999. The absolute magnitude of net transfers averaged approximately IR£700 million in the 1980s and IR£1.6 billion in the 1990s. (Braunerhjelm et al., 2000).

The investment program and the restructuring of the telecommunications system, co-financed with EU funds in the 1980s bear fruit in the 1990s. Investments in education, training, life-long learning (co-financed with EU funds) provided investors with a good business climate. FDI concentrated in sectors and fields where the Irish initial endowment of R&D and human resources was already good, thus developing a cluster of growth poles which largely contributed to the overall positive effect. 51 per cent of the jobs gained during the 1990s appear to have been in internationally traded and financial services, where telecommunication is a critical factor.

Ireland's use of EU funds is seen by many observers as exemplary. It supported the broad policy-mix by focusing on targeting the roots of competitiveness (for example, the lack of skills) rather than just developing infrastructure or channelling money to private-sector projects. Funds boost catch-up in two ways directly and temporarily by boosting demand through investment in buildings or machinery and equipment; indirectly and long-term by raising the stock of infrastructure and human capital and encouraging deeper structural reform (Bradley, 2005).

Besides, Ireland has been able to maintain good standards of administrative capacity. Strong social dialogue was also critical in the success of the strategy. The " Social Pact for National Recovery " introduced in 1988 with social partners has been re-conducted five times (Bafoil, 2007). In addition, the farm-related sector has been a large direct beneficiary of EU funds, contributing to restructuring the agricultural sector.

Source: Braunerhjelm et al., 2000; Bradley; Hill, Hoffmann, 2005; Bafoil, 2007.

In Poland, where cohesion policy is rather new, a right balance was to be bound between infrastructure investments and intangible assets; as local governments need to make the positive impact of EU funds visible and gain the support of local and private stakeholders. The frameworks developed by Poland since 2004 are well-designed and balanced in that respect.

## 2007-13: *Lisbon objectives, infrastructure, and enhanced decentralisation*

The 2007-13 strategy for regional development in Poland is crucial, as it may be the last time that Eastern and Central European countries receive such large aid transfers from the EC. For 2007-13, Poland faces the challenge of absorbing more than five times as much aid as in 2004-06, so it is important to use it effectively and fully from the beginning. The key document that sets guidelines for Poland's social and economic development is the National Development Strategy 2007-15 (adopted by the Council of Ministers on 29 November 2006), which is supposed to be the common umbrella for all sectoral policies.[4] The national development strategy foresees total funding of EUR 108 billion, with EUR 85.6 billion of EU funding and EUR 22.4 billion from national resources and private funds. Within this broad framework, regional development strategy has been developed in the *National Strategic Reference Framework* (NSRF) for the years 2007-13, which establishes the priorities for the use of EU funds.[5] In addition, a separate rural development strategy has been developed by the Ministry of Agriculture, and the policy approach has slightly evolved towards a broader understanding of rural development.

Polish strategy on regional development for 2007-13 (NSRF, Box 2.3)[6] reflects the directions of regional policy of the EU – with a focus on the so-called Lisbon objectives; *i.e.* the focus on growth-oriented activities (see Annex 2.A1). About 64% of the investments have been earmarked for Lisbon related expenditure, which is among the highest rates in the 10 new EU member states.[7] The driving role for growth of cities and metropolitan areas is acknowledged, and one of the key objectives is to enhance the spillover effect from poles of growth to lagging regions. Although the strategy is in continuity with 2004-06, several differences are noticeable: first, infrastructure is granted a higher priority; second, the strategy has a stronger decentralised component (more than 25% of funds are managed by regions in the "regional operational programmes"); third, the strategy is slightly more focused on lagging regions; with a specific programme targeting the development of Eastern Poland.

- The focus on infrastructure development is higher than in the previous financial period – with 41% of the allocated funds (28 billion euro, excluding co-financing) (OP Infrastructure and Environment) and 26.1% of allocated funds in ROPs. EUR 20 billion will be spent on transport infrastructure and EUR 8 billion on environmental infrastructure (particularly water management and sewage systems).It is planned to extend the length of motorways from 554 km to 1 754 km and to increase railways from 538 km to 1 566 km.

- Overall, the regional development strategy for 2007-13 relies more on local actors than between 2004-06. One of the main changes for 2007-13 is the decentralization of part of the EU funds management impulsed by the European Commission. The 16 Polish regions become managing authorities responsible for the formulation and implementation of regional operational programmes (ROPs). In total, regions are in charge of the management of

---

Box 2.3. **Regional development priorities in Poland 2007-13: Polish NSRF**

Poland's priorities for 2007-13, as set out in the NSRF, are to promote growth and job creation in order to reduce the gap between its GDP per capita and that of the EU27. The NSRF's strategic objective is to provide conditions for the growth of the Polish economy's competitiveness through knowledge and entrepreneurship, to increase employment and to enhance social, economic and spatial cohesion. 21 programs have been developed, 5 national ones (75% of the funds), with a strong regional dimension; and 16 regional ones (25% of the funds).

*For national sectoral programmes*, Poland will invest the largest part of the funds (41%) in infrastructure development, in particular by financing transport infrastructure and environmental projects (waste production, consumption of energy and water, sewage treatment plants). The programme for Infrastructure and Environment will include investments of nearly EUR 28 billion from the European Regional Development Fund and the Cohesion Fund. The second largest programme is the OP Human Capital with investments of nearly EUR 10 billion from the European Social Fund. The third one is the OP Innovative Economy (EUR 8.3 billion), the fourth is the OP Development of Eastern Poland (EUR 2.27 billion) and finally the OP Technical Assistance (EUR 517 million).

*For regional programmes* (ROPs), EUR 16.5 billion will be spent via 16 regional operational programmes, giving the Polish regions an opportunity to implement their own regional development strategies in line with EU priorities.

The ERDF will also contribute towards the financing of the "European Territorial Co-operation Objective" consisting of three strands: cross-border, trans-national and inter-regional. A total of EUR 731 million is allocated to Poland under this objective. The programmes will be the following:

● Cross-border (three programs Poland – Germany, Poland – Czech Republic, Poland –Slovakia, Poland – Lithuania, South Baltic).

● Trans-national (Baltic sea region, Central – East Europe Area).

● Neighborhood instrument (Poland – Belarus – Ukraine; Poland – Kaliningrad District of Russian Federation.

Poland completed negotiations of operational programmes in 2007. Poland has now moved to the next stage, which is the selection of projects; that will take place in 2008 and the following years.

Source: National Strategic Framework of Poland, 2007.

---

24.6% of the cohesion funds, *i.e.* more than 16 billion euro. In addition, the operational programme Human Capital (14% of the funding) is to a large extent regionalised, as regions are responsible for about 60% of the financial allocation.

- Although Lisbon objectives are the main priorities, the 2007-13 strategy also emphasises cohesion objectives, as a central programme for the development of Eastern Poland has been developed.[8] This programme, added to the criteria of allocation of funds of the ROPs[9] which favour lagging regions, contribute to give to Eastern regions the highest per capita EU funds in the European Union, when regional programmes only are taken into account. However, when all programmes are considered, this is not true anymore (see Chapter 3).

Figure 2.2. **Distribution of EU resources among operational programmes, 2007-13**

As a percentage of total allocation

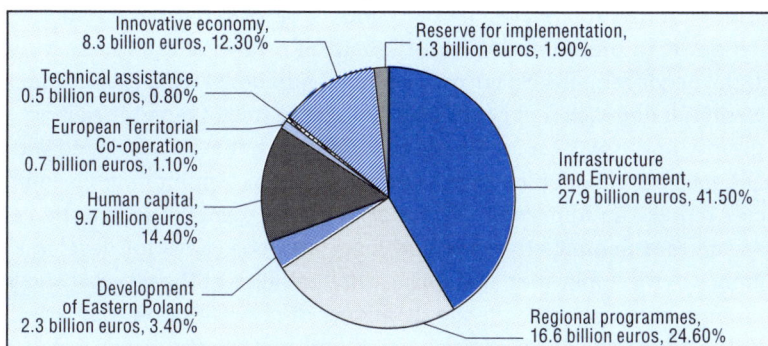

Note: Total represents 67.3 EUR billions.
Source: Ministry of Regional Development, 2007.

Figure 2.3. **Allocation of funds in Regional Operational Programmes (ROPs) for 2007-13**

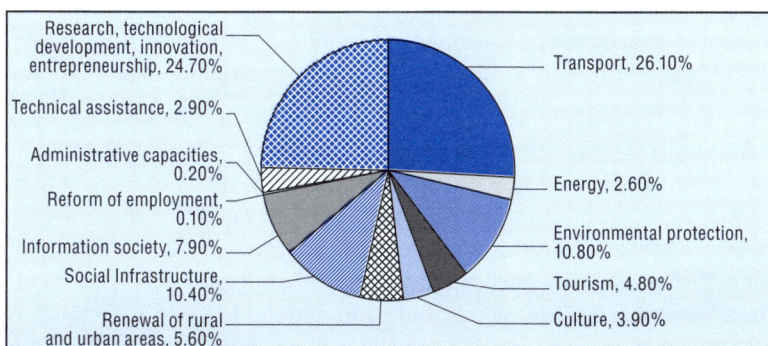

Note: Total represents 16.5 EUR billions.
Source: Ministry of Regional Development, 2007.

*Main challenges for Polish regional policy*

**Although the overall regional development strategy of Poland goes in the right direction, Lisbon objectives are very general and can potentially apply to many different types of policy options.** The comprehensive statements of intent in the NRSF give rich scope for policy formation. It is not clear whether the order of the priorities is intended to be significant in terms of timing, policies and funding. Much of the funding has yet to be spent, but it is important to respect a balanced allocation across the various priorities from the outset.

**The major challenge is the fact that the broad policy mix for regional development takes a predominantly sectoral rather than an integrated territorial approach.** Although there has been progress in inter-ministerial co-ordination (the role played by the Ministry of Regional Development), the challenge of implementing a multi-sectoral strategy tailored to various territorial needs remains. So far, only a limited number of tools exist to enhance the territorial dimension of policies. Although the role of large cities is set as a key priority in the NSRF, a metropolitan policy has not been developed yet; nor specific tools to enhance metropolitan co-operation. Appropriate place-based policies require an appropriate scale of planning, which needs to be better connected to economic strategies and long-term objectives for development. Coherence in the application of funds to different aims at the regional and local levels remains a major challenge. Problems of co-ordination may arise, for example between the regional development strategy and the rural development strategy. This reflects a broader issue of policy coherence at the EU level among the cohesion policy and the Common Agriculture Policy (CAP). Finally, the decentralisation of one fourth of the funding may help to tailor the policy mix to each region's needs; but this is not in itself a guarantee. Given the newness of the regions and disparities in management skills across these regions, a wide disparity of outcomes in the regional implementation is to be expected. Regional leadership and local capacity building will be essential to ensure efficient management of funds.

**Although Lisbon objectives are very general in principle, there is a risk that they be understood in a narrow way in some cases,** as a primary focus on enhanced research and technological development for example; which may not necessarily be the most appropriate choice for the needs of all regions. It is crucial to adjust programmes and strategies according to an in-depth assessment of local needs and to understand Lisbon objectives as all types of policies that contribute to enhance knowledge transfers (be it access to pre-school or tertiary education, support to medium tech industries, knowledge transfer between small- and medium-sized enterprises, etc.).

**There is a risk of focusing on rapid absorption of funds rather than their optimal use.** This is due in part to the constraints on the absorption of EU funds under the N+2 rule. The risk is greater for the infrastructure programme, given the challenge of organising the Euro 2012 soccer championship. The short time for absorption is an even greater challenge in a context of rising inflationary pressures, shortages of labour in construction and currency appreciation. Poland has to manage the challenge of the "crowding out" private investment because of rising interest rates due to strong public investment and enhance its capacity to absorb large sums. Reforms in governance and public management will be crucial for the implementation of the 2007-13 policies.

**The impact of EU cohesion policy on Polish public policies and governance system is much broader than purely financial.** In addition to empowering regional and local actors, cohesion policy has not only impinged on regional development policy per se but most sectoral policies (education, labour market, innovation, etc). The effects are multiple. Among others, the territorial dimension of sectoral policies matters more, as projects co-financed with EU funds are implemented by local actors to a large extent. Besides, sectoral policies linked to EU funding are subject to performance monitoring; thus new mechanisms of performance management have been introduced (see Section 3.5), which might have been much slower without the incentive of cohesion policy.

## 2. Spatial planning and infrastructure for competitiveness

Given Poland's major infrastructure needs (transport, telecommunications, environmental infrastructure),[10] the largest share of funds will be allocated to infrastructure development. More than 41% of funds of central programmes and 26.1% of the budget of regional programmes will be allocated to infrastructure development for 2007-13. Other major projects are linked to the development of the information society. Infrastructure development is crucial for regional development as it largely determines the appropriate allocation of public goods and services across the territory and provides the conditions necessary for the territories to develop. However, infrastructure policy will not by itself provide the conditions for long-term competitiveness; it has to be closely linked to dynamic spatial planning and to economic strategies and demographic forecasts. A proper strategy for infrastructure development may seem to be a "relatively easy and low-risk strategy for regional politicians" (Rodriguez-Posé, 2006), as it provides tangible results in the short term, but there are many challenges. This section will assess: the need to move to more strategic planning processes, in priority in large cities; the need to better link transport policy to strategic planning and to focus on urban transport systems (to complement the inter-city linkages approach); and the need to focus on broadband development throughout Poland.[11]

## 2.1. Deficiencies in spatial planning

### Polish spatial planning trends: a micro-focus

Although spatial planning is in principle a legal requirement and a prerogative of local governments (gminas and voivodships), most local governments do not have proper planning systems. The 2003 Spatial Planning Act requires that gminas[12] prepare a study on the commune's future physical development. Most municipalities have such plans, and 20% of the Polish territory is covered by the plans. In 2003, the Parliament abrogated all Poland's local development plans, but did not make the design of new plans for urban land use compulsory. Some municipalities lack the capacity (both financial and in terms of human resources) to make such a plan. When development plans are absent, exemptions for specific projects are possible through an administrative procedure, which involves some degree of arbitrariness (OECD, 2008a).

---

### Box 2.4. **Poland's spatial development laws**

Most of the planning activities in Poland are performed at the local and regional level by local governmental institutions. Spatial Planning Acts were introduced in 1961, 1984, 1994 and 2003. The basic regulatory instrument for spatial planning is the Spatial Planning and Spatial Management Act of 27 March 2003, which: defines the scope and procedures related to appropriation of land for specific uses and the principles for its sustainable development; and regulates the means of resolving conflicts of interest that might arise between citizens, self-governed communities and the state.

Other important acts of Parliament impose certain tasks and obligations on spatial planning actors, with the result that planning, building and environmental protection are regulated by completely different acts: the Environment Protection and Management Act (the framework for many detailed regulations concerning forests, water or waste management, protection of nature or arable land); the Building Code (in relation to construction and engineering activities); the Law on Real Property Management.

The lack of legal stability in planning systems over the past two decades has also contributed to an increase in "spatial chaos" (Spatial Planning in the Baltic Sea Region, 2001).

Responsibility for national physical (or spatial) development policy and other forms of planning at the central government level lies with the Ministry of Regional Development since 2006.

Source: Spatial Planning in the Baltic Sea Region (2001) and EIKN *www.eukn.org/poland/ polishurbanpolicy/index.html.*

---

Even when planning is well organised at the municipal level, it is weak, because of a narrow focus and lack of long-term vision. Physical development plans are not well connected with strategic plans and the planning focuses on administrative borders of gminas rather than on functional areas. Gminas do not co-operate enough in the planning process and have no incentive to do so, with the result that decisions on the use of space are sub-optimal. The upper levels of government (region, central government) are unable to enforce the implementation of strategic decisions. Regions (voivodships) have responsibility for planning systems, because they prepare the regional spatial development plans. However, these plans are not binding on municipalities and tend to remain quite general and superficial (Spatial Planning in the Baltic Sea Region, 2001). In particular, gminas have many ways to avoid unwanted programmes and projects, *e.g.* by prolonging procedures for preparing local plans, undertaking lengthy social and judicial processes, etc. There is no comprehensive spatial planning that encompasses physical and socio-economic developments at the regional scale, even though regions are encouraged to do this. The planning documents prepared at the different administrative levels are also often not coherent.

### Chaotic spatial planning and urban/rural development

The weaknesses of spatial planning systems have adverse effects on urban areas, particularly in terms of housing and public transport systems. The lack of functional spatial planning at city scale impedes the development of integrated transport systems and contributes to a rapid increase in the use of cars to the detriment of public transport. This increases congestion and pollution in cities. Besides, the lack of zoning has slowed the development of housing. Given the legacy of under-developed housing from the period of central planning, Poland now faces a shortage of some one million dwellings (Box 2.5), particularly for social housing. In addition to reducing labour mobility, the shortage of affordable housing reinforces a growing urban sprawl. The rural population started to increase again after 2000, especially in the neighbourhood of large cities, owing to the rise in housing prices. This new rural migration should continue until 2030 (the share of urban population is forecast to drop to 57%, while the share of rural population should reach 43% (CSO, 2007).

Although urban sprawl and migration to rural areas can provide new opportunities for rural development, the new mobility patterns, with increasing numbers of people commuting long distances every day, require better planning. However, because of the increase in land prices, especially around large cities, the surrounding *gminas* tend to speculate on land rather than develop a strategic long-term vision on its best use. The previous government therefore intended to amend the Law on Spatial Planning and the Construction Law. The process is still under way and the issue of co-ordination

---

### Box 2.5. **Shortage of affordable housing in Poland**

Housing prices in Poland have risen considerably in the past ten years, especially in large cities, making it very difficult for people in rural areas to move to urban areas. Residential property prices have been rising since 2003 at a annual pace of 10 to 20%. The post-accession period, especially from 2006, is marked by an unprecedented increase in housing prices. Poland probably led the property boom in Europe in 2006. Prices in Warsaw were among the highest in the Central and Eastern European countries and were even equal to levels reached in some western European countries. Given the dynamic demand, the housing supply has been quite inelastic (OECD, 2008a). Since the end of 2007 housing prices have however started to stabilise or even decline in major urban centres.

Despite policies adopted in 2003-04 (5 000 social dwellings and 500 beds in homeless shelters) to deal with shortage of social housing, problems remain. The limited access to affordable credit for individuals and large families limits access to housing. The shortage is not only quantitative but also qualitative, as a large proportion of housing is sub-standard. A consistent strategy for dealing with the problem (rental, promotion of first-time homeownership, etc.) has yet to be developed.

*Source:* OECD (2008a).

---

with transport infrastructure investments has not been fully dealt with in the draft legislation. The question of inconsistencies between the two acts has also been raised (OECD, 2008a). Two crucial challenges – for both competitiveness and cohesion objectives – are linked to the integration of housing and transport developments into broad strategic planning.

The concentration of housing problems in some areas pleads for a territorial approach to housing policy. Spatial planning needs to be linked to initiatives targeting enterprises and job creation. The neglected and degraded housing in many Polish towns also needs to be dealt with. Urban space in Poland has suffered from the construction in the 1960s and 1970s of gigantic complexes of block housing, usually forming a ring around Polish towns and cities. Today, such complexes represent sub-standard housing with high costs of exploitation and rapid depreciation. In some Polish cities such high-rise constructions are inhabited by 30-40% of residents, often low-income groups. In addition to creating adverse social consequences (lower educational levels, higher crime rates, etc.), this unattractive housing adversely affects competitiveness. As mentioned in the NSRF, rehabilitation of these post-industrial (and post-military) areas is crucial for both social and competitiveness reasons but will probably take decades. Management of town centres, where the housing stock is old and often run-down, presents another challenge.

Poor spatial planning also adversely affects rural areas. Because rural gminas do not enough co-operate on spatial planning, investment decisions are sub-optimal. For example, neighbouring gminas may build individual and thus more costly sewage systems. In the absence of strategic planning, the use made of rural areas creates negative externalities and the tourism potential of some rural areas is not well exploited. Although the price of land remains below the EU average in rural areas, it has increased rapidly since accession to the EU and there is a great deal of speculation. Additional difficulties arise from difficulties for changing the zoning of land from agricultural use to building purposes (OECD, 2008a).

Strategic planning needs to be understood as a key tool for competitiveness. Many OECD countries that have problems with planning and lack a multi-sector approach have moved in recent years to a more dynamic approach, often called "strategic planning". This more comprehensive approach has a multi-sector dimension and takes a broader perspective than municipalities' administrative areas. This is especially true for large metropolitan regions. Although there are many difficulties – given the frequent lack of multi-year and multi-sectoral budget for major projects – innovation in planning is crucial to better match public policy and local development needs (with concomitant changes in governance, discussed in Chapter 3).

Table 2.1. **Changes in spatial planning in OECD countries**

| | Old planning approach (managerial) | Transitional approach (incrementalist) | New planning approach (entrepreneurial) |
|---|---|---|---|
| **Main goals** | Allocation of land | Spatial redevelopment and infrastructure growth | Economic development Environmental and social sustainability |
| **Concepts (dynamics)** | Implementation and tactics | Open planning | Strategic vision |
| **Functions** | Provision of public services | Focus on project | Promoting innovation, risk taking and development |
| **Substantive aspects or forms (static)** | Centre/periphery rationale | Redevelopment of city centres, strengthening of rural/urban linkages | Poly-centricity Urban corridors |
| **Actors** | Public actors | Implication of the private sector | A broad set of stakeholders, numerous public-private partnerships |
| **Regional and local dimensions** | Hierarchical relationships between central/regional and local, central control | Emerging role of region | Strategic aspects increasingly decentralised |

Source: OECD (2007), Competitive Cities: A New Entrepreneurial Paradigm in Spatial Development.

## The need for metropolitan planning

An integrated spatial planning approach is more urgent for the large urban areas that drive Polish growth and face major challenges linked to housing, public transport and environmental problems (including water and waste management). Large cities would benefit from metropolitan planning to enhance their competitiveness and attractiveness. Integrated public transport systems are a key dimension of competitiveness in large cities (OECD, 2006a). They help reduce congestion and pollution, raise productivity, and enhance their attractiveness. Small cities and towns located near larger cities benefit from spillovers because growth spreads out from urban centres if there are appropriate linkages. In large cities, the lack of a metropolitan perspective also raises problems for the absorption of EU funds, as many projects extend beyond specific administrative areas and are more complex to prepare than in small towns.

Although the principle of supporting the leading urban areas is widely accepted, as these are considered the "dynamos" at the heart of the national economic system (as in the United Kingdom, Finland, France, the Netherlands and Switzerland), Poland does not yet have a specific strategy for large urban areas, to take into account functional economic areas. For many years there have been discussions about the need to work out a national urban policy to enhance co-operation at the metropolitan scale or increase the scale of urban powiats ("metropolitan powiats"); there are, however, no corresponding legal changes in this direction so far. Co-operation among gminas at the metropolitan scale is voluntary, and while there are some positive initiatives (Box 2.6), there is no tradition of voluntary co-operation between local governments (Furmankiewicz, 2002) (on this point, see Chapter 3). Incentives for metropolitan co-operation have not been introduced.

---

### Box 2.6. **Bottom-up initiatives for metropolitan development**

In 2006, the mayors of 14 cities in the *Upper Silesian Agglomeration* created the Upper Silesian Metropolitan Union. With more than two million inhabitants it is Poland's biggest agglomeration in terms of population. The main goals of the union are to: develop a common planning strategy, develop a common economic strategy to enhance competitiveness and attract FDI, develop common projects funded by structural funds, manage in common roads and water treatment infrastructure.

*Tricity* is an urban area consisting of three Polish cities: Gdansk, Gdynia and Sopot. It has a population of over a million people. A Tricity charter was signed in March 2007 as a declaration of the cities' co-operation. Tricity has essentially developed a common transport system, in particular inner highways.

---

Metropolitan policy can take many different forms, depending on how ambitious the goals are and whether the desire for integration is weak or strong (OECD, 2006a). One priority is to define the threshold and scope of

Poland's "metropolitan areas", based on economic criteria, local labour markets and functional linkages among gminas. So far, various official documents related to regional/urban development mention metropolitan areas, but the meaning of the term may differ. The National Spatial Development Policy Scheme of 2005, which does not have legal status and has not been adopted by the Sejm, identified nine so-called metropolitan areas, i.e. large cities with an aggregate population of more than 500 000.[13] The question is whether one or several medium-sized cities of eastern Poland (such as Lublin) should be included (even if they fall below the threshold of 500 000 inhabitants), as they would also benefit from better planning at the "metropolitan" scale. There is no best option; the choice of the instrument should be appropriate to the context. France's "agglomeration contracts" seem particularly appropriate for Poland, as they are based on the approval of a so-called territorial project, a five to ten year plan for infrastructure, economic development, social housing, culture and the environment at the metropolitan level. A contract is signed between the central government, the regional council and the *communauté*. Chapter 3 discusses various governance arrangements and describes the institutional tools for enhanced co-operation at the local level.

## 2.2. *Transport development and strategic planning*

Given the needs identified in Chapter 1, the development of transport to enhance labour mobility and accessibility to Poland is a priority both for Poland and for the European Union. Major investments in infrastructure are needed to upgrade the quality and density of most transport networks (roads, rail, air, sea). The Infrastructure and Environment programme is the largest ever funded by the European Commission (EUR 28 billion); and 71% of the money will finance investments in transport (EUR 20 billion). For 2007-13, it is planned to build 620 kilometres of motorway and 1973 kilometres of expressways, and to build and modernise 1 566 kilometres of railways. For the next few years, improving the infrastructure has become all the more urgent because Poland has been chosen to co-host the Euro 2012 soccer championship. As a result, the completion date for many investment projects has been moved up. Therefore, the challenge is not only to boost the quality of infrastructure but also to reach this objective on time (OECD, 2008a).

Although the sectoral programme for transport was the least successful in terms of funds paid out over the 2004-06 period, the sector's absorption capacity improved in the second half of 2006 and in 2007. At the end of 2006, it only amounted to 15.8% of the allocated budget. According to the Ministry of Regional Development, while the initial plan was to spend 78% of the budget by that date, many problems arose owing to poor preparation and, more specifically, to a lack of land, technical matters, environmental concerns or tender documentation (Ministry of Regional Development, 2006). Other difficulties related to the often-denounced rigidities related to EU funding. Nonetheless, by the end of 2006, Poland had implemented more than 12 000 infrastructural projects, and total assistance from structural funds exceeded PLN 34.4 billion (MRD, 2007). By the end of 2007, more than 50% of the ERDF funding had been spent and over 300 km of new motorways had been built. Given the N+2 rule[14] and given the substantial increase in funding for 2007-13, Poland will have to speed up the learning and absorption processes even more (OECD, 2008a).

### Place-based policy needed for investment in transports

The main focus of transport policy since 2004 has been road development (expressways, motorways, national roads). Major EU transport infrastructure investments have concentrated on Poland because it is crossed by four out of the ten pan-European transport corridors.[15] One of Poland's critical priorities is to create an effective network of motorways connecting the country's major urban centres and connecting these with the Trans-European Transport Networks and to improve road-bearing capacity and quality. The focus on roads has continued in the 2007-13 regional development strategy: 51.7% of total funds for the infrastructure programme (including co-financing) are allocated to road development (EUR 11.2 billion from EU funds and EUR 1.98 from national funds), while 21% is for rail transport and 13% for urban transport (Table 2.2). In the regional programmes, 26% of the funding goes to transport (EUR 4.4 billion out of a total of EUR 16.6 billion) (Table 2.3).

Table 2.2. **Funding details of the Operational Programme Infrastructure and Environment, 2007-13**

EUR billion, percentages

| | Overall | | EU funds | | Public funds | | Private funds | | Private funds | | Co-financing rate |
|---|---|---|---|---|---|---|---|---|---|---|---|
| | Amount | % | Amount | % | Amount | % | Amount | % | Amount | % | |
| **Road transport** | **14.38** | **51.78** | **11.20** | **57.68** | **1.98** | **33.53** | **0.00** | **0.00** | **1.20** | **70.59** | **22.1** |
| Rail transport | 7.67 | 27.60 | 4.86 | 25.04 | 1.90 | 32.28 | 0.40 | 53.06 | 0.50 | 29.41 | 36.6 |
| Sea transport | 0.71 | 2.57 | 0.61 | 3.12 | 0.11 | 1.82 | 0.00 | 0.00 | 0.00 | 0.00 | 15.0 |
| Air transport | 0.67 | 2.40 | 0.40 | 2.08 | 0.02 | 0.36 | 0.24 | 32.19 | 0.00 | 0.00 | 39.5 |
| Urban transport | 3.86 | 13.91 | 2.01 | 10.37 | 1.85 | 31.36 | 0.00 | 0.00 | 0.00 | 0.00 | 47.9 |
| Intermodal transport | 0.22 | 0.80 | 0.11 | 0.57 | 0.00 | 0.00 | 0.11 | 14.76 | 0.00 | 0.00 | 50.0 |
| Intelligent transport systems | 0.16 | 0.59 | 0.14 | 0.72 | 0.02 | 0.42 | 0.00 | 0.00 | 0.00 | 0.00 | 15.0 |
| Inland waterways | 0.10 | 0.34 | 0.08 | 0.42 | 0.01 | 0.24 | 0.00 | 0.00 | 0.00 | 0.00 | 15.0 |
| Total | 27.8 | 100.0 | 19.4 | 100.0 | 5.9 | 100.0 | 0.8 | 100.0 | 1.7 | 100.0 | 30.1 |

Source: Ministry of Transport, 2007.

OECD TERRITORIAL REVIEWS: POLAND – ISBN 978-92-64-04926-0 – © OECD 2008

Table 2.3. **Breakdown of funding for transport in the regional programmes (ROPs), 2007-13**

Percentages (total: EUR 4.4 billion)

|  | % |
|---|---|
| **Road transport** | **69.8** |
| Rail transport | 13.3 |
| Air transport | 6 |
| Municipal transport | 4.7 |
| Intelligent transport systems | 2.5 |
| Inter-modal transport | 1.5 |
| Cycle tracks | 1.3 |
| Seaports | 0.4 |
| Inland waterways | 0.4 |

**Linking the 16 regional capitals.** Care must be taken not to focus exclusively on inter-city linkages, but also on improving the connections of large cities with their surrounding gminas, as they are weakly developed. A main priority of transport policy is to establish links between the major urban centres, in particular the 16 regional capitals (including eastern Poland), as part of a network of motorways and express roads (NSRF, 2006). The projected motorway network will connect 10 of the 16 voivodship capitals.[16] The other voivodship capitals will be connected with the main network through expressways (this is the main purpose of the S19 expressway connecting three voivodship capitals of Eastern Poland). Although accessibility of regional capitals is important –for economic and political reasons – linkages among the 16 cities may not be the most efficient investment from an economic point of view, as some axes will have much less traffic than others. The improved north-south connections are clearly needed, but these inter-city linkages need to be balanced with "metropolitan roads" and better connections between large cities and their less developed neighbouring gminas. The economic benefit of intercity expressways will mostly come from the need to move freight, whereas the metropolitan roads facilitate mobility and local deliveries that stimulate local productivity and economic activity. Greater investment in metropolitan roads, including ring roads, which do not exist in most cities, not even Warsaw, might generate stronger economic outcomes. Connections between urban centres and their surrounding rural areas are crucial for making the most of the specific nature of Poland's territory: a balanced network of average-sized towns, which needs to be strengthened.

A link between rich and poor regions does not always benefit the poor region, as the classic example of Italy's Mezzogiorno shows. For example, improved expressways in eastern Poland will enable goods to reach overseas markets faster and at lower cost, but competition from other parts of Europe will also increase for eastern Polish regions. It is necessary to connect transport to overall policies to increase regional competitiveness, satisfying both labour market and housing needs. An improved east-west road network will not in itself ensure FDI attraction and increased employment. A number of studies have undermined the widespread conviction that motorways are essential to regional development and employment creation. The economic impact can be positive or negative, depending on the specific circumstances of a given region.[17] Other critical conditions to be met include the need for a qualified workforce and better telecommunications. Because roads have a long life span, they require a very careful economic appraisal.

**Roads vs. public transport.** Urban public transport represents only 13.9% of the allocation at the central level and 4.7% of regional operational programmes, a sign of its comparatively low priority. However, Poland's originally well-developed public transport systems have deteriorated in over the past decade, owing to inadequate spatial planning and limited investment by local governments. Since the early 1990s, the responsibility for urban public transport and urban roads has been delegated to local governments. Pressures to reduce urban public transport subsidies led to sharp fare increases (Brzezinski, 2003), which places a heavy burden on poorer people living in peripheral areas. Urban public transport does not offer enough alternatives to cars. In Poland, the car fleet increased from 5.26 million in 1990 to 9.28 million in 1999, while use of public transport fell by almost 50% (CEE Bankwatch Network, 2007). Although the share of passengers transported by public transport in Poland is still higher than in older EU member countries, it has declined in favour of personal cars in recent years. In Warsaw, there are now 450 cars for 1 000 inhabitants, one of the highest ratios in EU capitals. Rather than duplicating the vicious circle of increasing car dependency, noise and air pollution, urban sprawl, and congestion that Western Europe has experienced, care should be taken to ensure an appropriate balance between road development and alternatives modes of transport. The right balance between roads and public transports has yet to be found, especially in large urban areas. In their regional programmes, central and local governments have to carefully assess the economic advantages of investing in new roads as compared to other transport modes. For towns and the central government, urban public transport takes on added importance in a context of climate change and rising oil prices.

**A comprehensive plan is lacking.** A coherent long-term policy for the modernisation and development of the road network is lacking. There are no clear, systematic linkages between road networks, territories and economic, environmental and demographic development. Long-term objectives are not stated precisely, and an overall spatial scheme for transport (after 2013) has not been developed. The preparation of consistent medium- and long-term frameworks was undertaken but has been halted (it has only the approval of the board of the Ministry of Infrastructure), as is also the case of the documents "Strategy for transport development 2007-13" and the "National transport policy 2007-20" (OECD, 2008a). A detailed and publicly available strategy should address long-term prospects in the transport sector, provide an in-depth analysis of interdependencies among transport modes depending on underlying cost and revenue scenarios, and, finally, include, on that basis, a rigorous cost-benefit analysis of each project (OECD, 2008a). Cost-benefit analyses should state whether the decision is made on the basis of economic benefits or qualitative goals. In terms of strategies, the north-south links are crucial to the competitiveness of Poland's ports, the improvement of transport connections of large cities with Warsaw, closer relations between Slaskie and Warsaw, and the connection between Warsaw and Lodz.

The priority is to make the best use of funds by developing an appropriate place-based policy for transport investment, well linked to the economic strategies of regions and the development of the labour market. Cost-benefit analyses are essential to determine which investments will be optimal and to achieve the necessary balance. So far, there seems to be insufficient analysis of the benefits from proposed investments (OECD, 2008a). Without them, it is difficult to prioritise the various place-based investments and modes of transport (between road, rail [high-speed or standard] and air or sea ports). There seems to be too much emphasis on absorption of funds. A baseline list of 71 transport projects has been established, followed by an additional 46 projects from a "reserve list"; the main decision-making criterion for effective implementation is the timely availability of the relevant documentation.

Environmental issues may be one of the major challenges for transport policy. Poland has joined the EU's Natura 2000 programme, an ecological network aimed at protecting the best wildlife areas. The network has been extended to 18% of Poland's territory. However, it appears, as of now, that many of the approved road investment projects expected to be built in the near future fail to bypass protected areas. There may be as many as 100 potential conflict zones. There is a risk that payments for programmes and projects that are to be financed in 2007-13 may be blocked. The Ministry of Environment has not specified as yet the protected areas that take into account the areas indicated by non-governmental organisations (NGOs) on the so-called "shadow list". Poland's tardiness in completing strategic environmental assessments for all projects has resulted in the current problems. In addition, there are conflicts between the Polish government and the European Commission (Box 2.7). This results in legal uncertainties concerning the procedural requirements to be satisfied for carrying out many planned infrastructure investments in roads and railways.

> Box 2.7. **The case of the Rospuda River valley**
>
> The most important conflict relating to Natura 2000 between Poland and the European Commission is the construction of a trans-continental highway in the Rospuda River valley in the northeast of Poland. The purpose is to establish a major link between Warsaw and Helsinki through the Baltic States in order to increase trade between eastern and western Europe. In April 2006 the European Commission started an "infringement procedure" against Poland. Since construction has continued, EU authorities initiated legal action at the European Court of Justice in March 2007 which could lead to penalties and negatively affect the scale of EU funds to Poland.

### Risks of rising costs and inefficiency about public investment

There is a danger that projects will be carried out at maximum cost, particularly given the rising price of materials (in particular steel and cement) and the shortage of labour in the construction sector. Hiring problems are reported by close to 90% of firms in the construction industry.[18] Wages are accelerating on the back of increased demand and skill shortages (National Bank of Poland, 2007). As rising construction costs may accelerate inflation, it is likely that the central bank will contract monetary policy to meet inflation targets, particularly looking forward to the adoption of the euro. This will raise interest rates and appreciate the zloty, which will negatively impact private investment and exports. The long-run gains from improved transportation infrastructure may thus bring about in the short and medium-term a loss of competitiveness due to low private investment and loss of competitive business opportunities. To avoid or reduce these adverse effects, the large infrastructure investment plans must be carried out with much care as to their potential macro-economic impacts. The entry of foreign workers from Russia, Ukraine and Belarus was authorised in July 2007 and further extended in January 2008, but the employment period for temporary migrants should extend beyond the current maximum of six months. Further easing access to the labour market by foreign workers from other than neighbouring countries would help to reduce wage and price pressures and thus the rise in construction costs (OECD, 2008a).

The complex legal framework for absorption of EU funds in the transport sector has recently been simplified,[19] but some changes are still needed, in particular relating to public procurement and public-private partnerships (see Chapter 3). It is estimated that for linear infrastructure projects the time needed to prepare the documentation and obtain the administrative permits necessary to begin construction work exceeds five years (and in some cases several more) from the moment the investment decision is taken.

An additional weakness that may add to the cost pressure and negatively affect public investment is the lack of human resources qualified for the administrative work related to the investment process (local spatial management plans, environmental impact assessments), both at the central level (i.e. Ministry of Infrastructure and General Directorate for National Roads and Motorways) and at the local level (regions and municipalities). These essential services include planning, engineering, environmental assessment, architectural, legal (including courts), finance, and administration of permits. Capacity constraints on these services will keep productivity low in spite of the extra capital investment, drive up costs, and hamper the ability to meet construction timetables. Support services are crucial for major infrastructure projects, and in a context of limited human resources, strong prioritisation of investment is needed, especially to prepare for the Euro 2012 championship. Given staff shortages, the additional investment (for stadiums, etc.) must be a high priority. New Zealand, which is organising the 2011 rugby cup, has had to slow down its highway and road building programmes because it does not have enough planners and other support services (Box 2.8).

---

### Box 2.8. **New Zealand and the 2011 World Rugby Cup**

New Zealand needs to upgrade its national stadium to double its capacity in time for the 2011 World Rugby Cup. Though New Zealand is a completely open economy (harbour bridge built by the Japanese, power stations by Italians, etc.) only one Australasian firm has expressed any interest in the project and has therefore been selected. Competitive pricing and meeting the deadline will be a problem. Similarly, New Zealand has had to slow down its current highway and road building programmes because there are not enough planners and other support services available; those that exist are fully booked years ahead.

---

**Improve co-ordination across levels of government.** Poor spatial planning and lack of co-ordination among local governments also raise concerns for investment in air transport. Central authorities have decided to concentrate EU resources from the Infrastructure and Environment programme on the seven regional airports and the central airport in Warsaw, all of which are part of the TEN-T network. However, many other local authorities are eager to expand their airport facilities and argue for public and/or EU money from regional programmes, even though this infrastructure would not have national importance and is not warranted by distance and/or population density indicators. In some cases, rail (high-speed train) would offer greater economic returns than new regional airports. Overall, to avoid over-investment, it is important to better co-ordinate the different levels of government when designing airport infrastructure investment plans (OECD, 2008a).

Another important dimension of regional policy is the enhancement of co-operation among ports to achieve critical mass and better complementarities. This is particularly true for Gdańsk and Gdynia. This may be the role of the central government, or local governments, to stimulate co-operation as co-operation by harbours does not occur automatically, as they tend to compete with each other; which may not be in the interest of the region or country (Barzdukas *et al.*, 2000, in OECD, 2006). Investment in port-related infrastructure can have a high economic spillover for regional economies owing to the many activities involved in logistical chains. Improving intermodal transport is of vital importance, especially for port development, so as to facilitate links with the hinterland and improve container movement. The development of ports[20] and their surroundings as well as their accessibility from inland regions are important for competitiveness and the role of Poland in the Baltic Sea region, one of the world's most dynamic macro-regions.

### 2.3. *Digital infrastructure policies*

Although investment in hard infrastructure (transport or water management systems) is considered a priority by the different levels of government, as these systems correspond to immediate needs and are visible, investment in soft infrastructure, particularly Internet access and broadband, should be of comparable priority. As Chapter 1 shows, Poland lags behind other EU countries in Internet access and broadband development. EU expenditures on technologies in Poland in 2004 represented 2% of GDP;[21] the EU25 average was 3% (and more than 4% in Sweden and the United Kingdom) (NSRF, 2007). Polish telecommunications connection and service costs are among the highest in Europe.[22] The broadband penetration rate is 8% compared to 18% in the EU15. The slower progress in rural areas is due to the lower returns for private providers, and this raises the question of regional consistency in ICT investment. Investment in Internet and broadband development is urgently needed, both in urban and rural areas, as broadband offers a comparative advantage and can attract and retain businesses, train and educate individuals, and maximise the efficiency of public services (OECD, 2006h). Broadband is a crucial factor for the various regions and their different user segments: enterprises (multinationals, SMEs and micro-enterprises), local public institutions (hospitals, colleges, administrative departments) and the general public. Broadband technologies must thus be viewed as "local development tools" (Ullman, 2005) for creating new economic and social dynamics.

Although development of ICT has accelerated since 2004, in part with the support of EU structural funds, the rural-urban gap remains important.[23] The focus on telecommunications in rural areas– in particular Internet access and broadband – has received less support, in particular from local governments, partly because telecommunications have been privatised. However, without

Figure 2.4. **OECD broadband subscribers, by technology, December 2004**

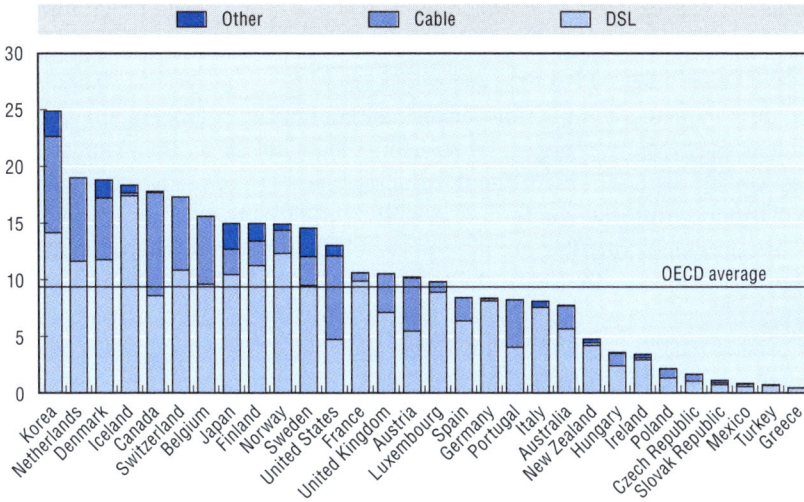

Source: OECD (2008c).

governmental policy intervention, land lines and broadband will not increase quickly enough, if at all, in remote areas. Projects relating to ICT development have been mostly concentrated in the Mazowieckie and Śląskie regions; they represent around half of the ICT expenditure co-financed by structural funds. In these voivodships, ICT outlays constitute the largest share of EU financial support. Development of Internet/broadband in the eastern regions remains limited, and the regional gaps in Internet and broadband access have so far not been closed.

Even if the 2007-13 strategy targets the development of ICT ("e-society") and the reduction of the digital divide among urban and rural areas and as a priority,[24] the strategy is rather fragmented among different programmes and is insufficiently linked to the broad infrastructure programme. Although ICT development is not confined to one sector, but affects all areas of public service, broadband development would benefit from stronger links with the infrastructure programme, as there can be economies of scale if transport and broadband projects are conducted hand in hand. Again, this reveals the insufficient connection between transport, spatial planning and broader competitiveness policies such as ICT. Planned investments in ICT are far more limited than for transport, with around 3% of the funding allocated so far for 2007-13 (EUR 1 598 million). However, as the list of projects is not yet complete, the final figure should be higher. One of the projects for 2007-13 is to establish an Internet network in the five eastern regions along with training to improve the Internet skills of inhabitants, SMEs and public agencies. The cost of implementing the project, which was prepared in the framework of the JASPERS initiative, is estimated at approximately EUR 300 million. The programme for the development of broadband Internet for the five eastern Polish regions should be strongly supported.

It is particularly important for regional authorities to understand the high value of the broadband project for reducing the digital divide. So far, most Polish local governments – in particular in rural regions – do not seem to acknowledge that broadband, like roads, has a role to play in the attractiveness and competitiveness of their areas. The development costs of broadband are relatively low compared with the costs involved in building a roundabout, a stretch of road or renovating a school; this thus becomes a question of local policy priorities (OECD, 2006h). In 2004, the European Commission recognised broadband as an essential local service. Better training of local governments on the benefits of digital infrastructure for local economies appears to be important.

### Conclusion

To sum up, transport policy needs to be better linked to strategic spatial planning and to sectoral policies such as ICT. Large economies of scale can be realised if integral territorial development is understood as a key tool for competitiveness and is better connected to long-term economic strategies. It is important to prioritise investment plans for transport, and complement the inter-city linkages with a stronger focus on metropolitan transports, as large cities are the main drivers of Polish growth. Greater coherence is needed, at both central and regional levels, in order to better co-ordinate transport and cohesion policies, and action must be taken to face construction cost inflation and to avoid crowding-out of private investment.

## 3. Building competitive regions: human capital, social capital and innovation

As argued in Chapter 1, the "knowledge" challenge, along with infrastructure, are the most important ones facing Polish regions. Although infrastructure development will provide for improved accessibility and mobility, enhanced competitiveness over the longer term will mainly require a focus on endogenous resources, i.e. development of human capital and innovation processes. Some regions are performing better than others in terms of innovation and tertiary education attainment (notably the five metropolitan regions of Mazowieckie, Slaskie, Wielkopolskie, Malopolskie and Dolnoslaskie), but all must face the challenges of knowledge, private research and development, and diffusion of organisational innovation. The key challenge for Poland and its regions is to understand innovation in its broader sense, as all types of knowledge transfers that can help improving the conditions for enhanced competitiveness on the longer term, rather than in a narrow sense focusing on R&D measures or high-tech developments. All sectors, all firms, all territories are concerned with innovation processes. The key question is to establish appropriate place-based policy-mix, for different types of territories.

The challenges are huge, but conditions are nevertheless favourable for change. There is a growing recognition within the Polish administration that innovation is important for future economic growth and that the regions will play a crucial role. EU structural funds, added to co-financing, present a major opportunity to reorient the policy mix to develop critical mass in research that is more closely linked to business innovation. For 2007-13, the programmes on the innovative/competitive economy and human capital, which receive a total of EUR 21.1 billion, including EUR 18 billion from EU funds (26.7% of the total allocation), will be the main means of accelerating the move to the knowledge economy in 2007-13, and regions will be key players. In addition, regions will allocate about 40% of their regional operational programmes to measures supporting competitiveness. This section will analyse the main policy measures to enhance the move to the knowledge economy in regions: i) human capital development; ii) social capital building; and iii) new priorities to finance innovation, in particular regional innovation strategies and the increased focus on SMEs.

## 3.1. Development of human capital

### Human capital programme (2007-13)

Although the "Human Capital" programme for 2007-13 provides opportunities for significant progress in the areas of initial and lifelong training; its impact will rely essentially on the identification of specific needs that vary greatly across regions. It accounts for EUR 11.4 billion, including 9.7 from the European Social Fund and 1.7 from national resources (see Annex 2.A2). The programme finalised in 2007 focuses mainly on increasing employment and participation rates, improving the match between labour markets and initial/lifelong training[25] and bringing 50-year olds back into the labour market (see Figure 2.5). Implementation of the programme will be partly decentralised, as voivodships' governments were appointed as intermediate bodies for programme management with other sectoral ministries (Ministry of Labour, Education, etc.). Regions have in fact the largest role to play with the human capital programme, as 60% of allocated funds will be implemented by regions while 40% by sectoral ministries.

### Enhance access to education of rural populations

Education is a key explicative variable behind regional competitiveness and to explain the rising territorial disparities in Poland. Improved access to education for rural areas, better matches among labour market needs and tertiary education graduates and improved life-long training are critical

Figure 2.5. **Priorities in the Human Capital programme, 2007-13 (total: EUR 11.4 billion, including co-financing)**

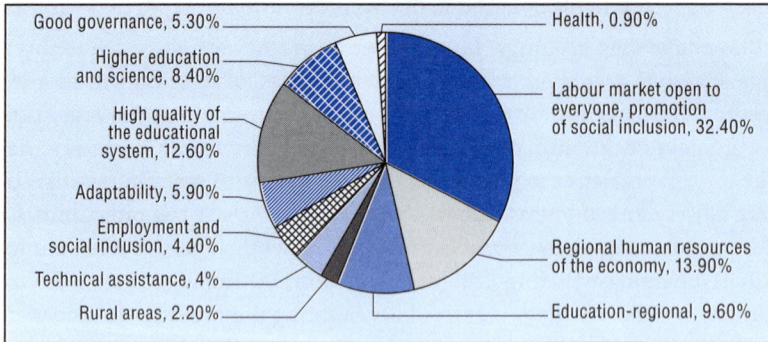

*Source:* Ministry of Regional Development, 2007.

priorities. As explained in Chapter 1, access to pre-school in rural areas remains much lower than in urban areas. On the demand side, there is a psychological/cultural obstacle, as parents see little value in sending children to pre-school; an appropriate campaign of information or incentives could be launched to change parents' minds. The Mexican programme *Oportunidades* which links family support and the obligation to send children to school and provide health care could inspire Poland (Box 2.9). On the supply side,

---

Box 2.9. **Mexico's *Oportunidades* programme**

Mexico has developed a specific strategy for poverty alleviation in rural areas, which is managed by the Ministry of Social Development, SEDESOL. The most important component is the *Oportunidades* programme, an inter-institutional programme which also involves the Ministries of Health and Education and seeks to fight poverty by improving the income, education and health of the poor. Its main innovation is the conditionality of support, that is, "eligible" families receive support as long as they meet certain obligations, *i.e.* send their children to school and provide them with a "basic package" of illness prevention and health care. It has three pillars, in each of which different ministries play an important role. The Ministry of Education is involved in the education pillar. The conditionality of the grants has been a crucial factor in the success of the programme, which has been labelled internationally as a "best practice" and has gained importance and budget in the Mexican administration. The programme has been expanded significantly during the Fox administration along three axes: territory, beneficiaries and scope. Territorially, the programme was gradually extended from rural localities (less than 2 500 inhabitants) to semi-urban, urban-intermediate and finally urban areas.

*Source:* OECD (2007h).

---

provision of pre-school education is currently the sole responsibility of the gminas, which need to find the necessary financial resources in their general budgets, as pre-school education is not included in the educational subsidy.

Other problems in rural areas are linked to the poor quality of some schools and to the lack of public transports. Educational offer of schools above the level of post-elementary schools (*gimnazjum*) tends to be poorer in rural areas. It is especially difficult to attract good teachers in rural schools (EIU, 2006). At primary and secondary level, teachers' relative salaries in Poland are very low by international standards and there are no specific incentives for teachers to teach in backward rural areas. Consideration could be given to options to reward teachers for getting some experience in rural regions. Another problem is linked to the lack of a good, affordable public transport system in rural areas. The choice of school above the post-elementary level depends on the network of schools in the immediate area and the travel and transport costs, which have risen considerably in the past few years (see Section 2.2 on infrastructure). For some rural families with little income, education has become a heavy financial burden. It is recommended to think of ways to offer cheaper public transport in rural areas and special school transport, such as western Australia's orange school buses which allow eligible students to attend the nearest government or non-government school. There could also be incentives to encourage urban schools to found branches in rural areas, perhaps rotating teachers for specialist subjects. Besides, although various programmes aiming at enhancing the use of ICT/Internet at school have been introduced since the early 2000s,[26] distance learning through e-learning should also be facilitated. In 2004, only 4% individuals (which is the lowest figure throughout EU) use the Internet in order to learn within the system of education (schools, universities). This is five times less than in the countries where such form of acquiring education is most common: Estonia (21%), Lithuania and Finland (20% each).

Last but not least, access of rural students to tertiary education should be improved. Financial obstacles are important, given the fees charged by private universities and the expenses of daily life in large cities. Although there is a student-loan scheme, take-up is extremely low, probably because repayment must start two years after the loan is taken out (*i.e.* often before students have completed their studies) and because a bank guarantee is required for students from the poorest families (OECD, 2006d). Student loans should be reformed to allow repayment as an income tax surcharge once, and only if, graduates are employed (as in Australia, New Zealand and the United Kingdom). A state guarantee could replace a bank guarantee for students from low-income families (a reform currently being discussed in France). In addition, special aids for housing of low-income students should be envisaged. In New Zealand and Australia, the university grant system includes provision for accommodation allowances for rural students, and universities have residence halls which give priority to out-of-town students and charge a price that is covered by the grant.

### Better match labour market needs and supply of students

In addition to numbers, it is essential to achieve a match between labour market needs and the supply of tertiary education graduates. In Poland, the links between the education system and labour markets are clearly insufficient (see economic model in Annex 2.A1 and OECD (2006d)). Tertiary education institutions are not sufficiently concerned with the employability of their graduates and undergraduates. Many students study communication/human resources fields but there is a shortage in sciences and technology. In addition, the school curriculum does not encourage entrepreneurial attitudes during the course of studies, particularly in technical courses. Priorities should include teaching programmes to develop entrepreneurial skills and competences and should match these programmes with industry requirements. An interesting example of training was developed in the Aviation Valley (see Box 2.10). The strong policy focus on the Regional Technical Colleges in Ireland in the 1980s-1990s (now entitled Institute of Technology), focusing mainly on business, engineering and science, has played a critical role in Irish growth (Burnham, 2005). Other initiatives might include work-based learning (i.e. coupling education and training in firms). These often lead to recruitment by firms (see the United Kingdom's knowledge transfer partnerships)[27] and there are great advantages to giving high priority to such programmes.

---

**Box 2.10. Training programmes in the Aviation Valley**

An interesting example of training is the "Aviation Valley" located in the Podkarpackie voivodship. To deal with skill shortages in the region, the Aviation Valley Association of Groups of Enterprises has organised special programmes in the region's schools to prepare specialists in this area. The initiative required tailoring the curricula of technical schools to the needs of the sector and providing extra education to school leavers.

*Source: Background Report, 2007.*

---

To help better match labour market needs and supply of students, local employment agencies should be more closely associated with secondary and tertiary education institutions in order to inform young people about employment opportunities in the region and to better match supply and demand (OECD, 2006b). Powiat labour offices retain large responsibilities in employment policy at the local level, but one can wonder whether the powiat scale is appropriate for such a policy (see Chapter 3). In addition, it is important to work towards the integration of regional labour markets and to facilitate the exchange of information and data on labour markets across regions.

## Training

Improving adult training beyond initial training is a key priority for Poland, especially in regions with high unemployment and less participation in adult training. Poland is not well ranked in terms of adult training and lifelong learning; its supply of overall training provision is similar to Hungary's but well below that of Nordic countries, the United States and the United Kingdom. Progress is also modest for older cohorts, particularly the 55-64 age group. There is also considerable regional variation in participation in adult training. In 2003, participation in Mazowiecke was almost twice that in Lodzkie (OECD, 2006b) (see Figure 2.6). Training appears to be more frequent in regions with low unemployment. In fact, no more than 4% of the unemployed receive any training provided by labour offices in a given year, even though these can finance training for an unemployed person for up to 12 months (24 months for the unskilled) (OECD, 2006b).

Figure 2.6. **Adult training, unemployment and unit costs, by voivodship, 2003**

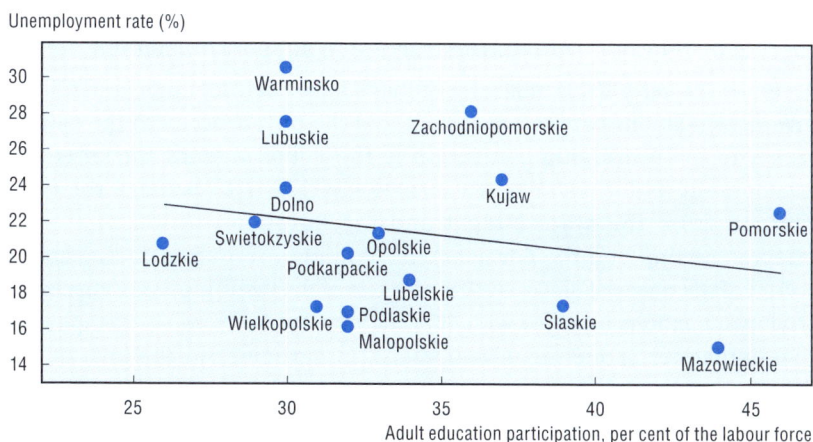

*Source:* OECD (2006b).

## Retain skills

Another crucial challenge for Poland is to retain skills, given the scale of out-migration since 2004. Staff shortages are particularly severe in the health and construction sectors, but they are also serious in the services sector in large cities (Poznan, Wroclaw, etc.). It is extremely difficult for public policy to limit out-migration of skills, as retention of knowledge workers mainly depends on Polish salary levels. Some measures have been adopted to try to limit out-migration or encourage Poles to return (in particular by raising the minimum wage).[28] Efforts have also been made by local governments; the municipality of Wroclaw's mayor launched an advertising campaign in London to encourage Poles living and working there to move to Wroclaw by promising good career development prospects. The city has achieved some success, with over 9 000 people returning.

### 3.2. Building social capital

On top of human capital, what makes the difference between regions that perform well and others on the long-term is the development of social capital, i.e. networks among actors, in particular between businesses and knowledge institutes, and knowledge transfers. To correct market failures, public policy has a role to play in helping public and private actors to collaborate and share knowledge. The "triple helix", or the collaboration between university, industry and government, has inspired reforms in several OECD countries (Finland, France, Norway, Sweden, among others). Poland has made progress in the development of infrastructure to support innovation, but major challenges remain, in particular for clusters development, involvement of Higher Education Institutes (HEI) in innovation processes, and active involvement of local governments in innovation processes.

### Progress in development of infrastructure to support innovation

Since the early 2000s, many institutions have been set up to underpin the network of relations between the public and the private sector at the national level. The main bridging institution is the Polish Agency for Enterprise Development (PAED) established in 2004. Its task is to manage the funds obtained from the state budget and the European Union to support entrepreneurship and the development of human resources, taking special account of the needs of SMEs. PAED is also one of the institutions responsible for carrying out actions financed with EU structural funds. Its role is to implement programmes for economic development, in particular in the area of SME support, exports, regional development, employment of new techniques and technologies, job creation, unemployment and development of human resources. Other national bodies include: the Foundation for the Promotion and Development of SMEs, the International Development Agency and professional associations such as the Chambers of Trade and Industry or the Polish Federation of Engineering Associations.

Local governmental institutions have also started to play a more active role in promoting innovation strategies, particularly in large municipalities (the Academic and Scientific Strategy of the City of Poznan; the European Institute of Technology in Wrocaw) (Box 2.11). The number of local governmental

---

### Box 2.11. **Examples of positive initiatives for innovation at the local level, 2004-06**

The Małopolska Council of Innovation provides a means of sharing ideas. Co-operation by a team of scientists, self-government representatives and the business environment in the framework of the Council contributes to the success of InnoRegioMałopolska, the Małopolska Innovation Strategy, a project under way since mid-2005. Another initiative proving that local entities can pursue innovative solutions is the Silesian Innovation Cluster for Clean Coal Technologies (Śląski Innowacyjny Klaster Czystych Technologii Węglowych), which is implemented by the self-government of the Śląskie voivodship, the cities of Jaworzno, Katowice, Gliwice, Rybnik, Jastrzębie Zdroj and Tychy and Społki Węglowe, power plants and scientific and research institutes. The entities involved in the project aim to develop technologies capable of making hard coal an environmentally friendly fuel and providing an alternative to natural gas and crude oil.

In Poznan, the City Council adopted in March 2006 the Academic and Scientific Strategy for the City of Poznan, which prioritises co-operation by higher education institutions, the City and scientific centres to facilitate the access of young people to relevant academic knowledge, to develop continuing and higher education, to improve the quality of teaching, the internationalisation of the learning process and scientific research, and to strengthen the city's position as a European academic centre.

As the third largest academic centre in Poland with more than 130 000 students studying in 29 higher education institutions, Wroclaw links its future development to the knowledge economy. One of the hallmarks of Wroclaw's future development plan is its bid to establish the European Institute of Technology (EIT) within its agglomeration as part of the Municipal Office's EIT Plus programme. The latter places knowledge and innovation at the heart of Wroclaw's metropolitan area development strategy and emphasises public-private partnerships. The programme will benefit from European funding and will focus on boosting knowledge industries, especially the biotechnology, IT and biomedicine sectors, on attracting knowledge-related investment and on promoting active citizenship in the knowledge society. Wroclaw has also recently been involved in a joint project with Opole, Katowice and Krakow, capital cities of regions crossed by the A4 motorway, called the Motorway of New Technologies Firms. The project aims to attract investment to an area which benefits from the country's best transport infrastructure (A4 and a rapidly growing network of international airports) by supporting the development of knowledge-based businesses and bolstering co-operation between them.

*Source: Background Report, 2007.*

---

institutions supporting innovation has grown by 91% since 2000. However, around 55% offer mainly training, advisory and information services; only one in ten is capable of supporting innovation activities of enterprises in terms of technology transfer. Their impact therefore remains limited. In addition, most local governments (around 50% of powiats and 75% of gminas, particularly in rural areas) still do not have specific institutions for addressing innovation-related issue (Background Report, 2007). In addition, there is a lack of workforce having suitable experience in supporting innovation, notably in technology transfer and commercialization in local governmental institutions supporting innovation.

Ten years after the creation of the first technology park in Poznan in 1995, there were 27 such initiatives, of which eight provide business support services to enterprises. 8 parks undertake training and information activities for enterprises and 11 parks are still at an early stage of development (Background Report, 2007). OECD studies show that science parks can have mixed results: the success of the long-term investments in science parks depends on careful prior cost-benefit analysis and evaluation of demand, which has not always been undertaken. Other linking institutions at the local or regional level include Centres of Advanced Technologies (CoAT) and technology transfer centres. In all, there were 77 active innovation centres in Poland and some 86 other initiatives at more or less advanced stages of organisation in the second half of 2005. The number of these entities has increased by over 60% since 2004.

At the voivodship level, regional development agencies are the most important public institutions for initiating and carrying out efforts to stimulate regional business and the development of SMEs; but their role as creators of entrepreneurship and support to local businesses could be further enhanced. They provide support to firms in the form of subsidies or loans, advisory services and training courses. A major aspect of their work is diffusion of information on policy developments and on more technical and market aspects. In many cases, these agencies serve as regional financing authorities and are in charge of transferring EU funds to entrepreneurs.

### Support to clusters initiatives

Until recently Polish economic policy paid little attention to the issue of clusters, but this has changed somewhat since 2004. The Gdansk Institute for the Market Economy and the Ministry of Regional Development, as well as other institutions, have worked to identify the main clusters (such as the Aviation Valley, the Plastics Valley in Tarnów, the maritime cluster in Gdansk and the food cluster in Lublin). Interestingly, some rural regions (like Lubelskie) have performed well in the development of clusters, with strong links among farmers and export firms (Box 2.12). Opportunities for cluster development have also been identified: the electronics industry in the Warsaw area; pharmaceuticals

---

### Box 2.12. **Rural clusters in the Lubelskie region**

Rural clusters in Lubelskie have proven effective in supporting the regional economy, as public and private actors have supported agricultural and wood production by developing the region's "natural" wealth. Lubelskie has managed to create a food cluster of natural agricultural products produced by small and medium farms. Strong links exist between farmers, export organisations, public and private actors. Local producers have set up a professional organisation to promote the "typical" Lubelskie products jointly with an export organisation and public actors which support this professional grouping by organising events such as festivals. Such initiatives should be strongly supported by regional authorities.

Like Poland's other "valleys" (the "plastics valley" or the "aviation valley"), the "food valley" is based on a grouping of farms specialising in quality food products. The goal of the association Ekolubelszczyzna, created in January 2007, Is to disseminate the region's agro-food products. The region is known for the quality of its eggs, meal, milk and other products cultivated in a "natural" manner. The organisation's participants are the firms in charge of collection and commercialisation, the suppliers of ecological products, the eco-agro tourism firms, the certification and qualification organisms, the high schools and research institutes, various advisory firms, pro-ecological NGOs, etc. The regional clusters are closely linked to other initiatives for supporting regional culture, such as the "cluster of the regional culture" which functions through workshops on cultural organisations, popular culture, protection of the national heritage, the forums on handicaps, universities and faculties of art, etc.

Other clusters exist, such as the "wood cluster", created in February 2007, which associates the primary sector (forests, logging) and the secondary sector (wood and wood products). At the end of 2007, there were 23 members closely linked to the municipality of Lublin, the region and the polytechnic.

Another cluster specialises in the production and commercialisation of fruit, in the gmina of Rybczewice, 30 kilometres from Lublin. At the beginning, in 1998, it was a co-operative of 42 members which developed common marketing activities. In 2002, they joined a business company (limited responsibility firm). Since then there has been investment in packaging and sorting activities, The total amount of land involved is 480 hectares, of which 240 of apple trees with more than 20 varieties (5 000 tons a year), as well as blueberries and hazelnuts.

---

and cosmetics in Krakow, Lodz and Warsaw; and the automotive industry in Dolnoslaskie and Slaskie (southern Poland). Cluster programmes should not seek to create clusters but to help latent clusters to emerge and expand. Central agencies therefore need to improve statistics and help region identify and map potential clusters.

Regional governments need to give more support to clusters; as the level of support is reported to be weak, in some cases. In Lublin, for example, the local wood and agro-food clusters have some links to the local technical universities but seem to lack strong regional support. In addition, it is difficult for clusters as a whole to apply for structural funds. Poland needs cluster facilitators able to work in regions and improve the culture of co-operation among entrepreneurs, particularly SMEs. The Klastry programme in the Czech Republic is an example of good practice in this area. It focuses on developing sectoral competencies and networking, mainly among firms, in all regions outside of Prague with support from EU structural funds. Providing training and cluster awareness sessions to clusters facilitators and regional governments, universities and the private sector is an efficient way to diffuse the concept and favour the strengthening of existing clusters.

Clusters development should also receive more attention at the central level. Although few concrete initiatives have been taken so far by public initiatives to support clusters,[29] the Polish Agency for Enterprise Development recently launched a call for developing and implementing training programmes to promote clustering. The main goal of the project is to give managers a chance to get acquainted through training with the principles and practice of co-operation within a cluster. The project also envisages the organisation of training for the public sector, especially for regional authorities responsible for enterprise policy at their level. This is a positive step ahead. As a next step, central authorities could launch a competitive selection progress to allocate specific funds to the best organised clusters. Most programmes targeting clusters with an innovation focus in OECD countries use a competitive selection process. Examples include Sweden's VINNVÄXT (150 applicants), the French *pôles de compétitivité* programme (105 applicants), and Germany's BioRegio, InnoRegio and BioProfile programmes. Even when lagging regions are an explicit target, some programmes include a competitive selection progress to identify the best public investments within the target group. Germany's InnoRegio, while targeting the lagging eastern *Länder*, selected only 23 out of 444 applicants. Other programmes open to lagging regions also included a competitive process (OECD, 2008b).

The focus on clusters regional innovation systems should be better linked to urban development, and the central government has a role to play in strengthening the various specialisations of metropolitan areas. Some OECD countries have developed integrated approaches focusing on metropolitan areas targeting both tangible assets (transport, housing) and intangible assets (innovation, economic policies) through incentives to enhance specialisations of cities. The Dutch government is increasingly seeking to enhance the specialisations of the four cities that form the Randstad metropolitan region (Amsterdam, Rotterdam, The Hague, Utrecht) through a national spatial planning strategy well connected with the national economic strategy. The French competitiveness poles introduced by the central government exploit the various clusters locations to strongly reinforce specialisations of territories. Finland has introduced an ambitious urban policy in 2005, aiming at increasing the competitiveness of the nine largest Finnish cities,[30] by enhancing their individual specialisation to bring about a better division of labour in the country (OECD, 2006f). These policies aim to ensure better co-ordination of existing programmes, by integrating all facets of urban development (infrastructure, housing, social policy, innovation, economic policies). These measures are ambitious, but they require proper co-ordination at the central government level.

### 3.3. New priorities to finance innovation: regional innovation strategies and SMEs

Polish innovation policy (Box 2.13) now pays more attention to regional aspects of development through the design of regional innovation strategies and the use of location-based instruments. The 2007-13 strategy for regional development focuses on innovation through a specific programme of EUR 9.7 billion euro, with EUR 8.7 billion from ERDF and 1.4 billion from national resources (see Annex 2.A3 for more details on the funding of the programme): the programme is thus co-financed with 85% of EU resources. In addition, the Ministry of Regional Development has recommended that regions allocate 40% of their expenditures (within regional operational programmes – ROPs) to innovation and enterprise support. So far, within the sectoral programmes, EUR 3 629 million have been allocated to specific projects linked to R&D and enterprise development, or slightly more than 7% of total funds (MRD, 2007).

---

### Box 2.13.  **Polish innovation policy**

After several years of piecemeal S&T policy reforms, Poland's entry in the EU in 2004 was marked by growing attention to innovation in order to help ensure future economic development and continue the process of convergence with other EU countries. The government's strategy for national development 2007-15 and the "innovation strategy" aim to rebalance the policy mix for innovation by shifting the focus away from basic research and towards innovation (STI/OECD). The National Reform Programme 2005-08 also recognised the importance of creating a business friendly environment and a special inter-ministerial team was appointed in February 2006. In the 2007-13 Strategy, one of the key instruments is the Innovative Economy Operational Programme which will mobilise EUR 7 billion of EU funds and an additional EUR 1.2 billion from national public sources. Because of the emphasis on structural funds, the focus on regions has been reinforced.

*Source: OECD (2007d).*

---

Most measures in favour of innovation in Poland are new and mainly financed through EU structural funds. A vast majority of the entrepreneurs surveyed in a study recently launched by the Ministry of Regional Development consider that these funds will significantly boost the innovation potential of their companies in the short term. This result is in line with other evaluations of the impact of structural funds on companies' competitiveness: improved product quality, an expanded offer and number of new products, and reduced dependence on external suppliers. Visible progress in improving innovation performance cannot yet be expected as the measures have been in place for a very short time.

### Regional innovation strategies (RIS)

The process of creating regional innovation strategies[31] began in 2002 and was completed with the approval of the voivodship councils in early 2005. Currently 15 regions (Mazowieckie is an exception[32]) have started to implement an RIS using EU structural funds and their own budgets. A positive effect of the RIS process was to elaborate, for the first time, clear, integrated strategies which acknowledged the role of SMEs in regional growth. Regional innovation strategies also correctly identified problems relating to co-operation between scientific units and enterprises, perceiving these as a major reason for the low innovation potential of regional economies.

Although this process has resulted in a positive step forward, it seems that, as in many EU countries, criteria for regional innovation strategies are too broad. Situations differ across regions and the RIS have been uneven in terms of quality and the methodologies used, but most RIS do not specify the policy instruments to be applied to encourage co-operation by scientific organisations and enterprises. It is difficult in the implementation of RIS to keep the integrated approach to innovation as the sources of financing are dispersed. In addition, the RIS tend to be inward-focused and disconnected from the situation in other regions. For 2007-13, expenditures will need to be looked at in detail for potential gaps between overall strategy directions and actual allocations of funds. The Ministry of Regional Development could help regions to develop their RIS with the use of specific analytical and methodological tools. France has recently developed such a toolkit to help regions elaborate their innovation strategies (Box 2.14).

Strategies need to be more focused, based on regional comparative advantages and discussed with private actors from the early stages of the process. OECD experience indicates that care needs to be taken not to make inappropriate policy choices by targeting fashionable objectives, such as creative industries or biotechnology. Care also needs to be taken to avoid transferring policies wholesale from regions with certain production models to regions with quite different characteristics. It is important to stick to regional

> **Box 2.14. Regional innovation strategies: toolkit for French regional authorities, 2007**
>
> When applying for structural funds, French regions prepare documents on their development strategies and forward them to the EU Commission. Brussels often considered that such papers lacked coherence and that the policy analysis could be more robust. The French government therefore decided in 2007 to create a guide that would help regions to assess their strengths and weaknesses and would improve the decision-making process. The guide was completed in November 2007 after discussion and consultation with several pilot regions. It has now been communicated to all regions.
>
> The guide provides an overview of the main factors determining regional growth in modern economies. It describes the overall components of the innovation system and indicates a number of regional indicators to calculate as well as benchmarks to consider. It provides methodological keys for establishing a regional strategy based on the diagnosis. Priorities are selected according to a number of criteria. Monitoring of programmes is made possible through the use of appropriate indicators and references.

comparative advantages and to target high value added niches cautiously and properly when embarking on high-technology strategies. In many regions, the shift towards competitiveness will work best if translated into incremental, medium- to low-technology organisational innovations rather than into efforts to develop high-technology industries *ex nihilo*. In addition, involvement of the business sector and other non-public stakeholders from the onset, not only in the design of the RIS but also in the management of the local and regional agencies or entities supporting innovation (including parks, incubators, etc.) will improve the governance of regional innovation systems.

Cross-border an international co-operation on regional innovative projects is important. The region of Mazowieckie has developed networks with other EU countries in the framework of pro-inno Europe, which is funded by the European Commission (*e.g.* involvement of SMEs in technology-based innovation clusters in Europe – Innet networking). Poland (in particular Northern regions) can gain from its proximity to the Baltic Sea region, one of the world's most innovative regions.[33] For example, the Pomorskie region participates in cross-border initiatives to enhance the innovation potential of the macro-region with the support of EU Interreg programme (see Box 2.15).

### Better involve SMEs

As in many other OECD countries, the diffusion of knowledge and its use by SMEs is not optimal in Poland, even though SMEs play a crucial role in innovation processes. The main problems for Polish SMEs are lack of awareness of the benefits of innovation and little access to information about services offered by

---

> Box 2.15. **The Baltic Sea region innovation network (BSR InnoNET)**
>
> The objective of the Baltic Sea region innovation network is to create links between innovation policy makers, implementing agencies and analysts in the Baltic Sea region. The goal is to help make the region a leader in creating an environment for policy makers and practitioners to establish joint activities, build strong industrial clusters and innovation poles to link national innovation systems and innovation programmes, and to develop methods to measure and evaluate cluster performance and policy success. The project started in 2006 and is planned to run until August 2009. In Poland, the West Pomeranian Regional Development Agency (ZARR) is a participant. This is one of four European projects with a new transnational perspective on development of innovation programmes and policies in Europe.
>
> *Source: www.proinno-europe.eu.*

the national SME network. Although some improvement in getting information to SMEs has been achieved since 2004,[34] thanks to EU funding; only about 10 200 SMEs have benefited from EU funding since 2004 (less than 0.5% of SMEs). SMEs have not played an important role for funds related to innovation *per se*, as demand for EU innovation funds came essentially from large enterprises, particularly the former state-owned enterprises. Besides, SMEs have benefited little from ICT development under the integrated regional operational programme (10% of the funds for ICT development went to SMEs). Few SMEs participate in training courses connected with innovation (*Entrepreneurship and Innovation in Poland*, 2007 IPREG report). Recent OECD research in three major global industries (ICT, automotive and pharmaceuticals) clearly shows that in major global industries, the role of SMEs has not diminished; on the contrary, small firms are often the prime source of innovative ideas that are integrated into other products or brought to the market in their own right by large firms (OECD, 2007k).

A priority for 2007-13 is to involve SMEs more in innovation and R&D and to ensure that information gaps and market failures in this respect are minimised. This requires, for instance, the creation of agencies or "brokers" specialised in support services for the industries of the local productive system. Knowledge vouchers have also been a success in a number of countries (*e.g.* the Netherlands, Italy), and Poland might consider introducing them. The principle is that a fixed amount of money is granted to (small) firms to buy knowledge from knowledge institutes (Box 2.16). Another subsidy regime could be considered to promote knowledge circles in higher education institutions on a regional basis. The knowledge circles developed in the Netherlands aim at increasing the outward focus of higher education institutions, especially towards SMEs.

Box 2.16. **Subsidy scheme for innovation vouchers
in the Netherlands**

In the Netherlands, the exchange of knowledge between SMEs and knowledge institutions is less than optimal. SMEs make far too little use of the knowledge available from other parties. Innovation vouchers were therefore introduced to allow knowledge held by knowledge institutions to play a role in developing new products, processes and services. An innovation voucher enables SMEs to get to know knowledge institutions by submitting research questions to them. The vouchers promote a transfer of knowledge between knowledge institutions and SMEs.

There exist two types of innovation voucher: a small one and a large one. The small voucher is worth EUR 2 500. Each SME may get a "small" voucher only once. The objective is to encourage the enterprise to approach a knowledge institution. A total of 3 000 small vouchers are available. The large voucher is worth EUR 7 500. It allows the enterprise to submit a more complex question to a knowledge institution. To qualify for these vouchers, the enterprise must contribute one-third of the total project costs. The government will provide an amount not exceeding EUR 5 000. In addition to the single small voucher, an enterprise may obtain one large voucher each year. A total of 3 000 large vouchers is available. Since 2008 it is also possible to use a (small or a large) voucher *once* to refund the cost for applying and obtaining a patent.

A voucher is valid for 12 months. Therefore, the knowledge institution must present the voucher to SenterNovem (part of the Ministry of Economic Affairs) for payment within twelve months of the date it was issued to the enterprise. Knowledge institutions that accept vouchers under the subsidy scheme for innovation vouchers are public knowledge institutions and few private institutions (universities, colleges, various higher education institutions, knowledge institutions established in other EU member states provided that they are similar or equivalent to Dutch knowledge institutions, and legal persons that carry out activities that increase general scientific and technical knowledge).

*Source:* Ministry of Economic Affairs of the Netherlands, 2008.

### Better involve universities in innovation processes

More marketable and industry-relevant R&D could be carried out in the tertiary education sector. Though its contribution is still modest (around 0.2% of GDP in 2003), the sector accounts for nearly one-third of all R&D spending in the country. Significant amounts of research funding are concentrated in some 30-40 institutions; thus, a large number of universities carry out no funded research. Another problem is the economic relevance of the research that is done; the decreasing importance of industry in funding higher education research (11.4% in 1994 and only 6.3% in 2003) is a trend that needs to be reversed. Deregulating some university activities would also facilitate their co-operation with the business sector. Poland does not allow the involvement of business representatives on university boards. In addition, universities cannot own or have equity stakes in spinoff companies. Relaxing this regulation would probably make it less difficult for university researchers and professors to find capital for their start-ups. It would also help universities and other higher education institutions to increase the employability of their graduates, improve their curricula and better anticipate regional labour market needs.

### Focus on strategic foreign direct investment

Polish regions should focus on strategies to attract FDI with the largest spillovers to local economies, rather than the maximum amount of FDI. Since the early 2000s, more greenfield foreign capital[35] (their share reached 58% in 2004, as compared to 37% in 2002) has been invested and has translated into a rise in employment (262 655 workers), essentially in manufacturing, mainly in the special economic zones (SEZ), which will operate to 2015-17. Poland is increasingly targeting FDI to technologically advanced sectors or the so-called rising sectors (Box 2.17). Through FDI spillovers and "sticky" activities (i.e. those that do not tend to move constantly to cheaper labour markets, but are more directly related to a country's resources and features), the government hopes to reverse the negative trend that characterised the innovativeness of Polish firms at the end of the 1990s.[36] Although it is too early to assess this policy, trends are encouraging; more than 30 multinational enterprises have recently set up R&D centres in Poland. However, the location of these centres in a limited number of places is an issue from the regional policy point of view.

---

**Box 2.17. Priorities for attracting FDI in Poland**

The priories outlined in the "Programme for the Economic Promotion of Poland until 2005" in terms of the structure of FDI were maintained in the "Assumptions of the Strategy for the Promotion of Poland's Economy for 2007-15" (Ministry of the Economy, March 2007). The document states that the most desirable type of investments are in high-technology areas, i.e. those aiming to establish the R&D centres of foreign enterprises in Poland. Other objectives for attracting FDI include: i) treating as priority sectors the automotive and related sectors (although these are traditional industry branches, with competitive positions and high exporting possibilities); ii) development of the chemical and pharmaceutical industry, using technical universities and medical academies as well as R&D units.

---

Foreign direct investment can play an important role in enhancing the competitiveness of local firms, increasing employment – through sub-contracting –, and exposure to overseas innovations and methods. The strategies for FDI seem to underestimate the role played by the presence of quality sub-contractors in international investors' decisions to locate in specific areas. In countries like Hungary, a charter was signed with a number of multinationals to increase local sub-contracting and enhance local demand-driven innovation programmes for SMEs (OECD, 2003). Poland might be interested in promoting the development of such often regionally based agreements.

Strong supportive services are needed at the local level to attract FDI, to complement the approaches developed by the central government. A major challenge is to co-ordinate the support system for FDI attraction at the local level, as there are many agencies dealing with FDI – regional development agencies, investors assistance centres, as well as regional governments, in addition to regional branches of PAIZ (Polish agency for Foreign Direct Investment). Western and southern regions seem better equipped in terms of institutions providing services for foreign investors (Regional agencies, SEZ) whereas Eastern regions lack a comprehensive institutional framework to attract FDI. The co-operation between public and private actors remains limited in Eastern regions, which seem to place most of their hope in central agency interventions.

### Conclusion

Poland has made great progresses to develop institutional tools and policies to enhance the move to the knowledge economy, at both central and local governments levels. The challenge is to evolve to a more integrated strategy to enhance innovation at the local level and to increase economic specialisations of various territories. Regional Innovation Strategies need to be more based on regional comparative advantages and discussed with private actors from the early stages of the process. Local strategies need to be place-based, and Lisbon objectives need to be understood in a broad way; for example the primary focus in rural areas should be education – including access to pre-school. In addition, a priority for 2007-13 is to better involve SMEs in innovation processes and R&D and to facilitate their access to EU funds, including from clusters.

## 4. Rural development policy

An appropriate policy focus on rural areas is crucial to balanced and sustainable growth in Poland, given the large rural population, employment in the agriculture sector and the rising disparities between rural and urban areas. As explained in Chapter 1, rural areas have benefited less from Poland's economic development during the past two decades. At the same time, positive new aspects of Polish rural areas include rising incomes for farmers, new outflows of population from urban areas to rural ones, especially near cities, which offer opportunities for new services activities; the need for recreational areas and second homes, as well as an under-exploited tourism potential in many rural areas with a well-preserved natural environment.

Given the decrease of agriculture in the share of rural incomes (20% in 2002, see Chapter 1), Poland faces the twofold challenge of implementing the new rural paradigm,[37] i.e. focusing on rural development beyond agriculture, while modernising agriculture through a reduction in the number of small farms and better productivity levels resulting from training and technological investments. The two dimensions are strongly linked and should not be separated as they were in the European Union in the first phases of implementing the Common Agricultural Policy (CAP). Poland's policy statements clearly show its wish to address both dimensions but it is less clear how to do so. The context in the late 2000s, with the increase in global prices for agricultural products and reforms of the Common Agricultural and Cohesion policies, provides a window of opportunity for smooth changes in agriculture and rural development.

Poland has increasingly moved towards a broad approach to rural development rather than a narrow focus on agriculture, but substantial progress can still be made, provided the territorial dimension is better taken into account and there is greater coherence with regional development policy. This section will analyse the need to i) take a more territorial approach to rural development; ii) focus on education and enhance rural-urban linkages; iii) modernise agriculture and enhance its productivity, as well as reduce the number of non-productive small farms; and iv) diversify the rural economy, particularly via tourism and services.

### 4.1. Take a more territorial approach to rural development

Although Poland has moved towards a broad rural development approach since the early 2000s, rural policy is still conceived top-down by the central level, with little involvement of local actors and redistribution measures still widespread. On paper, there was quite a good balance between agriculture and wider rural development in the rural development plan for 2004-06; the priorities were farm investment, food processing, with a focus first on direct payments and second on education, entrepreneurship, infrastructure development and environment protection. However, the allocation of resources still largely went for redistribution and compensatory measures (for pre-retirement measures for example). The approach taken was top-down, unlike the pre-accession SAPARD programme which promoted more local initiatives.

The 2007-13 rural development strategy, based on the 2005 CAP reforms (Box 2.18), is more oriented towards diversification of the rural economy, with 20% of the budget allocation (3.3 billion euro). Poland ranks fifth in the EU for

## Box 2.18. **The CAP and recent reforms to its rural development section (Pillar 2)**

The Common Agricultural Policy (CAP) has been one of the main tools of European integration. Most CAP support (over 95%) is distributed through Pillar 1 (market price support, direct payments to farmers, etc.). Thus it remains largely a sectoral policy. The beginnings of a territorial and integrated rural development programme emerged in 1999 when the EU agreed a Rural Development Regulation to establish rural development as the new "second pillar" of the CAP. This Pillar 2 is much smaller (less than 5% of support) and covers so-called "rural development measures", including support for farmers in less favoured areas, agri-environment schemes which pay farmers to manage their land in accordance with environmental objectives, and farm modernisation. In practice, virtually all these measures are available only to farmers, so they may still be regarded as sectoral rather than territorial in nature. In principle, the European Commission envisages that the emphasis of the CAP, in budgetary terms, will gradually shift from Pillar 1 to Pillar 2 – that is, from market support towards rural development (in this farmer-centric sense) – but this is strongly contested by farming interests in most, if not all, member states.

Following a reform of the first Pillar1 in 2003 and 2004, the Agricultural Council adopted in September 2005 a policy of fundamental reform of rural development (RD) for 2007-13. The following three major objectives for RD policy have been set for the period: increasing the competitiveness of the agricultural sector; enhancing the environment and countryside through support for land management; enhancing the quality of life in rural areas and promoting diversification of economic activities. A thematic axis was created to correspond to each core objective. The three thematic axes are complemented by a "methodological" axis dedicated to the LEADER approach (LEADER axis). In this way the reform integrates the LEADER Community Initiative (funded until 2006 through the European Fund for Agriculture Guarantee and Guidance [EAGGF]) into mainstream RD programmes and also brings rural development under a single funding and programming framework, the European Agriculture Fund for Rural Development (EAFRD):

Axis 1: Improving the competitiveness of the agricultural and forestry sectors.

Axis 2: Improving the environment and countryside.

Axis 3: Improving quality of life in rural areas and encouraging diversification.

Axis 4: LEADER approach.

While "a single set of programming, financing, reporting and control rules will simplify considerably the delivery of the policy" (EC fact sheet), in practice, the reform implies that LEADER has to compete with established agricultural interests for its funding. Moreover, the total sum available under Pillar 2 was reduced during the negotiations over the EU budget for 2007-13, leaving some financial pressure on member states, especially those that emphasise agri-environmental measures and payments to less favoured area.

Source: OECD, 2007 based on EU 2007.

allocations to Axis 3 (rural diversification), after countries like the Netherlands and Germany; 42% of total funds (7.2 billion) aim to enhance the competitiveness of farms; while 33% focus on the environmental dimension. However, less than 5% of the total is allocated to the LEADER programme (a successful programme for co-operation among local actors on rural development, see Box 2.18 below) compared to countries like Spain, Portugal, the Netherlands and Ireland which plan to allocate twice that share to LEADER (Figure 2.7).

Figure 2.7. **Comparative allocation of total public funds (EAFRD + national funds) to the four axes of their respective rural development programmes (2007-13) (2007-2013)**

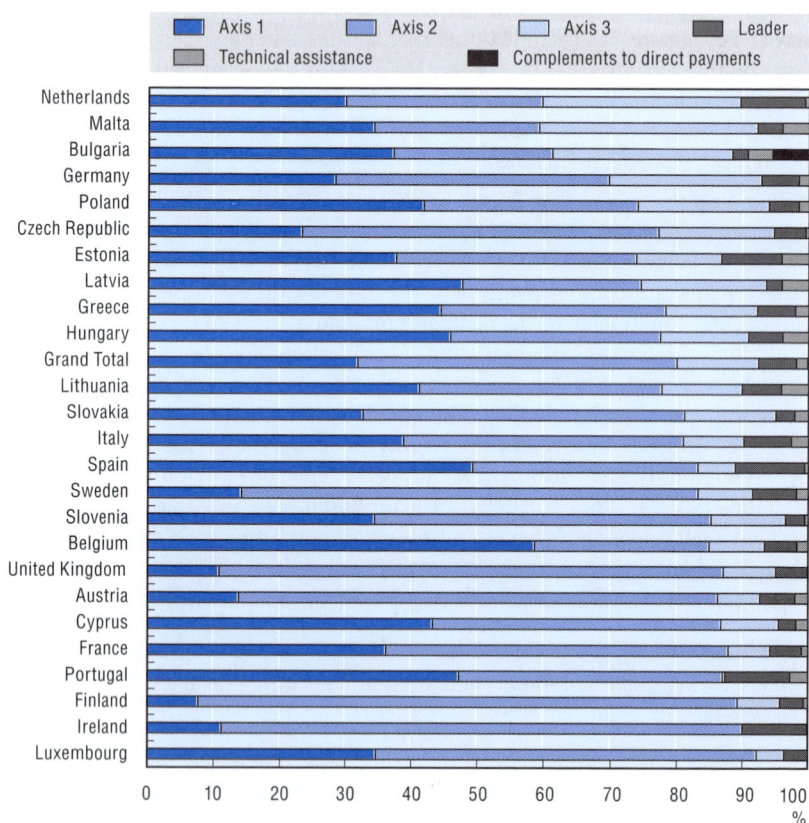

Source: OECD, based on EU, 2007.

The strategy for rural development 2007-13 is well balanced but has a weak territorial dimension (Box 2.19). One central operational programme for rural development has been set up by the Ministry of Agriculture in place of

> ## Box 2.19. **Poland's rural development strategy 2007-13**
>
> **Axis 1** with 41% of the budget is the most important. Its main objective is *improvement of competitiveness in the agricultural and forestry sector.* This should be achieved through support to the older population and to the reinforcement of mobility, infrastructures and educational programmes. Support for the older population involves early retirement, which makes possible a market in land by renting or selling farms in exchange for a pension. The second policy aspect concerns the infrastructure that encourages competitiveness through adjustment in the sector as well as to modernisation of agricultural holdings, support to the agricultural producer group, and to the integration of the farmers in food quality systems. The measures for education are those in favour of training and help for young farmers when setting up, advisory services for farmers and forest owners and lastly, information on and promotion of the sector.
>
> **Axis 2** with 32% of the budget aims at *improvement of the environment and rural areas*, in particular: i) the agricultural land within the NATURA 2000 network and payments associated with the Water Framework Directive; ii) the preventive reforestation of non-agricultural land' iii) mountain areas and less-favoured areas (LFA). Axis 2 both helps to prevent potential natural disasters such as those that occurred in the flooding of the Odra and Nysa at the end of the 1990s, and focuses on lagging southern regions (Tatras and Carpathen).
>
> **Axis 3** receives 20% of the budget and focuses on *diversification of the rural economy* through three measures: diversification towards non-agricultural activities; support for basic services for the economy and rural population to encourage the establishment and development of micro-enterprises and support for village renewal and development.
>
> The **final axis** corresponds to the **LEADER programme**.

16 regional ones, as it was considered useful to continue most of the 2004-06 measures and to reduce administration and management costs. The regional dimension of the central programme is quite limited, so that the same policy tools are applied in every Polish region, although the regions are in fact very diverse in terms of the rural challenges. Besides, local actors were little involved in the design of the strategy. This policy requires a stronger territorial dimension, owing to the wide differences in rural challenges across the country, as explained in Chapter 1. Moreover, the fact that funds for rural development are separated from cohesion funds raises governance challenges (see Chapter 3).

Figure 2.8. **Allocation of funds to rural development 2007-13 in Poland, billion euro (total: 16.6 billion euro)**

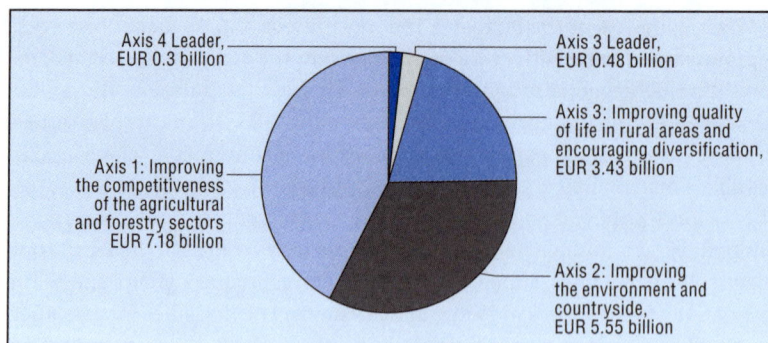

Axis 4 Leader,
EUR 0.3 billion

Axis 3 Leader,
EUR 0.48 billion

Axis 3: Improving quality
of life in rural areas and
encouraging diversification,
EUR 3.43 billion

Axis 1: Improving
the competitiveness
of the agricultural
and forestry sectors
EUR 7.18 billion

Axis 2: Improving
the environment and
countryside,
EUR 5.55 billion

Source: Ministry of Agriculture, 2007.

### 4.2. Reduce obstacles to mobility and enhance urban-rural linkages

The most important challenge for lagging rural areas is to become better connected to development opportunities and enhance their linkages to urban areas. This implies three main channels: education, access to capital and information, and better transport and telecommunications infrastructure. Enhancing access to education is a pre-requisite for any long-term rural development strategy, and should be considered as an absolute priority (see Section 2.3).

A network of agricultural consultancy services is distributed throughout the country's rural area, and consultants have vast experience working with farmers and residents, but there is limited focus on rural diversification. The advisory system for farmers and the rural population is dominated by agricultural activities. In addition, NGOs carry out very few activities in rural areas. Unions and professional groups should be trained to co-manage changes in rural areas. Psychological obstacles to mobility are important, and ready access to information is needed to overcome them. Good information flows are required to ensure mobility out of agriculture and the diversification of the rural economy.

Access to capital is an important pre-condition for mobility or changes in activity. Even if the inclusion of Polish farmers in the CAP has forced deep changes in relations between farmers and financial and advisory institutions (Wilkin, 2006),[38] limited access to capital remains a barrier for mobility out of rural areas. The amount of credit in Poland as a ratio of GDP is four times below the euro zone average. Also, the system for loan guarantee funds, micro-loan funds (particularly important for SMEs) and other means of supporting enterprises' development activities is still underdeveloped and under-capitalised. In addition, long-term loans are still very difficult to get:

with the rising cost of housing, this makes very difficult for rural people to move to urban (or semi-urban) areas. The Polish labour market is still far from achieving smooth mobility. The second problem is linked to farmers' limited micro-finance opportunities, as the financing system is still dominated by agricultural institutions.

Developing appropriate basic public services is a pre-condition for overall development in rural areas: increasing the competitiveness of rural areas and improving rural-urban linkages. In spite of improvements since the early 1990s,[39] Polish rural areas lag behind urban ones in terms of access to basic infrastructure such as transport, water, gas and sewage systems. The NSRF rightly points to the need to improve infrastructure development in rural areas. Together with the social policy and support for production, provision of basic infrastructure is an important part of overall rural policy. Infrastructure development is crucial for enhancing the quality of life of rural inhabitants, facilitating diversification, and attracting more foreign direct investment and tourism. It should focus on: cost-benefit analysis, co-operation among gminas and demographic planning (see the section on infrastructure). Mexico's experience with micro-regions promotes a multi-sector territorial approach to infrastructure development that could be relevant for Poland's lagging regions (Box 2.20). Importantly, the development of telecommunications and the reduction of the digital divide should be treated with the same urgency as the transport network (see Section 2.2).

### 4.3. Supporting competitive farms

Given the persistent high employment in the agriculture sector and its low labour productivity (17% of the population working in agriculture contributes to 4.6% of the national GDP, see Chapter 1); there is wide agreement in Poland on the need to rationalise agriculture and to increase the size of the average farm-holding. The NSRF mentions a target of reducing the agricultural population to 12% by 2020. Many policies have already been introduced to achieve this objective, such as pre-retirement measures, which are quite successful but costly. The agricultural population has already diminished significantly from 27% of the population in 1990 to 17% in 2008. However, this is largely due to the closure of large state farms in northern Poland, as well as changes in the statistical definitions of those considered as employed in agriculture. Surprisingly, small farms (even some of less than one hectare), mainly in south-eastern Poland, have strongly resisted structural change.

### The Common Agriculture Policy and Polish agriculture

The effect of the Common Agricultural Policy on Polish agriculture has raised many fears among Polish farmers.[40] Before 2004, given its focus on large enterprises (size of farms, yields and number of animals) and productivity,

---

### Box 2.20. **Mexico's micro-regions strategy**

Mexico's micro-regions strategy aims to provide basic infrastructure to the most marginalised rural regions. It involves many ministries and is led by the Ministry of Social Development SEDESOL. Its objective is to co-ordinate public policy for the least developed rural areas (263 areas of application spread across 1 334 municipalities in 31 different states) and to promote bottom-up participation in targeted communities. It is not a programme but a multi-sector, multi-tier strategy which relies on a multi-tier co-ordination mechanism.

The National Strategy for the Micro-regions was initiated in February 2001 as an effort to break the prevailing tendency towards "sectorialisation" in ministries and to enhance co-ordination and synergies among different ministries regarding investment in lagging rural regions. The strategy's micro-regions were chosen on the basis of the Marginalisation Index developed by the National Council of Population (CONAPO). The selected 263 micro-regions contain more than 99 000 localities and have a population of close to 20 million.

The strategy seeks to induce development through the provision of all basic infrastructure services in "micro-poles of development", called strategic community centres (CECs). Their function is to concentrate the necessary basic infrastructure for the local population and the surrounding settlements. Authorities expect these "centres" to help overcome the difficulties linked to the provision of basic services and foster a concentration of population around them to create larger rural hubs and contain migration towards urban areas. Objective criteria have been developed for validating progress in each CEC based on flag indicators. For each of the CECs, the stated objective is to reach eleven "white flags" or *banderas blancas*. A *bandera blanca* certifies that a target area has reached a certain level of infrastructure or service.

*Source:* OECD (2007h).

---

farmers feared extensive concentration of farms and the disappearance of small/very small farms (less than 5 hectares). On the other hand, the accession of Poland to the EU and more broadly the Eastern enlargement[41] has raised concerns about the sustainability of CAP funding. Indeed, Poland and Romania combined have almost as many farmers as the rest of the EU15. Implementing the policy in a context different from that in western European countries is a complex challenge. The key question is how to implement the CAP in a way that is consistent with other EU countries, while ensuring a positive impact on the competitiveness of Polish agriculture and a smooth transition for non-productive farms.

The impact of the CAP on Polish agriculture has been mixed. It has encouraged the specialisation and modernisation of large farms, but not the overall restructuring of small farms. The decoupling of the CAP has also allowed more small Polish farms to benfit from funding that focuses on "quality production" rather than quantity. In addition, the CAP has reinforced the focus on sustainable farming methods, through the second pillar and the decoupling. Overall, the impact of the CAP has varied with the size of farms:

- **Large farms (more than 50 hectares).** Subsidies from the Common Agricultural Policy have targeted large farms in priority, as in EU15 countries: 42% of CAP funding in 2005 went to the top 10% of recipients. This focus on large farms has strengthened some segments of Polish agriculture (in particular the dairy sector).

- **The intermediate group (farms between 5 and 20 hectares)** has suffered the most from the adjustment. They represented in 1988 40.5% of all farms; today they represent 21.1% (Halamska, 2005). They are too big to adopt the behaviour of small farms (semi-subsistence) and too small to buy land to compete with large farms.

- **Small/very small farms (less than 5 hectares)** have paradoxically resisted the structural changes intended by the CAP, for two reasons. First, the size of Polish farms able to receive these funds was reduced to 0.3 hectares (below the EU minimum size of 1 hectare). Second, the decoupling of the CAP has allowed many small farms to receive more funding to favour quality and sustainable development rather than productivity. Many small farms have in fact not used CAP funding to upgrade their equipment. Added to the pre-retirement measures, to the higher price of land, to welfare transfers and to the secondary activities of most farmers, small farms have been able to resist quite well at a semi-subsistence level. However, this will not be sustainable in the longer term and options for mobility out of non-productive farming are needed.

The key question relates to better link CAP funding to farms' modernisation and productivity gains, whatever their size. If large farms are the most competitive segments of the Polish agriculture and need to be supported as such, a few small farms increasingly have a multifunctional character and are engaging in organic farming. The relative success in some areas of the South-East (for example for strawberries cultivation) is mainly explained by quality increase due to FDI (Danish, French, Swedish FDI) in the downstream sector (food processing) which has modernized farms and help upgrade the quality of products. Provided they are large enough to compete at an economic scale, small farms – highly specialised and innovative– can be a potential strength, especially in the post-2013 CAP framework with its possible greater "rural development" component. Poland has significant market shares to win, particularly related to organic food, as demand has been growing[42] (the German market in particular offers potential growth opportunities for organic food).

### Reform the system of social transfers

The slow restructuring process is due to the ability of the majority of small farms to live on a semi-subsistence basis. Most farmers have secondary activities or work in the informal economy and receive pensions which are sufficient even for extended households (of several generations). These transfers, added to support for small farms constitute rents that present negative incentives for transformation effort and productivity. In addition, they constitute a heavy burden on Polish public finances that may become unsustainable with the ageing of the population.

The current situation of large inflows of EU funds, increases in direct payments to farmers as well as rising incomes for farmers due to the rise in global prices,[43] offer a window of opportunity to change the system of social transfers to farmers. Poland's membership in the EU has clearly increased the level of support for agriculture and rural areas. In 2005 the expenditure on agriculture, rural areas and agricultural markets in Poland tripled compared to 2003. Besides, the price for beef, milk and poultry has tripled since 2003. The price of land has also risen by more than 70% since the mid-1990s (Halamska, 2005), and this is especially significant in rural areas close to large cities. Now that the EU benefits are clear,[44] and revenues of performing farms have grown, there is an opportunity to modify the pension system (KRUS) and more generally the generous social and taxation systems for farmers. Although this is a sensitive reform, which may be costly in the short term, the long-term budgetary gains can be substantial, as they arise not only from the savings on transfer payments, but also from an increase in tax receipts (OECD, 2008a). Reducing subsidies to the KRUS and working towards merging it with the general system should be key priorities for the Polish government. Rural populations need to be deeply involved in the reform of social transfers.

### 4.4. Diversification of the rural economy and co-operation among local actors

Together with agricultural restructuring, the rural economy has to diversify towards non-agricultural activities. This implies the need for a more locally tailored or territorial approach and greater co-operation among local actors and has become an important objective of Poland's rural development and regional development strategies. Opportunities to diversify Poland's rural economy are numerous and so far under-exploited; they include tourism, forestry, rural services, energy and residential needs. Although land prices have increased strongly over the past few years, the average price of one hectare of land is still below the EU average; this gives Polish rural areas a competitive advantage. Moreover, the rural population near large cities is rising. Diversification of the rural economy also calls for improved spatial planning to ensure an orderly transition and to facilitate the changes that are in the best interests of the whole of Poland.

## Co-operation among actors crucial for rural development

Co-operation among farmers, export firms, foreign investors and public authorities is the essential determinant of rural development. It is the main lever of innovation in rural development and has positive externalities both for agriculture and other sectors of the rural economy. Rural clusters in Lubelskie are good examples of positive co-operation among public and private actors (see Section 2.3). An element which has not been fully achieved is the co-operation between wholesale markets and groups of agricultural producers. This is caused, *inter alia* , by the unwillingness of agricultural producers to act jointly. Hence it is necessary to take actions aimed to raise the awareness of the benefits of wholesale markets. These actions should be taken, among others, by agricultural advice centers, agricultural chambers and the already operating and successful organisations of producers.

Policies to enhance co-operation among local actors – such as LEADER+ – should be strongly supported (see Box 2.22). The LEADER+ programme seeks to support rural development through creation of social capital as well as mobilisation and proper utilisation of local resources. The Pilot Programme LEADER+, implemented in Poland in 2004-06, aroused much interest on the part of local governments and NGOs, and the value of applications submitted under the LEADER + programme substantially exceeded the amount of funds allocated to this purpose. It also provided an opportunity to popularise private-public partnerships in activities fostering rural development. The fact that the Leader approach will be employed on a much wider scale and apply to a much broader range of actions related to rural development in 2007-13 is positive. Although the LEADER approach will be employed on a wider scale during 2007-13, only 5% of funds for rural development will be allocated to LEADER+, less than in the Netherlands, Estonia, Spain or Portugal (Figure 2.7). More focus on the LEADER programme could help farmers and rural people to develop social capital, local groupings and farmers associations in order to embark on more value-added production such as niche products, bio-foods and local labels. The lessons of successful LEADER countries, such as Finland, should be kept in mind, in particular the need for a participatory tripartite LAG board, on which local governments, local businesses and associations, and local inhabitants are all represented on an equal basis. In addition, Higher education institutions (HEIs) should be more involved in rural development. Universities and research institutes can contribute to rural development by engaging students in rural development projects during their studies and by their participation in discussions of rural development in the LAGs, possibly on their boards (OECD, 2007i). This was done, for example, by Scotland's University of the Highlands and Islands.

> ## Box 2.21. **EU LEADER + programme**
>
> The LEADER Community Initiative is one of the better-known European rural development programmes and was conceived as an integrated and endogenous approach to rural development. The programme has been widely recognised as a success owing to its innovative character and because of the results obtained in many rural areas despite relatively limited budgets. The LEADER Initiative began in 1991 with LEADER I, continued from 1994 to 1999 with LEADER II and remains with LEADER + (2000-06 and 2007-13). The initiative has been implemented across the EU in both lagging and leading rural regions and has expanded rapidly: while LEADER I covered 220 areas, LEADER II reached more than 1 000 in the EU15.
>
> One important outcome of LEADER was the introduction of a LEADER method. This method implies co-operation across and within public administrations and the private sector and its application has had a notable impact on the governance of predominantly rural regions across Europe. Three main elements characterise the implementation of the LEADER method: i) a territory or LEADER area; ii) an integrated strategy relying on an endogenous approach and innovative actions; and iii) a local action group (LAG) characterised by decentralised financing, co-operation and partnerships between public and private stakeholders. These elements operate within two alternative approaches (Soto, 2004). The first is redistributive and perceives the programme as a partial compensation for the structural disadvantages of different rural territories. The second is more proactive and insists on the most innovative aspects of the LEADER method in order to facilitate the mobilisation of certain actors that elaborate and apply a development strategy in each territory.
>
> Source: OECD (2006h).

### Development of a huge natural potential

Although the potential for tourism in rural areas has been better exploited since the 1990s (with an increase of households in rural areas offering activities for tourists),[45] many regions, particularly in northern and eastern Poland, are not being effectively advertised to foreign tourist markets. However, their huge natural reserves can be an important drawing card for Polish regions. Poland's eastern regions are among the best preserved in the European Union: they contain 38.4% of the natural reserves of the EU (3.9 million hectares), lakes (in Warminsko-Mazurskie), forests (in Podlaskie), mountains (in Podkarpackie), with important populations of birds, animals, etc. The southern mountainous regions bordering the Slovak Republic contain biosphere reserves. "Natura 2000" pointed out large parts of the national territory which should be preserved. The tourism potential is under-exploited partly owing to limited accessibility and weak infrastructure for tourism, but also partly because of the lack of advertising by cities (Biaystok, Lublin and Rzeszow) which could rely more on the surrounding natural assets, wildlife and environmental qualities. Rural tourism in Austria, Spain and Italy has increased over the past decade and Poland could learn from these countries the best ways to promote regional products, environmental assets, etc. (see Box 2.22). Local initiatives in this area require the support of public authorities to help develop essential infrastructure – water, roads, recreation areas – to make such development options feasible.

---

### Box 2.22. **Examples of OECD rural regions with active tourism campaigns**

Many successful rural regions have been able to draw on public or quasi-public goods such as a clean environment, attractive landscapes and cultural heritage (including food). Rural areas have a range of natural and cultural assets that can be harnessed for economic development. Their increasing value is related to improved transport links that make recreation in rural regions increasingly feasible as well as offering more affordable residential locations. But most of all, it has to do with both a growing demand for rural areas on the part of urban dwellers and a local capacity to co-ordinate economic actors to supply and promote local collective goods.

Relying not exclusively but largely on its rural amenities, the **Italian province of Siena** has been able to improve its position relative to other Italian provinces in terms of per capita income through an effective policy to promote local products (nearly 70% of Siena's farms produce at least one certified product) which has also induced impressive employment creation (*OECD Territorial Review of Siena, 2002*). Siena is far from an isolated case: Tiroler Oberland (Austria), Mugla (Turkey) and Tasman (New Zealand) are regions that thrive on the tourism industry. Regions such as Engadina Bassa (Switzerland), Alpes de Haute-Provence (France) or Dare County (United States) also attract workers, enterprises and retirees.

**Rural tourism in Spain** is growing faster than tourism overall; it accounts for almost 6% of all national guests and 1% of foreign guests and has still plenty of capacity to grow in the coming years.

The **Cheese Route Bregenzerwald, Vorlarberg, Austria**. This was a strategic project for the LEADER II programme in Austria's westernmost province. The aim was to build on a well-established local product – cheese – in ways that ensured the livelihood of the rural population, reduced commuting and helped to create new jobs in tourism and trade. The concept involved multiple and multi-sectoral beneficiaries, a strong public-private partnership and co-operation between different sectors, including agriculture, dairies, accommodation providers, alpine pasture managers, trade and commerce. It has led to innovative products (such as Käsezwickel, Käseträger and Käse&Design) and the establishment of a new high-quality regional "brand". It has helped to maintain traditional alpine farming and the quality of the cultural landscape.

*Source:* OECD (2006h).

---

## Development of services in rural areas

There is increased demand for two types of services in rural areas: i) services needed in remote areas to upgrade the quality of life; ii) services needed because of migration to rural areas close to cities, as well as various forms of tele-work and e-business. With the new "urban migration" to rural areas, demand for services in rural areas will increase. This new patterns in migration should be amplified until 2030 (the share of urban population is forecast to drop to 57%, while the share of rural population should reach 43% (CSO, 2007). The number of newly created small and medium-sized enterprises (in services) has already increased in rural areas. This is particularly true in rural areas surrounding large cities (new areas of business activity, such as design and maintenance of gardens and parks, home and medical care for the elderly, etc.). However, peripheral and weakly developed areas have seen only limited growth in services, owing to the lack of potential clients/recipients (Banski, 2006). It is not conceivable to attract highly-skilled, high-income residents, still less businesses and their employees, without guaranteeing they will have adequate, quality access to a range of "basic" services (including health, education, security and culture). The focus should be primarily on financial services, postal and telecommunications access, local government services and health services. One-stop shops for services provision could be developed as in Scotland (Box 2.23).

## Conclusion

Balanced development of Polish regions requires a well-designed rural development strategy. Poland has increasingly moved towards a broad approach to rural development rather than a narrow focus on agriculture, but progress can still be made, to tailor the rural development strategy to local needs in a multi-sectoral approach targeting education (including pre-school), infrastructure, diversification of the rural economy, and specialisations in agriculture. Greater coherence is to be found between the rural development strategy and cohesion policy. Modernisation of agriculture should be pursued, and it is important to ensure that CAP funding is better related to modernisation and productivity gains, in particular for small farms in Eastern Poland. Overall, policies should focus on co-operation among local actors to facilitate the diversification of the rural economy to non-agricultural sectors; Poland could take more advantage of the LEADER+ programme in that respect; and higher education institutes could be better involved in the reform of the rural economy.

## 5. Development of eastern Poland and cross border co-operation

The development of Poland's eastern regions, the poorest in the European Union in terms of GDP per capita until the accession of Romania and Bulgaria,

---

Box 2.23. **Meeting public service delivery needs in rural areas**

**Australia** instituted the Rural Transaction Centres (RTC) Programme to help small communities establish locally run and self-funding centres that either introduce new services or bring back services that were no longer available in rural areas. Recently, the programme has been integrated into the Australian government's streamlined Regional Partnerships programme. Since its introduction in 1999, over 200 RTCs have been approved for assistance under the programme. An RTC programme field consultant assists in an initial community consultation and feasibility study. The RTC is tailored to meet community needs but not compete with other planned services, and usually includes: financial services, postal and telecommunications access, federal, state and local government services, insurance and taxation, printing and secretarial capacity. These centres employ from one part-time employee to four full-time staff. Funding from the central government covers the capital costs of establishing an RTC and subsidises its operating costs during its early years, if necessary.

In **Scotland**, as in many other countries, the idea of a one-stop shop has been applied in a wide range of fields of service provision, including education, social work, public services, information, business support and community services. A recent study on ten one-stop shops in different rural contexts found that: they are usually viewed positively by providers, staff and clients; they usually provide new or better services and make them more accessible; and that they sometimes tackle very difficult cross-cutting areas – such as social deprivation, youth and provision of services in remote and scattered communities – which would not be dealt with by existing service providers. They are therefore helping to join up government and other providers on the ground. The study also found that a number of important issues need to be considered in the design, layout, location, financing and staffing of one-stop shops, and that community involvement and ownership from the start is vital.

*Source:* Government of Quebec, 2004, Bryden, Rennie *et al,*, 2005, Aho *et al.*, 2004 (in OECD 2006h).

---

is a major policy objective of Poland and the European Commission. The five eastern regions[46] situated along Poland's eastern and northern borders are the smallest contributors to GDP (less than 3% each) and have the lowest growth rates in Poland (see Chapter 1). Their slow development is mainly linked to historical legacies, the predominance of low agricultural productivity in regional economies and their peripheral situation in the EU. They border on much poorer regions with economic difficulties and a different administrative context (Belarus and Ukraine). Cross-border co-operation is limited, especially with Belarus, and the informal economy prevails. The lack of large cities, with the exception of Lublin, is also a reason for their slower economic growth. In terms of FDI only 6% of firms in the eastern regions attract foreign capital.

## 5.1. *The macro-regional programme for eastern Poland*

For the first time, a macro-regional programme targeting the development of the five eastern regions has been developed with the use of EU funds for 2007-13. Previously, several programmes had been implemented for eastern regions, but they targeted specific regions/locations rather than the macro-region as a whole. For 2007-13, an additional budget of EUR 2.2 billion has been allocated by the European Commission for this purpose. The Development of Eastern Poland operational programme is managed by the central government (Ministry of Regional Development). It aims at enhancing the competitiveness and attractiveness of eastern regions, strengthening the metropolitan functions of cities and improving the quality of transport infrastructures (see Box 2.25). The programme is co-financed with EUR 401.2 million from the Polish budget and additional resources from the budgets of local governments for a total budget of EUR 2.2 billion (3.6% of the total allocation of the Polish NSRF).

The macro-regional programme is an opportunity for eastern regions, not only in terms of additional funding, but also in terms of co-operation and connections among the five eastern regions, to think about supra-regional interests, common public services and goods, and a common strategy for cross-border co-operation. The value added of the programme lies precisely in its macro-regional dimension, as it is a way to go beyond the administrative borders of voivodships. Eastern regions have under-utilised potential, such as one of the best preserved natural environments in the European Union, and a strong potential for human capital development, with Lublin's several universities. On the other hand, the risks of the macro-regional programme are linked to the fact that additional funds may only be perceived as an addition to the existing regional plans. If there is no "macro-politics" but only individual projects without connections among regions, the macro-regional programme will have limited value added as compared to regional operational programmes, and it adds the transaction costs due to another programme layer.

The macro-regional programme has a coherent and well-balanced strategy, with six priorities (Modernisation of the economy, Infrastructure and Information Society, transport infrastructure, support to cities, tourism and technical assistance) (Figure 2.9); but challenges are linked to the lack of cross-regional dimension of the various pillars:

● *Modernisation of the economy*: The overall directions are good, but the measures remain vague. Care must be taken not to build "cathedrals in the desert", to use an expression of José Andriguez Posé, that is, innovation centres with little connection to the surrounding socioeconomic environment. For example, as regards R&D and knowledge transfers between SMEs and services, creation of industrial parks and of centres for innovation, concrete measures for choosing which SMEs will be supported first are not spelled out and the rationale for building centres for innovation is not explained. The focus on education in the eastern regions should be highlighted as a key priority.

- *Development of roads:* It seems that this objective is more a complement to individual regional programmes than a "macro-regional" axis (investments below a certain threshold are included in the former, while above the threshold they are included in the latter).

- *Metropolitan development:* Along the same lines, the measures linked to "metropolitan development" are not precise and do not provide clear definitions of the concept (the perimeter of 100 kilometres around the city seems arbitrary rather than based on functional linkages). Also, the construction of business centres and conference centres is planned, but is not clearly explained with an analysis of demand.

Figure 2.9. **Development of eastern Poland: allocation of funds 2007-13 (total: EUR 2.2 billion)**

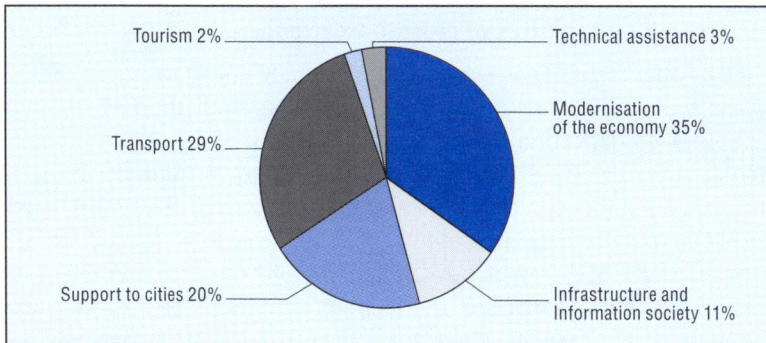

*Source:* Ministry of Regional Development, OP Eastern Poland development, October 2007.

Overall, the macro-regional programme does not seem to exploit well the *macro-regional* dimension and the potential for co-operation among the five eastern regions. Besides, the governance of the operational programme does not seem to include local governments, private actors and civil society. The elaboration of the programme has not led to regular co-operation among the five regions, and with other regions. Moreover, when issues would deserve a more differentiated approach, it is little developed. For example, cross-border co-operation is briefly mentioned, with the overall objective of "reinforcing" the border; however, the challenges are different at various points on the border (Russia, Belarus, Ukraine, Slovak Republic). Without greater involvement of local actors and stronger focus on the macro-regional dimension (which might imply a political/institutional dimension); the programme may not be effective.

The cross-regional dimension of the programme should be enhanced, with a focus on joint infrastructure projects, tourism and environmental issues. The creation of an agency for tourism in the eastern regions to promote their unique natural assets has been suggested. This proposal should be supported. Such an agency could train tourism professionals and develop agro-tourism. It could co-operate with universities to be at the forefront of international research in certain fields: agro-rural development; development of "natural" goods, etc. Connections with Ukraine should be targeted, especially in view of the 2012 Euro championship, when visitors will move between the two countries. In addition, developing cross-regional leadership through the creation of a supra-regional institution may be envisaged. It would be in charge of the follow-up of implementation of the various projects for connecting the regions. Finally, training of local governments and local elites is a priority in order to enhance exchange of experience with successful Euroregions (Box 2.24). A central data bank with the socioeconomic data of the five regions could be created to support the different policies.

### 5.2. Successes and failures of cross-border policies

The development of eastern Poland is strongly linked to cross-border co-operation with its eastern neighbours, as well as with the rest of Poland. Cross-border co-operation has been strongly pushed by EU initiatives, in particular Interreg[47] and Euroregions, which involve municipalities and regions that are not necessarily on the border, but also by the World Bank. In eastern Poland, these initiatives are valuable as a way to go beyond historical legacies. However, Euroregions have so far had limited success in the eastern regions. The western, northern and eastern borders present an important asymmetry in this respect. Experience with the German border is quite positive (Box 2.24), whereas co-operation with Russia (Kaliningrad) in the north and Belarus and Ukraine in the east, are more challenging. The factors that explain a rather successful co-operation on the western border of Poland are missing in the east, in particular the autonomy of local governments. In addition, the fact that Ukraine and Belarus do not have any short-term perspective to join the EU limits the impact of the European Neighbourhood Policy implemented in 2003.[48]

### Euroregions

Co-operation with Germany and the Czech Republic indicate some conditions for the success of Euroregions (Box 2.24). First, infrastructure development and linkages across the regions (by roads, rail) are important. The Polish and Czech borders are good examples of strong linkages, whereas connections with countries to the east are limited. Second, the existence of large cities in border regions is important, as cities usually play the role of

Box 2.24. **Cross-border co-operation between Poland and western partners (Germany and the Czech Republic)**

Cross-border co-operation between Poland and its western or southern partners has worked quite well. First, the bordering regions are quite close in terms of economic development and are complementary. Polish workers find jobs in the new *Länder* and the Silesian mines as well in Moravia, while the bordering German population can get oil or other products cheaper in Poland. Second, these regions share concern about environmental threats; the southern Polish region shares concerns with the Czech and German sides (for example the acid rain resulting from intensive coal mining industries in southern Germany (Saxony) and in the northern Czech regions (particularly Usti nad Labem).

**1) The Nyssa Euroregion** was the first to be created between the Polish, German and Czech borders. It has helped to develop the regions, essentially for environmental issues and tourism. Sulphur dioxide has been reduced by 92% and nitrogen oxide by 80%, and tourism has developed.

**2) The Viadrina Euroregion.** The frontier between Germany and Poland is 461 kilometres long, 135 of which are in the Pro Europe Viadrina Euroregion. From 1994 to 1999 it received EUR 45 million from the Interreg II EU initiative and EUR 75 million from the PHARE CNC programme (92 projects). Most of the money was invested in the traffic and transport realm and thus helped to improve cross-border traffic flow. Environmental protection targeted piping and sewage treatment facilities. Ten tourism projects were set up: six Oder barge moorings, two logistic platforms for a German-Polish port complex and two municipal infrastructure projects for water tourism. Finally, 319 small cross-border projects were supported (brochures to enhance co-operation, reinforce common knowledge, etc.). Activities for the 1999-2006 period concerned economic co-operation (by promoting innovation and improving cross-border logistics and traffic infrastructures) and the environment (by protecting the air, the water and the soil and by preserving natural resources). Agricultural and rural development aimed at proposing alternatives for the rural population by reinforcing the agro-tourism and tourism infrastructures. Finally the qualification and training programme aimed at adapting the regional population to labour market requirements, with support from educational and scientific institutions. However, the fact that Berlin is only 100 kilometres from the border limits economic opportunities in the border regions, as it is easy for Poles to go there to find jobs. In addition, industries set up along the Oder River during the 1950s-1960s are facing important difficulties (petrochemical complex, chemical plants closed down).

"leaders" for cross-border co-operation. The fact that Prague is less than 300 kilometres from Wroclaw, itself 193 kilometres from Katowice, creates a triangle for development. Last but not least, governance and institutional conditions on the two sides of the borders are crucial. The most active Euroregions are those which are supported both by strong NGOs (civil society) and by strong networks of central, regional and local authorities. If the Czech/ Polish borders have witnessed several conflicts among civil groups on environmental issues (also linked to flooding events), they are also the sign of the vitality of public debate and the involvement of local actors.

The governance dimension and the lack of autonomy of local governments in neighbouring countries are among the main reasons for the difficulty of co-operating with eastern neighbours and the limited success of Euroregions (Box 2.25). In addition, the new Schenghen legislation (since January 2008) which has reinforced border controls, makes crossing much more difficult. Tensions have grown, leading to pressures from groups such as lorry drivers or customs guards. The presidents of Ukraine and the Slovak Republic have recently signed an agreement called "the small trans-border co-operation" to facilitate internal mobility within the Caparthian Euroregion.

Finally, various programmes for cross-border collaboration have been developed, mainly funded by the European Union (Interreg, Euroregions, European Neighbouring Policy).[49] To simplify the administrative framework and clarify the political/economic objectives behind the co-operation strategies, it may be necessary to develop a single programme for cross-border co-operation in the eastern regions.

### Conclusion

The cross-regional dimension of the Development of Eastern Poland programme should be enhanced, with a focus on joint infrastructure projects, tourism and environmental issues; and cross-regional leadership of the programme could be introduced at the regional level. The window of opportunity for co-organising with Ukraine the 2012 Euro championship should be better exploited to identify precise points of collaboration on tourism and infrastructure development. Education should be the first priority in the eastern regions; and care must be taken not to build "cathedrals in the desert", innovation centres with little connection to the surrounding socioeconomic environment. Finally, a single programme for cross-border co-operation in eastern regions could be developed to simplify the administrative framework and give a sense of common vision.

The macro-programme on eastern Poland development reveals some of the main challenges for regional development, such as the difficulty to build multi-sector strategy tailored to local needs, involving strong co-operation among local

## Box 2.25. **Euroregions with eastern neighbours**

**The success of the Carpathian Euroregion has been limited so far.** This Euroregion includes four neighbouring countries: the Slovak Republic, Hungary, Ukraine and Poland. Some economic, cultural, educational and social initiatives have been launched, based on the experience of western Euroregions. However, they have met with limited success, mainly because Poland's administrative organisation is very different from that of Ukraine. Ukrainian municipalities have little autonomy, and Polish border gminas do not find partners to co-operate with. In addition, the informal economy is significant. Finally, the development projects are too small even if they have some positive local effects (cultural exchange); they are more formal than efficient. Finally, the Euroregion is too large, involving as it does four countries with very different capacities.

Even if a few positive achievements with **Belarus** are noticeable – such as a slight increase since 2003 in exports of Polish food products and imports of raw material from Belarus (salt, potassium, chemical products) – overall co-operation remains very limited. Belarus ranks only 24th in trade with Poland, despite its proximity. The main obstacles are political and linked to the lack of will to co-operate in Belarus. Crossing the border takes a long time, for example, because of customs duties and quotas.

**Co-operation with Kaliningrad is limited** and problems of corruption are reported. Kaliningrad is important for Russia because it is the only harbour that is free from ice year-long and is thus a strategic access to the Baltic Sea. Establishing positive relationships with its immediate neighbours is a necessity, not only to foster exports, but also to reduce the gap between the city of Kaliningrad and its regional environment.

In 2005, a joint programme was set up by Poland, Lithuania and Russia, and a **"Baltic" Euroregion** was created involving six countries (Russia, Sweden, Denmark, Latvia, Lithuania, Poland). A plan of joint development of tourism has been proposed based on a common strategy of three partners, which mainly supports the "amber route" project. In spite of these efforts, observers point to the lack of positive results, mainly owing to the lack of autonomous local actors and the limited economic exchanges.

actors and social capital building. Most challenges for the implementation of the Polish regional development policy are linked to governance; as improved horizontal collaboration across local governments and local capacity building will play a key role in the positive outcomes of the policy. Next chapter will focus on the governance needs to best implement Polish regional policy.

## Notes

1. Transfers subject to "additionality" cannot substitute for existing expenditure but should finance new projects.

2. In addition, other support came from the World Bank (mainly for rural development) and bilateral agreements with countries like Norway and Switzerland, for example.

3. However, Mazowieckie has now surpassed the threshold of 75% of the average EU GDP per capita.

4. Priority 6 of the national development Strategy for 2007-2015 is regional development.

5. European Regional Development Fund; European Social Fund and Cohesion Fund.

6. The Polish National Strategic Reference Framework (NRSF) was approved by the European Commission in May 2007.

7. For the EU27, 82% of the investments from structural and cohesion funds are earmarked to Lisbon related expenditure.

8. The Eastern program focuses on Lubelskie, Podkarpackie, Podlaskie, Warmińsko-Mazurskie and Świętokrzyskie Voivodeships.

9. The weighting of the Regional allocation has been done on a formula of Regional population, GDP per head, and unemployment, so that a higher percentage of the funds per capita have gone to the poorer regions than to the richer ones.

10. In this section, the definition of infrastructure will include ICT in addition to transport and environment.

11. Critical infrastructure challenges such as telecommunications and water management – other key components of the Infrastructure and Environment programme – will be discussed further in the rural section.

12. The Spatial Planning Act prescribes gminas' tasks as: identifying the commune's physical development preconditions and directions; establishing principles of sustainable territorial and economic development; functional zoning and indication of areas for housing and other direct investment; providing general proposals for technical infrastructure systems, the location of main roads and other technical networks; identifying the most important preservation areas due to their natural, economic (*e.g.* agricultural) and cultural value; establishing local planning policy (system of plans and monitoring); determining the boundaries of areas indicated for organised development or revitalisation and sites intended for implementation of public objectives (programmes). EIKN: *www.eukn.org/poland/polishurbanpolicy/index.html.*

13. These are: Bydgoszcz-Torun, Cracow, Lodz, Poznan, the so-called "Silesia" (includes Katowice and Rybnik-Jastrzebie), Szczecin, Gdańsk/Gdynia/Sopot, Warsaw and Wroclaw (see Chapter 1).

14. During the 2007-132007-2013 programming period, the N+3 is applied in the first four years and the N+2 in the last three years.

15. Poland is crossed by four out of the ten pan-European transport corridors, defined in 1994 and 1997 as routes in Central and Eastern Europe requiring major investment over the following 10 to 15 years. To this end, a set of trans-European transport networks (TEN-T) for providing high-speed, long-distance routes for moving people and freight throughout Europe was defined. Then, 30 additional

priority projects were identified in 2003 to be achieved by 2020, based on co-ordinated improvements to primary roads, railways, airports, seaports, inland waterways, inland ports and traffic-management systems.

16. This does not take account of the fact that two voivodships have two capitals: one hosting the voivod and the other the regional government.

17. SACTRA (1999), The Standing Advisory Committee on Trunk Road Assessment, Transport and the Economy, DETR, London, in CEE Bankwatch Network.

18. Construction firms have difficulties recruiting skilled (85%) but also non-skilled workers (27%) (National Bank of Poland, 2007).

19. The scope of the relevant laws on public procurement, construction work and protection of the environment have been simplified.

20. The Seaport Development Strategy to 2015 released by the Ministry of Maritime Economy in August 2007 aims at improving the competiveness of Polish seaports and hinges on four main pillars: improved port infrastructure and access to seaports; development of service offering in the seaports; improved co-operation of administration, management entities and seaport users; and building the image of seaports as important centres for sustainable development of coastal municipalities and regions.

21. *http://ec.europa.eu/information_society/activities/gothenburg_conference/doc/pdf/brief_poland.pdf.*

22. According to Gorzynski, the Office of Telecommunications and Post Regulation, the independent regulator, has to date not fulfilled its role, allowing TP S.A to continue its monopolistic activities and blocking the entry and development of fixed-line operators and mobile telephone operators (Gorzynski *et al.*, 2006).

23. Under the 2004-06 regional programmes, the main beneficiaries of projects related to the information society have been local governments.

24. The programming document which addresses the development of the information society is entitled the "Targeted strategy for IT development in Poland until 2013 and the long-term prognosis of e-society transformations until 2020" and the "Strategy for enhancing e-society in Poland until 2013".

25. Under the Human Capital programme it is possible to apply for support for projects related to human resource development in the region, management of economic change (support for restructured enterprises, training and re-qualification of employees) or transfer of knowledge (including co-operation between higher education institutions and enterprises). These will be supplemented by activities linked to promoting entrepreneurship and self-employment (Background Report, 2007).

26. Such as the initiative "internet in schools", Internet Education Service (IES), Interszkoła (Interschool) project.

27. The Knowledge Transfer Partnership scheme allows organisations to access groundbreaking research and the knowledge of a high-quality graduate.

28. The national government has launched in April 2008 a campaign of advertisement in the UK to encourage Poles to return to their country. There is evidence that many Poles are returning Poland, also linked to the current weakness of the British pound.

29. The necessity to support and enhance clusters in Poland was highlighted in a strategic document entitled the "Directions towards enhancing innovation of the

economy for the years 2007-13", adopted by the Council of Ministers on 4 September 2006, but few concrete measures have been taken.

30. Helsinki, Tampere, Turku, Oulu, Jyväskylä, Kuopio, Lahti, Lappeenranta Imatra and Vaasa.

31. Under EU auspices and with some assistance from the Commission (e.g. within the framework of the RIS/RITTS programmes and other initiatives), regional innovation strategies were set up in nearly 200 EU regions. The RIS is not only a document but a process which builds consensus in the region. Its main purpose is for all interested entities and institutions to contribute to maximising regional "innovativeness".

32. Although the Mazowieckie region is a leader with respect to innovativeness, it is the only region which has not completed a RIS. Work on the strategic document is in its final stage and its acceptatance by the voivodship regional parliament is expected during the first quarter of 2008. The regional innovation strategy of Mazowieckie will be implemented through different programmes including Mazovia Innovator, regional innovation centres, innovation traineeships, and programme of clusters support development.

33. The Baltic Sea region covers ten countries: Denmark, Estonia, Finland, northern Germany, Latvia, Lithuania, Poland, northwest Russia, Norway and Sweden. It has the world's highest penetration of mobile and Internet communication.

34. Assessment of the programme "Improving the Competitiveness and Innovativeness of Polish Enterprises" of 2004-06 indicates that 90% of the benefitting firms were SMEs. The Ministry of Regional Development indicates that, in relative terms, the regions of Podkarpackie, Podlaskie and Warminsko-Mazurskie attracted the most projects. 6 800 enterprises were said to have benefited from investment tax relief and 5 200 to have used advisory services. See Ministry of Regional Development, The Assessment of Poland's Progress on the Way to Cohesion with the EU, Report, Warsaw, August 2007.

35. Until the early 2000s, the impact of FDI on employment was limited as the FDI was mainly brownfield FDI (mechanics, metallurgy, raw material agro-industry) in restructuring industrial sectors, with reductions in employment.

36. According to the CIS survey, the index of innovativeness of Polish firms declined from 37.6% in 1994-96 to 16.9% in 1998-2000.

37. OECD (2006h). The transformation of the rural economy has led to a policy shift that privileges places over sectors and investments over subsidies.

38. In the late 1990s, less than 20% of farmers had bank accounts and used bank services. In 2004 almost 90% had bank accounts, which they needed in order to receive direct payments and other forms of Community support.

39. There has been substantial progress as regards the connection of inhabitants of rural areas to the collective water supply system. In 2004 2.3 million households were connected to the water supply system, but in 2004 the number had increased to 2.7 million (NSRF, 2006). There has been a threefold increase in the length of the water-supply network in rural areas (against a 2.5-fold increase in the country as a whole), a sixfold extension of the sewer network (against a doubling nationwide) and a fourfold increase in the length of gas pipelines (also against a doubling nationally). The number of telephone subscribers increased sixfold (against a threefold increase overall).

40. Poland has benefited since 2004 from direct funding under the CAP. To better control CAP funding and allow a learning process with the use of funds, as well as to compensate the price asymmetries among western and eastern Europe, the European Commission decided in 2004 to allocate CAP funds to new members at 25% of the rate paid to the older member states. This rate is rising slowly (with an increase of 10% a year) and will reach equality in 2013. With 2.5 million farmers, Poland is likely then to be a significant recipient of funds.

41. It has doubled the agricultural labour force and the arable area of the EU, and added over 100 million consumers of food to the internal market.

42. Soil purity (in terms of its heavy metals content), extensive methods of cultivation and agricultural use of land are other advantages of Poland in comparison with many other EU member states.

43. The value of exported organic products has increased tenfold over the past nine years. The global milk market grew by 5.5% in 2006. In 2011, the market is forecast to increase by 27.2% compared to 2006.

44. Polish farmers now strongly support the EU; although before 2004 they were the most hostile group. If in 1999, only 23% of farmers were in favour of integration, in 2007, 73% support the EU. To explain their strong support, farmers mention the opening of the borders, their ability to find jobs abroad, the huge demand from abroad (particularly Germany) and the EU funds (CAP). Following Maria Halamska's results, 61% view the CAP positively but believe that the level of distribution should be equal to that of the EU15.

45. According to the Ministry of Agriculture and Rural Development, in 1993 some 1 000 household farms in rural areas offered tourist services; there were 11 260 in 2000. Around half of the latter were agri-tourist farms, while the remainder engaged in agricultural production. The most agri-tourist farms are in Małopolska and Warmia-Mazury voivodships, and thus in areas appreciated from the point of view of nature, landscapes and culture (Banski, 2006).

46. Podkarpackie, Lubelskie, Podlaskie and Warmińsko-Mazurskie voivodships plus the Świętokrzyskie voivodship which is also classified in this group.

47. Interreg III has supported different cross-border co-operation programmes.

48. This policy, launched in 2003, invites countries outside the EU to be part of a partnership, making possible the respect of common norms of economic trade and political values in exchange for EU funds. The four European freedoms (people, goods, financial and services) can be delivered to the new neighbours provided they commit themselves to adopt the acquis communautaire.

49. In the 2007-2013 period, the European Union has launched a new instrument – the "instrument of neighbourhood and partnership" which is focused on 17 countries neighbouring with the European Union, and involves the allocation of EUR 17 billion.

ANNEX 2.A1

# Activities Eligible under the "Lisbon Earmarking" Requirement

Cohesion Policy 2007-13 regards the activities in the following spending items as eligible for meeting the "Lisbon earmarking requirement" because they have been identified as contributing to one of the 24 priorities of the Lisbon strategy:*

- Research and technological development (R&D), innovation and entrepreneurship: R&D activities in research centres, R&D infrastructure, technology transfer between small- and medium-sized enterprises (SMEs), assistance to R&D in SMEs, advanced support services for firms, assistance to SMEs for environmentally-friendly products and production processes, investment in R&D-related equipment, other investment in firms, other measures to stimulate R&Ds or entrepreneurship in SMEs.

- Information society: telecommunications infrastructure, information and communication technology (ICT) equipment, services and applications for the citizen and SMEs, other measures for the use of ICT by SMEs.

- Transport: railways, motorways, multimodal transport, intelligent transport systems, airports, ports, inland waterways.

- Energy: trans-European networks for electricity, natural gas and oil; renewable energy; energy efficiency.

- Environmental protection: promotion of clean urban transport.

- Adaptability of workers and firms: development of life-long learning systems and strategies, design and dissemination of productivity-enhancing organisational practices.

---

* See EC (2005) for the list of and more details on the 24 priorities. *Source:* Council Regulation 1083/2006, Annex IV.

- Improving access to employment and sustainability: modernisation and strengthening of labour market institutions, implementing active and preventive measures on the labour market, measures encouraging longer working lives, support for self-employment, measures to reduce sex-based discrimination in the labour market and to reconcile work and private life.

- Improving the social inclusion of less-favoured persons: pathways to re-entry into employment for disadvantaged people, promoting diversity in the workplace.

- Improving human capital: reforms in education and training systems to develop employability, measures to increase participation in lifelong learning, and develop post-graduate studies and networking activities between universities, research centres and businesses.

ANNEX 2.A2

# Financial Table for Operational Programme Human Capital 2007-13 with Division to Priorities and Sources of Financing in Euro by Current Prices

| Priority | Community input | National input | | | Total | EU funds indicator | For information purposes | |
|---|---|---|---|---|---|---|---|---|
| | | Total | National public input | Private input | | | EBI loans | Other financing |
| | 1 | 2 = 3 + 4 | 3 | 4 | 5 = 1 + 2 | 6 = 1/5 | 7 | 8 |
| I. Employment and Social Integration | 430 260 954 | 75 928 404 | 75 928 404 | 0 | 506 189 358 | 0.85 | 0 | 0 |
| II. Development of Human Resources and Adaptability of Companies and Improvement of Health of the Working People | 661 310 120 | 116 701 786 | 116 701 786 | 0 | 778 011 906 | 0.85 | 0 | 0 |
| III. High Quality of Educational System | 855 300 828 | 150 935 440 | 150 935 440 | 0 | 1 006 236 268 | 0.85 | 0 | 0 |
| IV. Higher Education and Science | 816 311 813 | 144 055 026 | 144 055 026 | 0 | 960 366 839 | 0.85 | 0 | 0 |
| V. Good Governance | 519 225 980 | 91 628 114 | 91 628 114 | 0 | 610 854 094 | 0.85 | 0 | 0 |
| VI. Labor Market Open for All | 1 918 389 821 | 338 539 380 | 338 539 380 | 0 | 2 256 929 201 | 0.85 | 0 | 0 |
| VII. Promotion of Social Integration | 1 319 970 145 | 232 935 908 | 232 935 908 | 0 | 1 552 906 053 | 0.85 | 0 | 0 |
| VIII. Regional Staff of Economy | 1 350 207 670 | 238 271 942 | 238 271 942 | 0 | 1 588 479 612 | 0.85 | 0 | 0 |
| IX. Development of Education and Competences in Regions | 1 447 911 629 | 255 513 817 | 255 513 817 | 0 | 1 703 425 446 | 0.85 | 0 | 0 |
| X. Technical Assistance | 388 287 040 | 68 521 242 | 68 521 242 | 0 | 456 808 282 | 0.85 | 0 | 0 |
| **TOTAL OP HC:** | **9 707 176 000** | **1 713 031 059** | **1 713 031 059** | **0** | **11 420 207 059** | **0.85** | **0** | **0** |

OECD TERRITORIAL REVIEWS: POLAND – ISBN 978-92-64-04926-0 – © OECD 2008

ANNEX 2.A3

# Presentation of Financial Obligations for the Innovative Economy Operational Programme, 2007-13 Broken into Priorities and Sources of Financing (Current Prices in Euro)

| Priority axis | Community contribution | National contribution | Indicative division of national contribution | | Financing in total | Level of co-financing | For information purposes: | |
|---|---|---|---|---|---|---|---|---|
| | | | National public unds | National private funds[1] | | | Contribution of the EIB | Other sources of financing |
| | 1 | 2 = 3 + 4 | 3 | 4 | 5 = 1 + 2 | 6 =1/5 | 7 | 8 |
| 1. | 1 104 380 000 | 194 890 589 | 194 890 589 | 0 | 1 299 270 589 | 0.85 | | 167 293 790 |
| 2. | 1 104 380 000 | 194 890 589 | 194 890 589 | 0 | 1 299 270 589 | 0.85 | | 45 658 132 |
| 3. | 289 000 000 | 51 000 000 | 51 000 000 | 0 | 340 000 000 | 0.85 | | 16 666 667 |
| 4. | 2 915 254 000 | 514 456 588 | 514 456 588 | 0 | 3 429 710 588 | 0.85 | | 1 704 076 303 |
| 5. | 339 148 000 | 59 849 647 | 59 849 647 | 0 | 398 997 647 | 0.85 | | 33 528 997 |
| 6. | 349 038 080 | 61 594 955 | 61 594 955 | 0 | 410 633 035 | 0.85 | | 46 588 927 |
| 7. | 670 000 000 | 118 235 294 | 118 235 294 | 0 | 788 235 294 | 0.85 | | 139 100 346 |
| 8. | 1 203 485 200 | 212 379 741 | 212 379 741 | 0 | 1 415 864 941 | 0.85 | | 266 429 018 |
| 9. | 280 200 000 | 49 447 059 | 49 447 059 | 0 | 329 647 059 | 0.85 | | 0 |
| Total | 8 254 885 280 | 1 456 744 462 | 1 456 744 462 | 0 | 9 711 629 742 | 0.85 | | 2 419 342 180 |

1. Amount of private funds involved has not been presented since, in accordance with the provisions of the Council Regulation (EC) No. 1 083/2006 of 11 July 2006, whenever state aid is provided, the share of structural funds is counted in relation to public funds.

ISBN 978-92-64-04926-0
OECD Territorial Reviews: Poland
© OECD 2008

# Chapter 3

# Making the Most of Regional Development Policy Through Multi-level Governance

The window of opportunity of EU funding has to be exploited as much as possible, not only for territorial development, but in the perspective of broader public governance and management changes. The impact of European cohesion policy on the Polish multi-level governance system goes well beyond financing. The design and implementation of EU operational programmes – not only regional ones – has led to enhanced decentralisation and collaboration with private actors and civil society. Regional and local actors are engaged in a strong learning process. To further improve the effectiveness of regional development policies, three broad governance challenges are critical to address: i) enhancing co-operation across levels of government and with private actors; ii) strengthening capacities of sub-national governments, to design, implement and monitor development programmes; iii) supporting accountability, at all levels of government and monitoring the performance of regional as well as sectoral policies. Poland also needs to think about longer-term options for better matching competencies and resources in some areas after 2013, when Polish regions may no longer benefit from the same level of external funding, and for further increasing the strategic role of regions. This chapter explores these different cross-cutting governance challenges, and proposes policy recommendations.

## Introduction

The window of opportunity of EU funding has to be exploited as much as possible, not only in the perspective of regional development, but in the perspective of broader public governance and management changes. Governance arrangements are the key levers to improve the effectiveness of regional development policy. As explained in Chapter 2, one of the major challenges for regional policy is to move to a more integrated territorial approach, with appropriate scale of planning and stronger social capital, i.e. co-operation among public and private actors at the local level. The challenge for governance is a twofold one: i) to enhance central and local capacity to implement place-based policies instead of one size fits all; and ii) to build long-term arrangements that go beyond the focus on the absorption of EU funding. Changes in the Polish multi-level governance system has to be forward looking since beyond 2013, most Polish regions may not benefit from the same level of financial support from the EU.

Governance challenges for Polish regional development policy can be summarised under three broad items: co-operation, capacity and accountability:

- **Enhancing co-operation,** both across levels of government, local governments and public and private actors. This might imply new institutional tools to foster collaboration across municipalities, in particular in metropolitan areas; improved co-ordination at the central level, and enhanced involvement of private actors in planning and monitoring regional programmes. Building social capital is an important pre-requisite to improve the implementation of regional development strategies, as the historical inheritance of Poland has resulted in low level of social trust.

- **Improving capacities of sub-national governments.** Poland has developed in the late 1990s a multi-level governance framework in which regions play a strategic role for the implementation of regional development policies. There is still a need for both more effective regional leadership and clear allocation of responsibilities and budgets among sub-national authorities. Flexibility into the implementation of regional development policy would gain from a better match between responsibilities and resources. This requires also enhancing local competencies.

- **Supporting accountability as regards regional development policy,** at all levels of government. The current system has become increasingly complex –

especially with the management of EU funding – and the distribution of competencies across the different actors, at both central and local levels, is sometimes unclear. Monitoring the performance/impact of regional policy is a key tool for sharing information across levels of government, for helping local actors to reveal their knowledge, and for building trust. Poland has made significant progress since 2004 in developing infrastructure for performance monitoring, but the impact of such systems will largely depend on the improved data collection at both regional and central levels and the use of such information in policy-making.

This chapter explores these different cross-cutting challenges. i) The first section focuses on promoting sustainable relations across levels of government, keeping in mind that EU funding will be available for a limited timeframe. ii) The second section analyses the need for greater collaboration across municipalities, in metropolitan areas in particular. iii) The third section highlights the needs for improved co-ordination at central government level and enhanced place-based dimension of both the regional development strategy and the rural one. iv) The fourth section explores the needs to improve programming and managing capacities of regions by reinforcing public-private collaboration and strengthening local public capacity. v) Finally, the fifth section analyses the ways to enhance accountability for results and performance.

## 1. Poland towards multi-level governance for regional development

Regional policy in Poland is implemented in a multi-level governance framework developed in the 1990s. Municipalities (*gminas*) have significant responsibilities and large budgets, while regions (*voivodships*),[1] created in 1999, increasingly play the role of strategic partners with the central and local governments to decide the needs and priorities for local development, and the use of EU funds. Overall, after almost a decade of existence, this decentralised policy framework is perceived as a success, even if challenges remain for enhancing the efficient implementation of regional development policies. While many challenges are linked to the need for more collaboration across local governments, with private actors and local capacity building (focus of Sections 3.2 and 3.3), this section focuses on the challenges linked to the repartition of competencies across levels of government and the fiscal capacity to conduct regional/territorial development policies. Poland has introduced an extended decentralisation process, especially compared to the other countries in Central and Eastern Europe. However, it is important for Poland to think about longer term options to better match competencies and resources in some areas; and to further increase the strategic role of regions.

## 1.1. *Extended decentralisation process in Poland*

In the 1990s, Poland undertook reforms with a view to decentralisation, and it is probably the country of Central and Eastern Europe that has gone the furthest in this direction. It started with municipal autonomy in 1990, seen as consubstantial with democracy after four decades of centralisation under communism. The communes were to play an essential role in shaping a democratic Poland (Stoker 1991). Municipalities (*gminas*) have the largest responsibilities in terms of spatial planning, infrastructure development, housing, social services and education (see Annex 3.A1).[2] Mayors are directly elected, which gives them high political visibility. Municipalities are of three types: urban, rural and urban-rural.[3]

The creation of the 16 Polish regions in 1999 was an important step in the establishment of multi-level governance. The regions (*voivodships*) have an elected regional assembly and are responsible for regional economic development, higher education, hospitals and facilities beyond municipal boundaries, the labour market and job creation. The borders of regions generally correspond to historical units: they result from an endogenous process of institutional change (Hughes *et al.*, 2003; Swianiewicz, 2004). A decade after their emergence as part of the Polish administrative framework, their existence, as regions, is widely recognised. Although they play a relatively limited role in providing public services (mainly higher education and transport); their strategic role is important and increasing, owing to the elaboration of regional development strategies and the management of increased inflows of EU funding.

---

### Box 3.1. **Newly created Polish regions in 1999**

Poland now has a three-tier governmental system: 2 478 municipalities (*gminas*), including 65 with the status of district (*powiat*); 314 powiats; and 16 voivodships. There had been 49 rather small regions (voivodships) under the communist regime and a reduction in their number was considered necessary. The main difficulty was the loss of status of the previous capitals of the voivodships. The design of new regions was therefore rather delicate and has resulted in a few trade-offs (for instance the small *Opole* voivodship with only 1 million of inhabitants, which was justified owing to the small German minority). The number of regions – 12, 16 or 22 – was strongly debated. The main criteria adopted for the design of regions were historical boundaries and functional linkages.

---

314 powiats were also created in 1999 (they had been abolished in 1975). Compared to regions and municipalities, they have a more limited role and influence, as they are essentially funded by the central government. Their main responsibilities include secondary schools, public health services, social

welfare, economic activity and job creation (employment offices). At the head of the powiat, the *Starosta* is elected by the powiat council, itself directly elected for a four-year term. The largest municipalities (above 100 000 inhabitants) also have the status of powiats and combine the responsibilities of both. This was mainly seen as compensation for the former regional capitals that lost their capital status in the 1999 administrative reform. Overall, the role of the powiats is increasingly questioned, as many of their functions could be moved either to the voivodship or the municipality level. This could improve the efficiency of the decentralised framework.

The reform of the Polish administrative system was inspired in part by the French system. As a consequence, institutional trends in France's decentralised system are particularly relevant for Poland, and this chapter will focus particularly on the French benchmark. The *marshal* is the head of regional local government, whereas the *voivod* represents the interests of the state (the equivalent of the French "prefect"). The voivod is responsible for security and defence in the voivodship, in particular for public order in crisis situations, and, as the representative of the state treasury, for the region's use of funds. The different levels of government de not represent a hierarchy: regions, powiats and municipalities are on the same hierarchical level. The state plays an important role at local government level through state grants and regional contracts. A notable difference between Poland and France is the number of local governments (36 000 municipalities in France but only about 2 500 gminas in Poland). Despite the many changes in Poland over the past century, the number of municipalities has remained relatively constant, so that Poland has avoided the jurisdictional fragmentation that has complicated decentralisation processes in many OECD countries.

Table 3.1. **Territorial organisation in Poland**

| State territorial administration | Sub-national governments |
| --- | --- |
| 16 voivod offices (prefectures) | 16 regions (voivodships) |
| | 314 counties (powiats) |
| | 2 478 municipalities (gminas) |

## Fiscal decentralisation: limited revenues for regions and powiats

The 1999 reform was accompanied by a significant devolution of expenditure responsibilities from the central to sub-national governments in the areas of education, roads and healthcare. Municipal expenditure is by far the most important component of sub-national expenditure (79%), followed by county (13%) and regional expenditure (7%) (Dexia, 2008). Sub-national expenditure has increased twice as fast as total public expenditure over the past ten years. This is largely due to the fact that education and health are the responsibility of local governments. The share of sub-national level in total public spending is slightly above 30%, *i.e.* at the same level as Italy or the United Kingdom (see Figure 3.1). When considering the entire sub-national sector,[4] expenditure reached EUR 32 billion in 2005 and represented 13.2% of GDP. However, the share of sub-national governments in general revenues is slightly below 20% (OECD, National Accounts).[5]

Figure 3.1. **Share of sub-national governments in general government revenue and expenditures (2006)**

Share in general government revenues and expenditure, 2006[1]

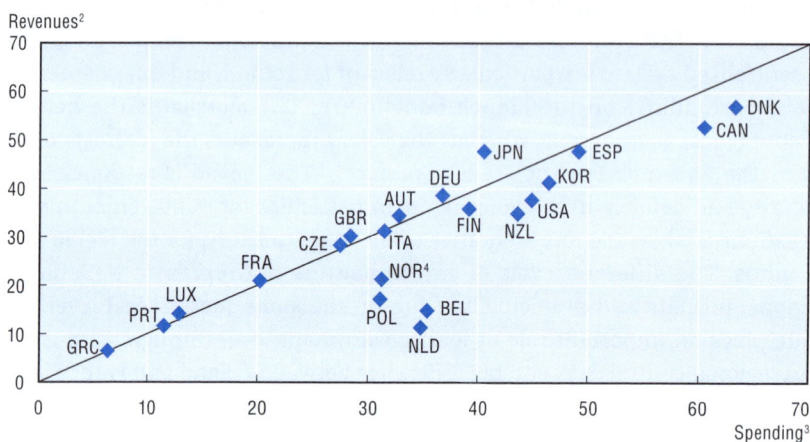

1. Or latest year available: 2005 for Korea, New Zealand and Poland.
2. Excluding transfers received from other levels of government.
3. Excluding transfers paid to other levels of government.
4. The share of subnational revenues is expressed in per cent of total government mainland revenues.
*Note:* Decentralisation is measured by the changes in the share of sub-national governments in total public revenues and spending.
*Source:* OECD *National Accounts database*; Statistics Norway; Statistics Canada; US Bureau of Economic Analysis.

Revenues and fiscal autonomy of newly created *powiats* and regions have remained limited. Regions and *powiats* rely mostly on grants distributed by the central government. Municipalities also rely heavily on the grants system, but they have higher tax autonomy, as they perceive ten times more tax revenues than regions for example (Figure 3.2).

- **Grants:** Nearly half of local government revenues (47%) come from grants (mostly from general grants, 32% of which are earmarked),[6] while tax revenue represents around 38% of sub-national revenue (see Annex 3.A2). The general grant was EUR 8.1 billion in 2005. Municipalities received 75%, counties 21% and regions 4%. It constitutes the main grant for sub-national governments. *Earmarked grants* amounted to EUR 3.9 billion in 2005 (32% of all state grants), of which municipalities received 73%, counties 20% and regions 7% (see Annex 3.A4).

- **Taxes:** Polish local governments received 11.5% of total tax revenues in 2004, slightly below the average of 13.5% for OECD unitary countries (OECD, 2008a).[7] Municipalities' main sources of revenue are property taxes and the proceeds of various excise taxes.[8] *Shared tax revenue* brought in EUR 5.7 billion for sub-national governments, with the lion's share going to municipalities (74.4% of all shared revenue). It represented 51.5% of municipal tax revenue, as well as the totality of county and region tax revenue (see Annex 3.A2).

Figure 3.2. **Structure of sub-national revenue by type (2005)**

EUR millions

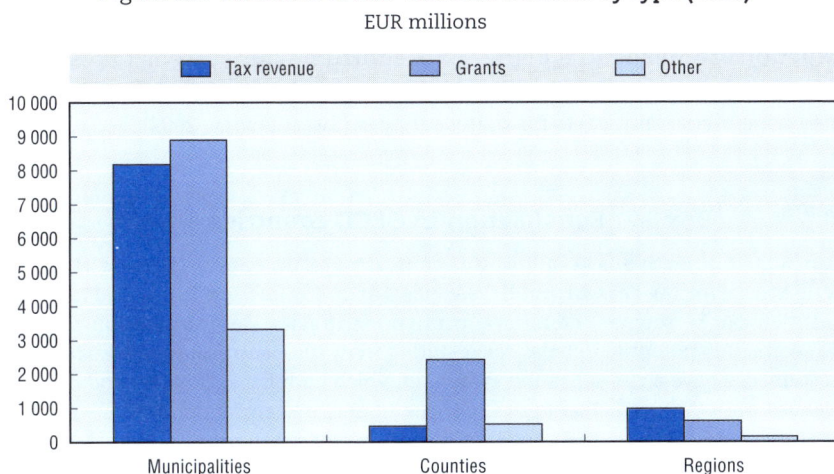

*Source:* DEXIA, 2008.

Although fiscal autonomy has increased in Poland since 2004, following the reform of local finances (and increase of shared tax revenues going to powiats and regions), it remains very limited at the powiat and regional levels. The tax system of Poland is hampered by the fact that social security contributions for both employers and employees are very high. Poland has one of the highest tax wedges in the OECD, despite relatively low personal income tax rates.[9] The system also relies heavily on consumption taxes, whereas relatively little revenue is collected from such bases as environment externalities, inheritances and, in particular, property. The taxation system as a whole is one of the least redistributive among OECD countries (OECD, 2008a).

## Limited focus on redistribution

Like many OECD countries, Poland has an equalisation system, *i.e.* a transfer of fiscal resources across jurisdictions with the aim of offsetting differences in revenue raising capacity or/and public service cost (OECD, 2007c).

The focus on redistribution in the allocation of grants remains however relatively limited in Poland; compared to countries like Denmark, Finland or Japan.[10] Polish equalisation system is mixed: although it is essentially based on tax capacity, it also takes into account some expenditures needs. The equalisation grant amounted 1.2 billion euro in 2005, i.e. 4.6% of sub-national revenue. The formula for each level of sub-national government was modified by the 2004 Act. It is mainly based on criteria linked to tax revenues, population and unemployment rates.[11] Although Polish equalisation system is first and foremost for equalisation of revenues, there are some attempts to take expenditures needs into account, through the population criteria (the assumption is that large cities provide more services and therefore their expenditure needs are higher). In addition, the system takes into consideration that the smallest local governments (less than 5 000 population) may have higher unit costs for many services (Swianiewicz, 2004).

---

### Box 3.2. **Equalisation in OECD countries**

Its principal objective is to allow sub-central governments to provide their citizens with similar sets of public services at a similar tax burden. Fiscal equalisation can be seen as the natural companion to fiscal decentralisation as it aims at correcting potential imbalances resulting from sub-central autonomy. Many OECD countries have an equalisation system in which both fiscal capacity and cost differences are equalised. The consequences of this system depend on several factors, but in many cases the contributions of metropolitan areas outweigh the benefits they receive on the basis of cost differences.

In OECD countries, fiscal equalisation makes up around 2.3 per cent of GDP. Across countries, the size of equalisation transfers varies between 0.5 and 3.8 per cent of GDP, between 1.2 and 7.2 per cent of government expenditures.

Fiscal equalisation serves several potential roles. Its primary policy objective is horizontal equity among the residents of different jurisdictions, i.e. ensuring that, subject to local decisions, all persons or firms in a country can obtain comparable public services at comparable tax rates. Fiscal equalisation may also correct for inefficiencies that might arise if households choose their location based on fiscal rather than productivity considerations, although equalisation itself may reduce labour mobility and hence adjustments between regions. Finally, fiscal equalisation may help support macroeconomic stabilization, insuring regions against asymmetric shocks they may not be able to cope with if left alone. Equalisation is a passive, corrective fiscal policy with no growth and development strategy behind it, and there is a case for concomitant policies aiming at productivity increases, such as transport, research and education. Fiscal equalisation aims at equalising regional public revenue, not GDP or individual household revenue. Like any other redistributive programme, fiscal equalisation policy can result in potentially adverse fiscal and economic incentives for sub-central governments.

Source: OECD (2007c), Fiscal Equalisation in OECD Countries.

---

The focus on redistribution has been slightly enhanced by regional contracts, which financing takes into account the GDP per capita criteria and also with the way EU funding has been distributed since 2004. About one fourth of the EU funding has been distributed since 2004 on the basis of territorial criteria (23% between 2004-06 and 25% between 2007-13, as well as 3% on the programme for eastern Poland development). Cohesion criteria are prominent in the territorial distribution of funds. All regions participate in the distribution of 80% of total funds according to their population. The remaining 20% of funds is distributed only among those regions whose GDP per capita is less than 80% of the national average and in which the cross-powiat unemployment rate is higher than 150% of the national average.

Although EU funds clearly play an equalisation role, it is not clear whether in the end richer regions will not benefit more from EU funding than lagging regions through sectoral programmes. This is because the majority of EU funds have been allocated through sectoral programmes (75% of funds), independently from territorial criteria. It is the case in 2007-13, and it was also the case in 2004-06, when a substantial portion of structural funds and the entire the Cohesion Fund were implemented via national programmes. A complete evaluation for the first financial period will be possible only at the end of 2008, but analysis so far shows that Eastern regions received the smallest amounts (in terms of value per capita) of the EU funds in 2004-06, as they have not managed to "attract" larger amounts of the EU funds from sectoral programmes.

## 1.2. Increasing strategic role of regions

Although regions have a much more limited fiscal capacity than municipalities, they have played an increasingly strategic role for regional development, as they are the main partners of the central government in negotiating regional contracts and they play an increasing role in the allocation and management of EU funding.

### Regional contracts

Regional contracts were introduced in Poland in 2001, partly inspired by the French state-regions contracts. They consist in an agreement between the government and self-government authorities, through which regions receive from the state budget a specific budget for capital investments, among others, in the area of road infrastructure, health-care system, educational facilities, sports infrastructure, and tourist and leisure or cultural facilities. Regional contracts represented in 2005 more than EUR 165 million in terms of total investment. Regional contracts are co-financed by the central budget and local government budgets (Box 3.3). The marshal decides the allocation of funds, while the voivod controls the spending of the funds.

---

### Box 3.3. **Regional contracts in Poland**

The first contracts were in 2001-03. The initial assumption was that their main role would be to prepare the public administration to manage the absorption of structural funds. Self-governments had to become acquainted with procedures for obtaining and allocating] funds from external programmes.

In 2004, contracts were treated by self-governments as complements of initiatives undertaken under IROP, in particular in areas in which community assistance was more complicated. Under the activities covered by the contracts, small projects prevailed. Another set of contracts was prepared for 2005-06.

In 2005, the government financed 62% of regional contracts and local governments 38%. The contract stipulates the method for implementing investments proposed by the regions and financed from the state budget. Under the 2005 contracts, 786 projects were implemented, including 32 multi-year investments of local self-government units.

Source: Background Report, 2007.

---

Within the overall envelope, regions determine which projects will be funded in priority under the regional contract; they do not negotiate the amount of funding with the central government. The breakdown of the funds by voivodships is determined by a pre-established algorithm[12] that favours cohesion criteria, as it takes into account criteria such as GDP per capita and the unemployment rate. By preparing the regional contracts, the marshal plays a strategic role within the region, as most projects are defined (and in certain cases co-financed) by municipalities and powiats. Hence, the marshals influence the territorial development of gminas/powiats through the priority they give to local projects in contracts, as this is the formal basis for project selection and prioritisation. In 2004, contracts for all voivodships contained approximately 1 500 tasks, including 39 long-term investments of territorial government units.

Regional contracts constituted the main operational dimension of regional development strategies until 2007, when Regional Operational Programmes co-financed by EU funds were developed. On the positive side, it is clear that regional contracts helped regions to prepare for the management of EU funds and enhanced their role as partners of local governments (gminas, powiats), the national government and the European Commission. Regional contracts have been the main tool for enhancing the accountability of voivodships and a learning tool for local governments. There is, however, a gap between the broad long-term objectives of regional strategies and regional contracts, which have a much more short term (one year) and practical dimension. Overall, the focus in contracts has been on investments for major public service needs, essentially health and education, rather than support for economic development (support to enterprises represented less than 10% of the budget of regional contracts for 2005). Contracts mainly address small projects (often not exceeding the value of several hundred thousand zlotys). This tendency was particularly visible in the area of education, where the amount awarded often did not exceed PLN 10 000 (EUR 2 600). Economic development efforts mainly took the form of regional and local loan funds.

### Regions and EU funding

The most important change related to the role of regions is linked to EU funds. As explained, one-quarter of EU funds has been decentralised since 2004, and the programme Human Capital is also partially regionalised. If regions had little say in the allocation of the funds during 2004-06, as there was one integrated regional operational programme at the national scale, the situation is different for 2007-13, as regional/local governments are in charge of the preparation and implementation of regional operational programmes. 16.5 billion euro are allocated to finance ROP, which is six times more than the amount of regional contracts on a yearly basis.

For 2004-06, although priorities were set by the Ministry of Regional Development, regions had an important role in the selection of projects and management of the funds (see Section 3.4). The 16 regions received EUR 4 billion under the IROP (Integrated Regional Operational Programme); and regions (marshals) have played an important role as they help to prioritise and select projects. Regions have been very actively engaged in the implementation of regional development policy in the first financial period. Local governments have been the major recipient of EU funds, in particular municipalities, which have received 44% of EU funds for 2004-06. More than two-thirds of municipalities co-financed projects benefiting from EU funding.

EU funding has played an important role in the increase of capital investments by local governments. Although local public investment rose at a slower pace than total public expenditures in the early 2000s, the inflow of EU funding after 2004 has reversed the trend. In Poland, only 4% of national government expenditures are spent on investment but 13% of local government expenditures are for capital improvements, and local governments carry out more than 58% of total public investments (DEXIA, 2008).[13] About 14% of sub-national investments made in 2005 were co-financed by EU funds. Transport and communication are the main areas of sub-national capital expenditure: they represent 25% of municipalities' investment expenditure, 47% of those of counties and 50% of those of regions (DEXIA, 2008). Sub-national capital expenditure is likely to increase faster in 2007-13.

Figure 3.3. **Structure of sub-national expenditure, by type (2005)**
**(In percentage of total expenditures)**

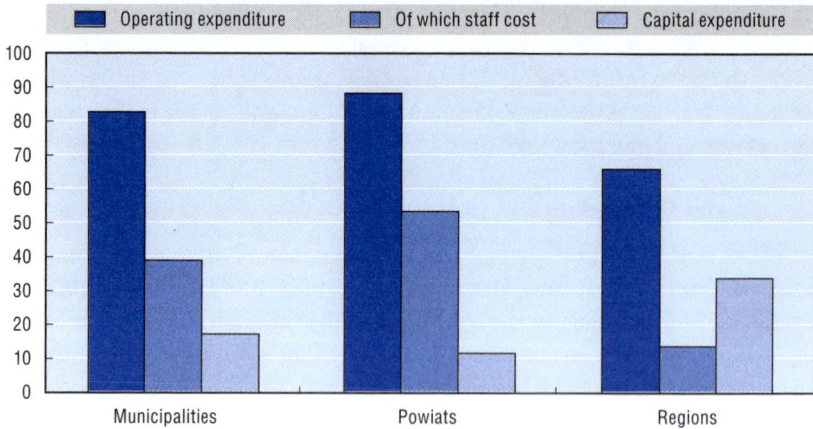

Source: Ministry of Finance (in DEXIA, 2008).

## Cohesion policy and broader impact on public governance

The impact of the European cohesion policy on Polish multi-level governance system goes well beyond the financial dimension. European cohesion policy has not only brought additional funds to be delivered, but a longer term impact on Polish multi-level governance system. The design and implementation of EU operational programmes – not only regional ones – has led to a new dynamic process of decentralisation and enhanced collaboration with private actors and civil society, where regional and local actors are becoming empowered and engaged in a strong learning process. Cohesion policy thus strongly influences the decentralisation process. In the long-term, the main impact of cohesion policy may well be the in-depth changes in governance and public management, on top of the support to growth and reduction in territorial disparities.

## 1.3. Promoting sustainable decentralisation for improved regional development

### Long-term challenges for Polish multi-level governance

The question is not so much to go further in decentralisation, but rather to clarify the current framework and make it more efficient and functional. Decentralisation is a learning process and is not set once for all. Permanent adjustments are necessary: relationships between levels of government exist and have to evolve beside constitutional arrangements (with EU funds and regional contracts for example). Drawing an optimal matrix that would define to which scale competencies and resources for each public good should be decentralised (or centralised) might be ideal but highly complex (OECD, 2008b). Besides, challenges for regional policy are also not to necessarily adopt the same solutions or institutional tools for the entire territory. Although it is acknowledged that Poland has done reasonably well in assigning service responsibilities to the appropriate levels of government (Kopańska and Levitas in Swianiewicz, 2004); the division of responsibilities across levels of government is not always clear, or may lead to overlaps and additional costs.

For example, there are overlaps both across local governments and with state agencies/voivod offices in particular for rural development, transport, health and employment policy. i) For rural development, regional local governments retain some responsibilities while rural agencies, not dependent on the regional government, are in charge of implementing EU funding linked to rural development: this constitutes a dual framework at the regional level for rural development issues. ii) This is also the case for roads,[14] as road maintenance formally is the responsibility of local governments and various tiers of the state administration at the regional office and voivodship levels. Given the large investments in road infrastructure that are currently planned in Poland and the high operating costs that will result from them; clarification of the different responsibilities is needed. iii) Besides, there is an artificial division in social care/health between municipal level, powiat and regional level. iv) Finally, accountability remains unclear concerning employment policy. Although 16 regional labour offices have been created, regions (marshal offices) have also taken some responsibilities in the fields of scholarships and life-long training. In addition, powiats retain some responsibilities in labour market policy, through the powiat labour offices. This results in a lack of coherence across the various responsibilities on labour market policy at the local level, which may affect its efficiency. For example, there is a critical lack of data on labour mobility at the local level, as no agency is officially in charge of collecting these data.

## Fiscal gaps

Although EU funding will provide significant additional resources in the next few years for local governments, they do not constitute a long-term answer to the fiscal gaps at the local level in Poland. Post-2013 solutions need to be found well in advance to improve the functioning of decentralisation. Local government expenditures have grown faster than public revenues. Sub-national expenditures are heavily constrained and there appears to be a mismatch between the spending responsibilities of local governments and their ability to effectively allocate resources to meet the needs of their population. The major fiscal gaps are related to local governments' capacity to finance health services (in particular regional hospitals)[15] and education. Education represents by far the largest item of sub-national expenditure, much higher than the OECD average for unitary countries, owing to large sub-national responsibilities in this area,[16] especially the payment of teachers' salaries (paid out of a non-earmarked grant received from central government). Wages in the education sector and debt service costs account for 65% of sub-national expenditure. Another 10% is linked to the maintenance of basic state institutions (armed forces, police, the judiciary, public administration). The structure of local expenditures limits the margin of manoeuvre for local development-related actions.

Figure 3.4. **Sub-national government expenditures by main category, as a percentage of total (2005)**

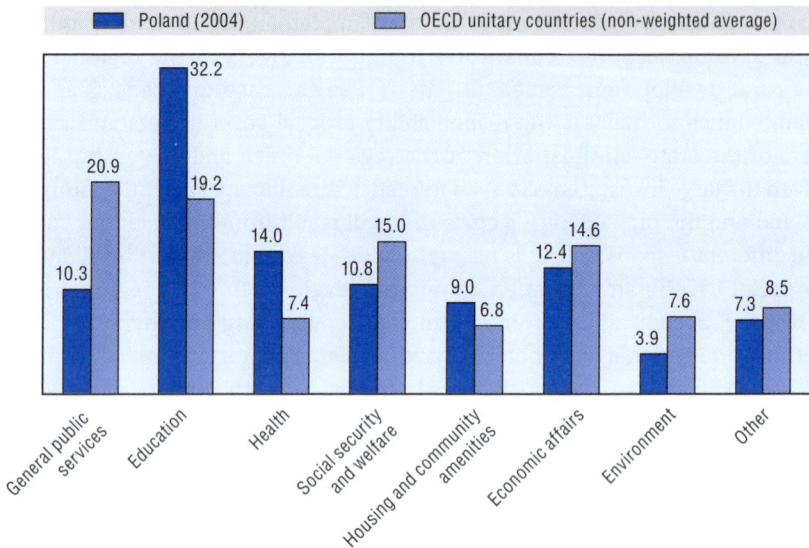

Source: OECD National Accounts, 2008.

The fiscal gaps appear more challenging for the regional and municipal levels. Although the region is supposed to address regional economic development, spatial planning and public transport at the regional scale, the resources for the voivodship to fulfil these competencies are limited, when EU funds are not taken into consideration. This is also due to the fact that regions have responsibilities in health care. Sub-national expenditures on health are much higher in Poland than the OECD average. Health care services are financed from centralised National Health Fund. However, regions own hospitals and policlinics, which are currently highly indebted and operational costs cannot be financed. According to some experts, health care is the biggest problem of public services in Poland today. The room for manoeuvre for broader development policies is limited. A disproportion exists between the scale of prerogatives to conduct regional policy and the level of financing at the disposal of voivodship self-governments (Szchlacta, 2004).

Municipalities are also confronted to important fiscal capacity challenges, in particular related to education, housing and public transport:

- For education, the challenges concern both urban and rural gminas. The "algorithm" used for allocating central government funds for education does not take into account the needs for pre-school education (OECD, 2006), thus many rural gminas lack sufficient resources to develop pre-school, contributing to further problems in educational attainment in rural areas (Chapter 2). In urban areas, there is a risk in some places to under-finance certain schools, as the number of pupils in schools is not taken into account when allocating the education grant, even though there are three times more pupils in urban schools (*Gdansk Institute of Market Economy*, 2008).

- For housing, municipalities lack sufficient budgetary resources to realise necessary investment in housing construction, in particular in industrial and medium size cities. Housing expenses are especially high in cities with developed industrial sectors, where nearly all housing belonged to large state enterprises until recently but was transferred to municipalities in the early 1990s. Since many of these buildings are in poor condition, their repair and operation are very costly (Kowalczyk, 2003, World Bank). The fiscal gap for housing investments has contributed to enhance the housing shortage in Poland (see Chapter 2), estimated to a million units in 2002, and contributing to limit labour mobility.

- Local governments are in charge of urban public transport; but municipalities have tended to reduce urban public transport susbsidies, leading to the degradation of the public transport system in many cities, and increasing use of cars.

**Rural gminas** have a specific challenge of fiscal capacity, linked to the fact that the agricultural sector is taxed at a markedly lower rate than other sectors of economy, and as farmers do not pay income tax. The own revenue of rural gminas comes from the very small agricultural tax (decreasing) and some income tax from civil servants (employees of the commune and teachers). Hence there are large differences at the local level between gminas which can benefit from professional taxes and rural gminas. Public revenue per capita in Mazowieckie (region of Warsaw) is nearly five times that of Swiętokrzyskie (Eastern region), and the differential has increased since 1999 (Background report, 2007). Rural gminas have problems financing basic public services, and in the medium term (2010), experts estimate that they may have problems for co-financing projects under regional operational programmes.

## Promoting a sustainable repartition of competencies for improved regional development

To improve effectiveness of regional development policies and promote an improved functioning of the multi-level governance framework, the following challenges may be tackled:

- **Further clarifying the repartition of competencies between regions,** povias and gminas is needed, in particular on education, health and labour market policies;

- **Securing additional revenues for gminas and regions:** i) *Regions:* To enhance fiscal capacities of regions, it could be envisaged to increase the shared taxes that go to regions; ii) *Gminas:* To enhance revenues of gminas, the property tax could be gradually expanded. Two options could be envisaged to enhance fiscal capacity of rural gminas: *a)* revise the taxation system for farmers – this would provide the advantage as well to enhance labour mobility outside of agriculture; *b)* revise the criteria for allocating grants, with a different funding for rural, urban and mixed municipalities. However, care must be taken not to reduce tax and development effort from poorer gminas.

- **Exploiting the strategic role of regions: Enhance political legitimacy and capacity of regions to arbitrate.** The strategic (and arbiter) role of voivodships for regional development is complex to play, as they lack sufficient own resources, flexibility in budget management, political visibility and enforcement power on spatial planning (see Chapter 2). There are frequent tensions between voivodship (marshal offices) and large municipalities, which have a much larger budget than the region. Regions do not have any capacity to influence intra-regional spending through transfers across different levels of local governments. Each transfer decision has to be agreed by the ministry of finance. Given that the highest disparities are intra-regional and not inter-regional (as explained in Chapter 1), the fiscal system should provide more flexibility to adjust to intra-regional needs. Besides, the executive power of the marshal is not strong, as he is not directly elected by the population – contrary to the mayor. The marshal's visibility and legitimacy could be enhanced if he/she were elected directly.

- **Better exploiting the role of contracts for regional economic development:** Although regional contracts have played a positive learning process, their use could be optimised in a longer term perspective (post-2013). Their timeframe could be longer, in order to help partners overcome the drawbacks of the annual budgetary principle. Contracts should include an important focus on proactive development/competitiveness approaches, negotiated in inter-ministerial collaboration.

- **Facilitating local public investment.** Local public investments are currently hampered by strict rules on borrowing. Two prudential rules apply to sub-national government borrowing: credit cannot be contracted either if it results in local indebtedness exceeding 60% of total annual revenues, or if the future debt service would be higher than 15% of total annual revenues. However, borrowing related to EU grants is not included in these prudential rules according to the new Act on Public Finance adopted in 2005. Sub-national debt amounts to 2.1% of GDP, much lower than the EU average (5.8%). The borrowing regulations applicable to sub-national governments may soon be modified. A bill presented in April 2007 proposes to abolish the two general prudential rules: the limit of borrowing would be related to the individual financial situation of each sub-national government. Moreover, the legal regulations on co-financing and long-term liabilities have not allowed for flexible financing of long-term investments so far.

## 2. Improving co-operation at local and metropolitan levels

Improving co-operation at local and metropolitan levels is a key priority to implement effective territorial development strategies. As explained in Chapter 2, the current lack of co-operation across municipalities (*gminas*) makes it difficult to reap economies of scale and to implement appropriate place-based competitiveness policies. Experience in OECD countries indicates that several options can help enhance horizontal co-ordination. An important criterion is the extent to which one option is politically more feasible than another in a limited timeframe, as co-ordination across local governments is always a sensitive issue. This section shows that co-operation across gminas and particularly at the metropolitan level needs to be promoted through specific incentives and an integrated approach to spatial planning, not only to improve public service delivery but to implement long-term competitiveness strategies.

### 2.1. Encouraging co-operation across gminas

The implementation of regional policy in Poland suffers from a lack of co-ordination across local governments, particularly in terms of spatial planning. In the Polish institutional system, one single municipality has the power to block projects related to infrastructure development for example. Individualistic behaviour prevails among gminas, reflecting a kind of extreme conception of decentralisation in Poland. The political culture of Polish local leaders is characterised by a reluctance to co-operate and the lack of a strategic long-term vision of development able to transcend the borders of a gmina (Dabrowski, 2007). Weak collaboration across gminas and the quasi-absence of spatial planning result in an under-optimal allocation of collective goods and services, which undermines competitiveness at an aggregate regional or national level. The challenge of horizontal collaboration is shared by all OECD countries and many countries have recently introduced institutional changes to improve co-ordination mechanisms at the local scale. Although Poland has acknowledged this need, specific reforms targeting horizontal co-ordination across local governments have yet to be implemented.

The existing upper level – *powiats* – could have played a more important role to facilitate co-ordination, but it has not been the case so far. *Powiats* have relatively limited competencies and no specific authority in terms of spatial planning. Some of the powiats combine both municipal and county responsibilities with a single budget, as a result of the Counties Act (1999) which converted into *powiats* those cities with more than 100 000 inhabitants and the former regional capitals that lost their capital statute in the administrative reform.[17] However, the current allocation of responsibilities does not allow *powiats* to tackle the challenges linked to urban transport and housing at the functional scale. The overall efficiency of *powiats* is currently under debate, especially regarding counties located close to municipalities having county status (Dexia, 2008).

Although the Polish legislation introduced voluntary mechanisms for inter-municipal collaboration, no specific financial incentives are available at present. Sub-national governments can work together in three ways: by setting up a syndicate; by signing an agreement; and by setting up an association (Box 3.4). For example, syndicates mainly focus on joint service delivery, such as public transportation (as in the Upper Silesia industrial region) and water supply or waste removal (common in rural areas); associations collaborate on the construction of utility infrastructure (*e.g.* water and sewage systems). Although 60% of gminas are engaged in some kind of inter-municipal collaboration scheme, voluntary co-operation between local self-governments in Poland does not have a long tradition and remains relatively limited (Furmankiewicz, 2002).

The context of large inflows of EU Structural Funds calls for effective ways of co-operation between neighboring communes. Gminas are the largest recipients of EU funding (they received 44% of total European funding in 2004-06). During the 2007-13 period, they will need to learn how to co-operate efficiently in order to perform an even wider variety of tasks (ranging from the construction of roads and the refurbishment of historical monuments to the management of professional training programmes and the setting up of technological clusters). So far, it still happens sometimes that part of a road renovated thanks to the Structural Funds stops right at the border between the gminas it crosses (Dabrowski, 2007). Changing individualistic mindsets is certainly a long-term effort but it is fundamental for an effective delivery of regional policy (Grosse, 2004).

## Which type of intervention to promote economies of scale?

Economies of scale and horizontal collaboration need to be promoted through increased incentives or a more coercive approach in order to facilitate the absorption of EU funds, and more broadly for the efficient implementation of regional policy in Poland. International experience indicates that

Box 3.4. **Co-operation of local governments in Poland**

The 1997 Constitution authorises sub-national governments to join forces to carry out their missions. Specific regulations are set out in the different Local Government Acts. Sub-national governments can work together in one of three ways:

i) By setting up a syndicate (*związek*). Syndicates are the most frequently used form of co-operation. They are established to fulfill sub-national governments' tasks such as water provision and treatment, public transport, gas distribution, telecommunications and environmental protection. A syndicate must adopt a statute, established by the participating sub-national government councils, and be registered by the Ministry of Interior and Public Administration. It is a legal entity with its own right. Syndicates are financed by fees or grants from its members, and by revenues from its activity. In 2006, there were 280 municipal syndicates and 1 county syndicate.

ii) By signing an agreement (*porozumienie*). Municipalities decide to give one of them the right to fulfill a particular task.

iii) By creating an association (*stowarzyszenie*). The association operates under the Act on Association adopted in 1989 and it is mainly financed from members' fees. The 1990 Municipal Act allows sub-national governments to co-operate and create an association (*stowarzyszenia*) "to provide backing for a local government project or protect and promote common interests". There must be at least three participating sub-national authorities.

*Source:* Dexia, 2007.

co-ordination rarely results from a bottom-up dynamics; the central government has a key role to play. Two broad approaches have commonly been developed to promote economies of scale in OECD countries: amalgamation of municipalities and co-operative arrangements. Amalgamation reduces duplication of tasks and improves accountability, but it tends to be politically more sensitive and therefore more difficult to achieve.[18] Co-ordination mechanisms between municipalities tend to blur accountability, but they are more flexible and easier to tailor to different types of functional areas.

In Poland, amalgamation of municipalities is clearly not the best option. The number of municipalities in Poland has remained relatively stable over the last twenty years (2 452 units in 1993, compared to 2 375 units in 1975). The average size of municipalities (around 15 500 inhabitants) is not that small compared to other OECD countries (Figure 3.6). Very small municipalities are relatively few compared to France or the Czech Republic for example. Besides, municipal autonomy is guaranteed by the Polish Constitution. Mergers would require time-consuming constitutional reforms, when the absorption requirements related to EU Funds call for urgent solutions to co-ordination dilemmas. Finally, municipal amalgamation offers no guarantee of economies of scale since functional areas may differ from one public service to another (*e.g.* water supply and education).

Figure 3.5. **Average size of municipalities in selected OECD countries (thousands of inhabitants)**

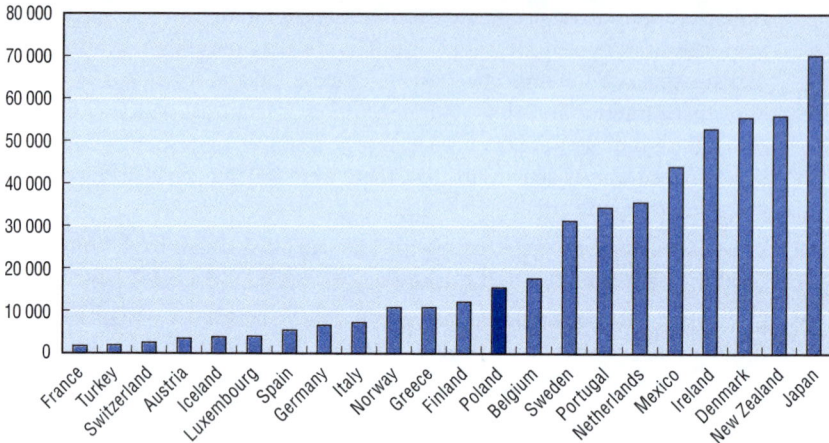

*Source:* OECD, 2006.

Enhanced co-operation is unlikely to occur without the involvement of the central government. While various forms of co-operative arrangements exist in OECD countries (Box 3.5), financial support to inter-municipal co-operation has been provided by the central government in countries like France or Norway.[19] The French experience in inter-municipal co-operation is probably one of the most advanced in the OECD area, as 88% of municipalities have been integrated under some kind of inter-municipal structure (also due to the very small size of French municipalities). Inter-municipal co-operation in France can bring important experiences and help Poland to adapt the system to its own needs.

Although inter-municipal co-operation is not a specifically rural or a specifically urban phenomenon, it is important to make the distinction. Challenges are particularly significant in large Polish cities, which are driving national growth (see Chapter 1). Different institutional solutions may be necessary in order to take into account the specificity of different places. What is considered appropriate for urban areas may not help much in dispersed rural communities, where the delivery of public services is an important tool

Box 3.5. **Various forms of co-operative arrangements in the OECD**

Co-operative arrangements can cover very different situations according to the context in which they are introduced and the goals pursued. One possible form is the single-purpose or sectoral authority devoted to one specific public service, aimed at increasing co-ordination and economies of scale. This framework is common in countries where local autonomy is strong (OECD, 2006).

A second form of inter-municipal joint collaboration is the multiple purpose body, which performs a wide range of functions such as planning and co-ordination, and sometimes delivery of public services. Multiple purpose bodies can be created by an upper level of governments (*e.g.* Montreal Community of Montreal) or through voluntary co-operation (*e.g.* Greater Vancouver Regional District), sometimes with incentives from upper levels of governments (*e.g.* French Urban and Agglomeration Communities). Some receive grants from upper-level government, and/or fees from members local governments, and can even levy their own taxes. An advantage of multi-purpose agencies is that they preserve local autonomy, diversity, and the distinct identity of its member municipalities. However, popular legitimacy can become an issue when the institution takes on increasing responsibilities and fiscal revenues. In addition, problems may arise for policy implementation when the municipalities are not bound to respect the decisions (OECD, 2006a).

for regional development objectives (*e.g.* Norway). The case of the Canadian Province of Quebec also illustrates the importance of developing differentiated policies for urban and rural areas.[20]

Horizontal co-ordination in Poland should be considered as an instrument to develop a shared strategic vision for the area through integrated approaches of spatial planning ("project territories") rather than to improve only the efficiency of public service delivery. Institutional mechanisms for horizontal co-ordination therefore need to be complemented by a specific focus on the spatial planning dimension in Poland.

### Spatial plans in urban and rural areas

Given that horizontal collaboration *per se* does not necessarily foster place-based integrated approaches to spatial planning, a further challenge consists in creating new processes through which competitiveness strategies are elaborated. In this regard, the example of French spatial planning could be relevant. In France, the central government has instructed sub-national government to build up a special scheme called SCOT (*Schéma de cohérence territoriale*: Territorial Coherence Scheme) (Box 3.6). The SCOT aims at ensuring a balance between urban renewal and the rural periphery, preserve the diversity of urban functions and social mixity, and achieve competitive and sustainable development. It is also expected to ensure coherence between the various sectoral policies (housing, facilities, mobility, etc.) at a larger scale than that of the municipality.

---

Box 3.6.  **The example of SCOT (*Schéma de cohérence territoriale:* Territorial Coherence Scheme) in France**

The SCOT are elaborated by local governments within a functional area, and in particular within urban areas (*i.e.* covering city centres and their periphery). City plans (*plan local d'urbanisme*), local urban transport plans and housing plans must be compatible with the SCOT in order to be valid and enforced. The SCOT sets the main orientations of the organisation of a group of adjacent communities (*intercommunalité*) for a 10-year period.

The elaboration of a SCOT is decided under the initiative of the municipality or a coalition of municipalities. The decision is made by the resolution of each municipal assembly in the area, with a two-third majority in the area. The coalition of municipalities is the main actor and the national government, the Region, the Prefecture etc., can participate in the elaboration. In addition, opinions are heard from the Prefect (*Préfet*), the Chairperson of the Regional Assembly (*Président du conseil régional*), the Chairperson of the Departmental Assembly (*Président du conseil départemental*), and the mayors (*Maires*) of municipalities. After taking necessary steps in the Public Hearing System, the SCOT is approved by the the coalition of municipalities. The SCOT consists of: i) Diagnostic part and orientation report; ii) PADD (Project of development and sustainable development).

---

Poland could also introduce a flexible approach to spatial planning in rural areas, based on territorial strategies transcending administrative boundaries. Rural gminas need closer co-operation at the local scale to reach a more efficient size for the delivery of public services and to play a more effective role in local economic development by exchanging information, sharing responsibility for certain investments and programmes and dealing with territorial externalities (OECD, 2006i).

Pooling resources and achieving economies of scale require an adequate spatial organisation that gives reality to the small functional region, usually organised around one, maybe two, small to medium sized towns. Many OECD countries have developed such groupings of rural municipalities, with large variations across the different systems. In linking rural municipalities together, the main town often acts as a public and private service centre for the whole area (social services, sometimes a hospital, banks) while representing a sizeable portion of employment. In optimal situations, this hub is adequately linked to the domestic transportation network. The examples of Ireland, France or Mexico could inspire possible changes in Poland. The Irish Spatial Strategy retains these rural hubs as major elements in efforts to foster the development of rural areas and links these, in terms of infrastructure development to "Gateway" cities at the regional level, to which the former need to be properly connected (OECD, 2006h). In France, the delimitation of a "Pays" follows a certain number of guidelines to ensure that the small territory responds to a degree of economic logic linked in particular to employment.[21] In Mexico, rural Micro-regions are defined through a top-down approach based on socio-economic indicators, combined with other spatial indicators through the use of Geographic Information Systems (GIS).

### 2.2. Toward metropolitan governance in Poland

Co-operation in large urban/metropolitan areas (defined in Poland as above 500 000 inhabitants)[22] needs to be promoted through more proactive measures. Although the contribution of large urban areas to national growth is widely acknowledged in the Polish NSRF, a specific policy has not yet been developed for them (see Chapter 2). Bottom-up initiatives for co-operation exist but the central government has a key role to play. Whether in the case of merging municipalities, creating sectoral or multi-sectoral co-ordinating bodies or even metropolitan governments, rarely have the reforms of metropolitan governance emanated from purely local initiatives in the OECD countries. The national government has played a leadership role either by imposing or by encouraging reform, in the conviction that the emergence of metropolitan authorities is necessary to promote the growth of cities and thus national growth (OECD, 2006a).

A metropolitan planning Act endowed with fiscal incentives could give large urban areas flexible institutional tools to co-operate at a functional scale. Several discussions on this topic have been conducted in Poland since the 1990s, but incentives to enhance co-operation are yet to be adopted. This also reveals strong resistance from gminas, especially those located close to urban powiats, which fear a certain loss of autonomy. More recently, there have been discussions about the creation of "metropolitan powiats". Along with national zoning planning, some work has recently been done on urban/metropolitan planning, but with no legislative change so far. A new spatial development strategy is expected to be prepared by mid-2008. The availability of EU Funds could also be made conditional to enhanced collaboration, especially with regard to transportation and environment issues.

Many OECD countries have developed specific incentives to enhance metropolitan co-operation, suggesting that there is no best practice or a "one size fit all" solution (Box 3.7). Centrally instituted metropolitan governance reforms are typically implemented through a national law, which gives legitimacy to the process. However, in the absence of any form of incentive and leadership, the laws rarely lead to any concrete reform in practice (OECD, 2006a). The French experiment has worked better than the Italian proposal because the related laws involved fiscal incentives for inter-municipal collaboration. While in Italy the creation of metropolitan cities (*Città Metropolitana*) was optional

---

**Box 3.7. Broad types of metropolitan governance in OECD countries**

Many cities have placed greater emphasis on voluntary instruments for co-ordination and co-operation. Even the few examples of strong metropolitan governance through metropolitan governments and amalgamated cities coexist with other forms of network arrangements. In terms of efficiency, it may be second-best to rely on a co-operative mechanism rather than a self-financed and directly elected administrative organ, but it has its own merits of fostering communication and possibly limiting the tendency to bureaucratic mission creep.

New modes of metropolitan governance, involving reform of traditional institutional and financial structures of major urban centres, are an arduous task. They pose a multitude of problems relative to the roles and responsibilities of different levels of government operating in metropolitan regions, intergovernmental co-ordination, and new relationships with the private sector and civil society. In this context, there is a strong interest in developing an adequate formula that will respond to metropolitan challenges now visible everywhere. The discussion of how to manage metropolitan regions better revolves principally around a spectrum of models that range from relatively "heavy' to relatively" light' in terms of the scope of the reform they imply.

i) At the relatively heavy end are functional models whereby governance structures are re-shaped to fit or to approximate to the functional economic area of the metropolitan region. Examples include the creation of a metropolitan government and the amalgamation of municipalities.

ii) At mid-position are a wide range of co-operative arrangements through inter-municipal joint authorities, most often on a voluntary basis, such as sectoral or multi-sectoral agencies whose main functions generally include transport, urban planning or economic development (sometimes on *ad hoc* basis).

iii) At the light end are informal co-ordination bodies such as platforms, associations or strategic planning partnerships, often relying on existing networks of relevant actors, without necessarily following the logic of territorial boundaries. Also to be included here are purely fiscal arrangements such as equalisation mechanisms and tax-base sharing whose main purpose is to deal with fiscal disparities and territorial spillover within the area as well as public-private partnerships and contract services.

*Source:* OECD, 2006a.

---

**194**

and was not implemented in practice, in France certain powers (mandatory and optional) were transferred to supra-municipal authorities, urban communities or agglomeration communities. The French central government offered an incentive grant to the participating municipalities in addition to their existing block grants entitlements. One of the conditions, however, is that the municipalities accept to adopt a unique business tax system within the area (the business tax is the main local tax in France) (OECD, 2006a).

Poland could draw particular inspiration from French *communautés d'agglomération*, which offer the advantages of both enhancing horizontal collaboration across municipalities and improving vertical collaboration with the central government (Box 3.8). Although some problems remain (such as unclear accountability mechanisms *vis-à-vis* the citizens and conflicts on the political leadership of the *communauté*), the *communautés d'agglomération* have constituted valuable tools to promote territorial development strategies and to implement strategic spatial planning.

### The case of Warsaw

Although it is not the purpose of this report to enter into the detail of the many co-operation projects needed at the metropolitan scale in Poland, the case of Warsaw deserves specific attention. Although Warsaw is the first pole of growth in Poland (see Chapter 1), it seems that the potential of the metropolitan area has not been fully exploited. Warsaw enjoys a specific institutional organisation: in 2002, a single entity was created unifying the municipality, gminas and the powiat. The mayor of Warsaw is now directly elected. While these reforms go in the right direction, the Warsaw functional area could be further promoted. It is estimated that the Warsaw functional area (which consists of around a hundred municipalities) could in practice be larger than its current 2.2 million people. Housing density is quite low compared to other OECD capitals, and it is decreasing. The right side of the Vistula, in particular, seems to have under-used potential for housing development, which suggests potential room for further collaboration among neighbouring gminas. The metropolitan policy also facilitates environmental policies, for example to make necessary investments on water treatments.

In addition, co-operation between Warsaw and Lodz (which together gather 4 million inhabitants) is important for the long-term competitiveness of both cities. Co-operation between these two cities (the two largest in Poland) and the two voivodships has remained very limited so far. The construction of an express train is expected to reduce the commuting time between the two cities from 2 hours today to only 40 minutes by year 2011. The A2 motorway will also link Warsaw to Poznan (and Berlin) through Lodz. It is thus essential to think about the long-term development of this large urban pole, which could become a strong economic centre in Central and

Box 3.8. **The French *contrats d'agglomération***

France has been one of the OECD countries most consistent in pursuing the creation of specific institutional arrangements for metropolitan areas. This process has accelerated since 1999 when the central government established metropolitan authorities in the 150 largest urban areas. In addition to creating the *communautés urbaines* and the *communautés d'agglomération*, central government drafted specific model agreements that urban areas must adopt and projects that urban areas must undertake if they want to receive government grants. These have been specified in two Acts on National Territorial Planning and Inter-municipal Co-operation in 1999.

Following these two acts, councils for *communautés urbaines* and *communautés d'agglomération* must approve a so-called territorial project. This territorial project is a five to 10-year plan which concerns infrastructure, economic development, social housing, culture, environment, etc at the metropolitan level. But it is more than a plan since it specifies the amount of funding and all the operations to be performed in order to achieve the plan's objectives. Once approved by the *communauté* council, the project is then discussed with the central government. When it is approved by the central government, an agreement is signed between it and the *communauté*, called a *contrat d'agglomération*.

This agreement guarantees that the central government will finance some of the actions decided in the territorial project (there are therefore negotiations between the central government and the *communauté* regarding government funding). In addition, the law states that the *contrat d'agglomération* must also be signed by the regional council. This means that the actions envisaged in the *contrat d'agglomération* will also be financed by the region, and as such, will be part of the *contrat de Plan*, a larger five-year agreement signed by the central government and the region. Moreover, this means that EU Structural Funds will feed the general budget of the territorial project.

For instance, the Bordeaux *contrat d'agglomération* amounts to EUR 1.2 billion over a seven-year period. It has been signed by the *communauté urbaine* of Bordeaux (CUB), the provincial (*département*) council of Gironde, the City of Bordeaux, the regional council of Aquitaine and the central government's representative (the regional prefect). The central government contributes 17% of the total funding while the CUB contributes 36% and the regional council, 15%. Other contributors are the EU, the Department of Gironde, municipalities and national public agencies such as the National Railways (SNCF) or the National Centre for Aerospace (CNES).

Eastern Europe with complementary specialisations and functions. More effective co-ordination could also allow for a better use of natural and cultural assets located between Lodz and Warsaw (Lowicz, Arkadia, Nieborow, Zelazowa Wola) (Markowski, 2008). Co-operation needs to aim at yielding benefits for both cities and not only for Warsaw to reap additional housing possibilities in Lodz. It should not be simply considered as a local government issue; exploiting the major pole of growth in the country is a national concern and raises a key priority in terms of strategic planning over the next few years.

Table 3.2. **Main purposes of a selection of metropolitan co-operative arrangements**

| | Tax-base sharing and redistributive grants | Informal co-operation networks (association/platform/ metropolitan conferences) | Metropolitan authority/agency | | Metropolitan government | Amalgamation |
| --- | --- | --- | --- | --- | --- | --- |
| | | | Single-purpose | Multi-purpose | | |
| Examples | Minneapolis Saint-Paul Stockholm County Some municipalities within Paris Ile-de-France Busan/Seoul | Regio Randstad (Plateform) Lyon Urban Region, Council of Stockholm, Mälar Region, Bilbao 30 – Metropolitana, Torino Internazionale (Associations), Regional conference (Rhin-Rhur) | Many US cities Mexico City (large number of sectoral agencies) Athens transport agency | Montreal Metropolitan Community Greater vancouver District Communauté d'agglomération in France | Greater London Authority Stuggart Verband Association Portland Communidad de Madrid Région Ile-de-France (Paris) | Montreal, Toronto Busan/Seoul in the 1950s Madrid in the 1960s Melbourne in the 1990s |
| Administrative boundaries | No change | No change | Possible creation of a new layer | | Building on a regional tier or creation of a new a regional tier with elected body | Disappearance of municipalities. Possible creation of sub-local units |
| Economies of scale (cost saving) | No | No | For one public service only | For certain public services only | For certain public service only Expected | Expected |
| Sharing of public services | In a limited way | No | Yes, for one public service only | Yes, for certain public services only | Yes, for certain public services only | Common |
| Specific advantage | Reduce fiscal disparities Still allow some variety | Great flexibility. Might provide impetus to further co-operation Weak implementation capacity | Cost saving for a particular service Better management of a metropolitan function | Idem to single-purpose + Integration and co-ordination of sectoral policies | Integration and co-ordination of certain sectoral policies Better equalisation of costs Stronger political power | No fiscal disparities One decision centre |
| Specific disadvantage | Separate the costs and benefits of local public services | Does not tackle issues such as territorial spillover/negative externalities/equity | Emergence of sectoral constituencies | Emergence of the funding and legitimacy issues | Democratic cost? | Lack of creative diversity Democratic cost? |
| Long term strategic vision | No | Yes, in many cases | Yes, in many cases for economic development agency Risk of avoiding the multi-sectoral aspects or urban development | In some cases only | Yes, will depend on the administrative boundaries of the new structure | Yes, will depend on the administrative boundaries of the new structure |

Note: This table provides a typology of metropolitan governance arrangements previously discussed according to the different objectives that calls for horizontal co-operation. This typology is not exhaustive. The selections of different options that it includes are not mutually exclusive, as some metropolitan regions combine several options (e.g. Montreal experienced an amalgamation of 27 municipalities whilst a multi-sectoral agency was created at the wider metropolitan level).
Source: OECD (2006a), Competitive Cities in the Global Economy.

## 3. Towards an integrated territorial policy approach at the central level

In addition to better co-ordination among local governments to achieve an optimal scale of territorial development, it is important for *central policies* on regional development to have a territorial dimension. There are five key conditions for promoting integrated territorial approaches to regional policy at the central government level: *i)* high visibility/priority on the political agenda and long-term commitment; *ii)* efficient mechanisms for inter-ministerial co-ordination; *iii)* appropriate co-ordination of regional and rural development strategies (which are separate under the cohesion policy and CAP); *iv)* promotion of place-based rather than one-size-fits-all policies at the central level; *v)* involvement of local actors in the design of central strategy. Although Poland has made good progress on the first two of these conditions, the three others still present challenges, in particular co-ordination of rural and regional development strategies and the need to enhance the place-based dimension of central policy. The Ministry of Regional Development increasingly needs to encourage differentiated territorial place-based approaches, with appropriate incentives, rather than one-size-fits-all policy. This section analyses these challenges and describes how certain OECD countries, confronted with the same challenges, have responded.

### 3.1. High priority on the political agenda and long-term commitment

High visibility and priority on the political agenda and long-term political and budgetary commitment are needed to implement regional development policy. Without strong political leadership, regional policy is likely to suffer from inadequate co-ordination from spending ministries, such agriculture or transport; and from low priority in terms of budget allocation by the Ministry of Finance. Regional policy design and implementation also requires an arbiter at the highest level of the executive to arbitrate among different policy objective and priorities, within what is by nature cross-sectoral policy.

Poland benefits from a strong political commitment to regional development, owing in part to the large inflow of EU funds for cohesion and rural policies. Regional development is a major policy objective of the current Polish government. In institutional terms, regional policy gained recognition with the creation in 2005 of the Ministry of Regional Development (MRD). Poland is one of the few OECD countries with such a ministry (see Box 3.10). Although the ministry's first objective is to ensure co-ordination of the management of European structural funds,[23] it helps to enhance inter-ministerial co-ordination of regional development issues and to move towards more multi-sectoral approaches. It highlights regional development as a key priority on the political agenda and ensures that regional policy is recognised as a structural policy in

Box 3.9. **Co-ordination of regional policy in OECD countries: various models**

In OECD countries there are several different models for improving the co-ordination of territorial policies at national level. The spectrum of instruments ranges from bodies charged with co-ordinating the activities of sectoral ministries to full-fledged ministries with broad responsibilities and powers that encompass traditionally separate sectors. The simplest and most common instrument is co-ordination through inter-ministerial committees and commissions. Some co-ordinating structures are relatively informal, others are more structured. Austria, for example, has developed an informal approach that emphasises consensus building among ministries, while Switzerland uses a more formal approach in which ministries dealing with territorial development issues have to convene regularly in an inter-ministerial body.

Several countries augment cross-sectoral co-ordination mechanisms through special units or agencies that provide planning and advisory support to help ensure policy coherence across sectors. In Norway, the Regional Development Unit of the Ministry of Local Government and Regional Development has responsibility for co-ordinating the regional dimension of policies of other government departments, principally through inter-ministerial groups. In the United Kingdom, the Regional Co-ordination Unit – currently in the Office of the Deputy Prime Minister – was set up to implement cross-cutting initiatives and advise departments. In Japan, the National and Regional Planning Bureau in the Ministry of Land Infrastructure and Transport has developed a new view of territorial/regional policy and provided a network for local authorities as well as other local actors. In France, the DIACT (*Délégation interministérielle à l'aménagement et la compétitivité des territoires*) is an inter-ministerial body directly linked to the office of the Prime Minister (which co-ordinates national territorial policy and handles planning contracts and the European structural funds) and receives information from the different ministries regarding their regional priorities and the strategic objectives identified by the regional prefects.

While co-ordinating bodies represent an important tool, decision-making power remains principally in the hands of the individual sectoral ministries that implement policies. As such, while the planning stage is more or less well integrated, implementation is potentially compartmentalised. To overcome problems relating to sectoral implementation and in line with the increasing importance accorded to regional development policies, inter-ministerial co-ordination bodies have sometimes been given some responsibility for implementation. The DIACT in France is an example of an inter-ministerial body that is charged with ensuring co-ordination but also has a formal role in territorial development planning, decision making and policy implementation. The Office of the Deputy Prime Minister in the United Kingdom has also evolved towards a broader and more active role than its original policy co-ordination remit. In Italy the Department for Development and Cohesion Policies in the Treasury Ministry has broad competence for programming and co-ordinating investments with particular reference to the Mezzogiorno region.

In addition, these co-ordination bodies also function as the interface with regional government in the area of economic development – allocating funding, setting the guidelines for drawing up regional strategies, advising on and authorising the strategies, and ensuring value for money.

*Source:* OECD (2005), *Building Competitive Regions.*

Box 3.10. **Mechanisms proposed in the Polish NSRF for inter-ministerial co-ordination**

In order to ensure effective co-ordination of the implementation of the NSRF, it is planned in the Polish NSRF that the Prime Minister will appoint an inter- ministerial committee chaired by the minister in charge of regional development. It would be composed of representatives of all managing and intermediary authorities and ministers in charge of particular areas covered by operational programmes, the minister in charge of public finances, the head of the Office for Competition and Consumer Protection, the head of the Central Statistical Office and the head of Public Procurement Office. The committee will be assisted by a permanent secretariat created within the Ministry of Regional Development.

Source: Polish NSRF, 2007.

itself, not simply a complement to sectoral policies. Other former EU accession countries, such as Hungary and the Czech Republic, have also introduced regional development ministries, with broad responsibilities for different aspects of regional policy design and implementation, and management of EU regional aid. However, the existence of a dedicated ministry cannot guarantee knowledge sharing among central, local and private actors.

Poland also benefits from long-term political commitment to regional policy, in part under the influence of EU policy with a target date of 2013. All EU countries have been requested by the Commission to develop National Strategic Reference Frameworks (NSRF) covering the 2007-13 period, as well as long-term objectives for regional development. In Poland, the centralisation of regional policy management in the MRD has helped achieve greater co-ordination and coherence in policy objectives. This long-term commitment gives a sense of vision to all levels of government. Poland has also developed a long-term development strategy that goes beyond cohesion policy to include all areas of policy development, the national development strategy (NDS) for the period 2007-15.[24] This helps to improve policy coherence as it is meant as the umbrella under which all policies are developed. It influences regional development programmes and strategies, as they must take into account the times frame specified for the NDS. A major goal is to achieve the greatest possible coherence in the programmes and sectoral strategies implemented under the NDS.[25] However, the NDS remains a strategic document, the implementation of which may depend on the government in place – political cycles are of course shorter than the 2007-15 time frame of the NDS.

Long-term commitments under regional policy may require greater coherence. At EU and national levels, the timelines of the different strategies are quite varied. For example, the cohesion policy has a seven-year timeline

(2007-13), whereas the NDS has a nine-year timeline (2007-15), owing to the N+2 rule. The Lisbon strategy (the basis of cohesion policy) targets 2010 as its main objective. Other tools of regional policy in Poland – the regional contracts – have a one-year timeline. Moreover, Poland's budget process is still largely an annual one, apart from some exceptions involving co-financed EU projects, which have a three-year timeline. Poland's provisions for multi-annual budgeting are limited and the authorities need to move increasingly towards a multi-year budgeting framework (see Section 3.5).

## 3.2. Inter-ministerial co-ordination and arbitration

Although the institutional framework for regional development was improved with the creation of the ministry, the policy framework has become increasingly complex since 2004-05, owing in part to the EU funds to be managed and to the multi-sectoral dimension of the policy, as well as the number of sectoral agencies and levels of governments involved in implementing regional policy. The will to increase co-ordinating bodies relies on a real concern for the workload involved in an ambitious regional development policy; however there is a risk of creating parallel administrative structures that might complicate rather than facilitate the interaction of the different actors in planning and implementing regional development policies. While co-ordination is a critical component of coherent regional policy, the mere presence of co-ordinating mechanisms does not guarantee coherence (OECD, 2007h). In fact, too many overlapping co-ordinating mechanisms can cause inefficiencies through duplication of effort, particularly if information is not shared in a way that enhances synergies. The effectiveness of different co-ordinating mechanisms must be assessed regularly.

For 2007-13, co-ordination is a challenge for all programmes as they are thematic and do not correspond to particular ministries: their wider scope requires inter-ministerial co-operation. Although the Ministry of Regional Development is the managing authority for all programmes for 2007-13, with the exception of the rural development programme, numerous intermediary institutions are involved in their implementation; in principle, they must follow ministry guidelines for implementing each operational programme. There are 45 intermediary institutions (public agencies) in charge of implementing the different operational programmes. In addition, there are about a hundred intermediary institutions of second rank, also involved in the implementation (see Table 3.3). In all, about 150 public institutions – including local governments are involved in implementing regional policy.[26] This myriad of authorities means that information flows are not easy, accountability mechanisms are not clear, and decision-making processes are complex and time-consuming. Besides, investment resources may be fragmented into many small projects with less impact on overall

Table 3.3. **Poland: managing authorities of regional policy**

| Operational Programmes (OP) | Managing authority | Number of intermediary institutions (II) | Intermediary institutions of second rank (II2) |
|---|---|---|---|
| OP Infrastructure and Environment | Ministry of Regional Development | 6<br>Minister in charge of transport<br>Minister in charge of environment<br>Minister in charge of economy<br>Minister in charge of health<br>Minister in charge of culture and national heritage | 28 I |
| OP Competitive Economy | Ministry of Regional Development | 3<br>Minister in charge of economy<br>Minister in charge of science<br>Minister in charge of IT | 10 I |
| OP Human Capital | Ministry of Regional Development | 21<br>Minister in charge of social security<br>Minister in charge of labour<br>Minister in charge of education and upbringing<br>Minister in charge of higher education<br>Minister in charge of public administration<br>Minister in charge of health<br>Self-government of voivodships | 33 |
| OP Eastern Poland | Ministry of Regional Development | 1 | |
| Regional Operational Programmes (16) | 16 voivodships (Marshal Office) | 13 institutions | |
| OP Technical Assistance | Ministry of Regional Development | | |
| Operational Programmes European Territorial Co-operation | Ministry of Regional Development | | Minister in charge of regional development and with participation of relevant ministers self governments of voivodships |

Source: Polish NSRF, 2007.

competitiveness. In a long-term perspective, it is important for the Ministry of Regional Development to maintain a central position and ensure leadership in managing regional policy.

In practice, it is difficult for the Ministry of Regional Development to act as arbiter. Although it is the managing authority for all programmes (except one: rural development), all ministers have equal status in the council of ministers, so line ministries often resist decisions taken by the MRD and put forward their own agenda. The challenge is greater from ministries with large budget allocations (such as the Ministry of Infrastructure) or from the Ministry of Agriculture which is the managing authority for the rural development programme. The problem also comes from the fact that rural and cohesion policies are separated under the new framework for 2007-13; resulting in duality of strategies, which can raise obstacles for the effective implementation of rural development policy. Challenges also come from within cohesion policy itself, since for 2007-13 there are now two separate implementation systems for ERDF and ESF (mono-fund systems). This creates challenges in terms both of the design of strategies and operational co-ordination, as operational programs cannot be funded simultaneously from the European Regional Development Fund and from the European Social Fund.

There is also a need for greater coherence between the transport plan and regional development policy. There is a low co-ordination between the transport plan and the regional development strategy, which reflects to some extent the difficulty of co-ordinating the Community's transport and cohesion policies. Better prioritising investment plans for transport at the central level is important (see Chapter 2); this implies better co-ordination of the transport plan with the NSRF, the spatial planning strategy and the environment ministry. It is important to complement the inter-regional dimension with a strong intra-regional focus, in particular to make transport systems coincide with the functional scale of urban areas. It is crucial for Poland's balanced development and for enhancing sustainable long-term competitiveness.

An arbiter is needed at the central level which is able to facilitate and foster the decision-making process on regional development at the Cabinet level. Such an authority existed previously: for example, until 2006, a commission headed by the Deputy Prime Minister was in charge of arbitrating potential conflicts regarding the use of EU funding and taking final strategic decisions. So far, no new arbitrating authority has been put in place. However, it is envisaged to create an inter-ministerial committee chaired by the minister in charge of regional development to co-ordinate the implementation of NSRF (Box 3.10) and a co-ordinating committee[27] that would oversee the coherence of sectoral strategies with the National Development Strategy for 2007-15.

Co-ordination and arbitration on regional development policy at the central level is a challenge throughout OECD countries, but some options have emerged. The task of managing co-ordination across ministries – i.e. chairing co-ordination bodies – is often a responsibility of the head of state, prime minister or cabinet. In France, the CIADT (Comité interministériel à l'aménagement et au développement du territoire) prepares the decisions of the Council of Ministers in the field of spatial planning. It brings together experts in the field from relevant ministries: Planning and Building, Environment, etc. In the United States, the President's Cabinet is responsible for cross-sectoral co-ordination, in Mexico, the Presidency, in Ireland, the Office of the Taoiseach, in the United Kingdom, the Office of the Deputy Prime Minister, in

Austria, the Federal Chancellery. The participation of finance/ treasury ministries and the link between the outcomes of co-ordination processes and budget allocation procedures is another important aspect (OECD, 2005).

### Enhance inter-ministerial dimension of regional contracts

It is also important to enhance inter-ministerial collaboration on the design and monitoring of regional contracts and regional operational programmes (ROPs) for 2007-13.

- In the case of regional contracts, the minister competent for regional development enters into an agreement with the voivodship's managing authorities; however, there does not seem to be extensive involvement of other ministries. Cross-sectoral co-ordination may be lacking in the implementation of regional contracts.

- In the case of the ROPS it is not clear to what extent ministries (other than the Ministry of Regional Development) have been involved in their preparation. In France, it was decided to involve ministries (Ministry of Industry and the Ministry of Research) as well as representatives of the business sector and universities more closely in the monitoring of the regional operational programmes dealing with innovation and competitiveness.

### 3.3. Enhancing co-ordination between regional and rural development strategies

The co-ordination of regional development policy with rural policy is particularly crucial, given the importance of the latter in Poland, as explained in detail in Chapters 1 and 2. The rising urban/metropolitan-rural gap is one of the most important challenges facing Poland, and supporting the development of rural areas is crucial both for social/cohesion reasons but also to enhance their competitiveness and make better use of their untapped potential. When agriculture is not a common denominator, rural areas become a heterogeneous array of regions where one-size-fits-all policies no longer apply. Appropriate governance mechanisms for rural development are thus needed to ensure the best policy outcomes. Moreover, the migration of the last decade from urban areas to rural ones (close to cities) makes clear the need for interaction between urban policy and planning and rural policy. In this context, rural policy would strongly benefit from being framed not as an extension of agricultural policy but as a dimension of regional policy, together with a (yet to be elaborated) urban policy.

The governance framework for rural development in Poland is closely linked to the separate EC policies on cohesion and agriculture (and the related financial instruments – ERDF and EAFRD). The Polish Ministry of Agriculture is in charge of the design and implementation of the rural development strategy. Experience in OECD countries indicates that a body chaired by a single sector (in the rural area, agriculture) may have difficulty pursuing multi-sectoral objectives and may hinder full involvement by other ministries in a national rural strategy. So far, co-ordination with the Ministry of Regional Development seems to have remained largely institutional, rather than an attempt to reach common objectives. Logically, the two ministries hold different views, as the Ministry of Agriculture still has a predominantly agricultural focus even if progress has been made in incorporating broader objectives, whereas the Ministry of Regional Development sees rural development in a broader perspective. In fact, both ministries have responsibilities for framing rural development strategie(s) for Poland. Under the 2004-06 framework, rural issues were part of the cohesion policy; and in the new financial period 2007-13, rural development is included in some of the regional operational programmes. In addition, the policy approach is different, as the Ministry of Agriculture has developed a single operational programme for rural development with very little place-based dimension, whereas 16 regional operational programmes have been developed under the cohesion policy. This results in a complex policy framework for regions, and a kind of duality in policy implementation: regions manage part of the funds for rural development within their ROPs (managed by the Ministry of Regional Development), but the funds for agricultural and rural development are managed by regional agencies (ARMiR) and not by voivodships, and their focus is different from the regional priorities. Duality may lead to both overlaps and contradictions across policy objectives.

There is a need to enhance the territorial/place-based dimension of the rural development strategy and its co-ordination with the regional development strategy, at both central and local levels. So far, there is no inter-ministerial structure for rural development, despite its importance for the future of Poland. A number of OECD countries have developed a new integrated governance approach to rural policy that might serve as inspiration for Poland. The Finnish Rural Policy Committee has been a key actor and force for change in Finland (Box 3.11). In Canada, the "rural lens" approach aims to ensure that rural priorities are taken into account in the various sectoral policies of the federal government (Box 3.12). Many other OECD countries have developed new governance approaches to rural development at central/federal levels. The micro-region policy developed in Mexico (mentioned in Chapter 2) is another possibility. It is important for central ministries to establish criteria and shared strategies in order to synchronise the decentralisation of programmes and resources to local governments with a view to the complementarities that can be generated at the local level.

Box 3.11. **Governance of rural policy in Finland**

The Finnish situation show the need to look not only at the position that rural policy occupies within the government but also at the legitimacy that rural policy has earned among the different actors involved in rural affairs, including politicians, government officials at all levels, academia, and the rural population and its organised civil society. The place that rural policy has earned in Finland is largely due to the Rural Policy Committee (RPC), established as the Rural Advisory Committee in 1992, but not recognised by law until 2000. This 29-member committee representing nine ministries and 18 other organisations has not merely been a device for policy integration and bringing together diverse actors but has also been a prominent actor and a force for change. The place that rural policy occupies within the government, however, is still (as in many countries) secondary. Originally, rural policy was framed within regional policy to highlight its cross-sectoral dimension and mark a clear distinction with agricultural policy, and the institutional advances of broad rural policy have been leveraged by regional policy. However, EU rural policy influenced the decision to place the Rural Policy Committee and the Rural Development Programmes under the Ministry of Agriculture and Forestry. As in other countries, this has created competing agricultural and rural policy priorities and constituencies, as witnessed by the relatively low priority that rural development measures obtained as compared to agri-environmental support in the preparation of the EU Rural Development Programme.

The RPC has among other functions the role of assisting the government in drawing up and implementing the Rural Policy Programme under which different government bodies take specific decisions as part of what is called "Broad Rural Policy". The Rural Policy Programme has been reasonably successful in achieving coherence among sectoral policies oriented to rural areas.

Key strengths of the process are; i) the involvement of civil society and academia as providers of local and technical knowledge, thereby reducing the knowledge gap that many central governments suffer for targeting the priorities of rural policy; ii) the ownership of the programme by the different government and non-government actors, resulting from a long process of multi-arena negotiation and aligning the actions of all key stakeholders; and iii) the clarity in allocating roles and responsibilities within the government and the biannual monitoring and evaluation of proposals/decisions.

*Source:* OECD, 2007j.

Box 3.12. **Integrated governance approaches to rural development in OECD countries**

Canada's "rural lens" aims to ensure that rural priorities are taken into consideration in the development of government policy and that there is policy coherence over rural objectives across ministries. The Community Futures Programme promotes bottom-up economic development in rural areas.

Finland's multi-year Rural Policy Programme also seeks to draw attention to the specific needs of rural areas. "Broad" policies proactively integrate these needs into central government decision making in different sectors. "Narrow" policies specifically target rural areas.

Germany developed the "REGIONEN AKTIV" programme to address inadequacies in existing agricultural and other sectoral policy approaches. A number of small model areas (*Regionen*) were selected and local partnerships established to improve the focus of public policy for the region.

In the United Kingdom, DEFRA (Department for Environment, Food, and Rural Affairs) was created in June 2001 to broaden the focus of rural policy and to eliminate policy "silos" by gathering under one department several rural functions. The Rural Strategy, published in 2004, reinforced the change to a more broadly based and locally focused rural policy. Several recent initiatives, including Rural Pathfinders and Local Strategic Partnerships (LSPs), are piloting some of these changes.

The Mexican micro-regions strategy adopts an overall approach to rural development by co-ordinating policy initiatives for 263 rural micro-regions characterised by a high level of marginalisation. Every micro-region contains a Strategic Community Centre around which actions are focused based on priorities established through a highly participatory process including all sectors of the local communities.

The Netherlands' "Agenda for a Vital Countryside" published in 2004, introduced important changes in the Dutch approach to rural development. While this document details the national policy targets and budgets for the countryside, regional and local authorities translate these policies into action and integrate them into local and regional development plans.

*Source:* OECD, 2006h.

## 3.4. *Enhancing the territorial dimension of regional development policy*

Poland has made progress in enhancing the multi-sectoral dimension of the regional development strategy (which relies on various pillars such as human capital, innovation and infrastructure, see Section 2.1). However, progress has yet to be made to enhance the territorial dimension of the strategy. Apart from the programme on the development of eastern Poland (3% of total funding); central programmes lack a strong territorial orientation. No distinction is made, for example, among the needs of metropolitan areas, medium-sized cities, mountainous areas, coastal areas, and so on. The fact that 25% of the funding has been decentralised may help to tailor the policy mix to each region's needs, but this is not in itself a guarantee, as it depends on various regional capacities to implement appropriate place-based policies. In any case, the regional policy mix should be complemented by place-based approaches at the central level, with appropriate incentives for local actors. There is a need to further enhance the place-based dimension of the different pillars of the regional development strategy, to link urban and rural considerations and provide a "call to action" for actors at other levels of government. It also implies involving more local actors in the design of national strategies, as so far their involvement seems to have been limited, even in the specific territorial programme on the development of eastern Poland.

To gain more visibility in the central institutional structure and promote regional policy as a key structural policy, essential for the competitiveness and cohesion of the country, the Ministry of Regional Development should promote differentiated place-based approaches in its national strategy. The various needs and objectives among places could be distinguished, along with incentives for local actors to reveal their knowledge. In Sweden, for example, a typology of regions has been set up to help the central government apply different types of regional policies according to the type of region. Some regions still enjoy traditional support from the central government with respect to equity in terms of access to essential public services, while other regions benefit from specific support addressing competitiveness targets. In Japan, differentiation is based more on infrastructure policies and goals to mitigate income disparities: rural areas benefit from central government investment, while metropolitan areas, which are not subject to the same market failures, are able to use private investment to finance their infrastructure. In France, the DIACT has adopted different policy approaches for metropolitan areas (metropolitan contracts), urban areas (urban and agglomeration contracts); rural areas ('pays' and rural poles of excellence), but also coastal and mountainous areas.

The Ministry of Regional Development should increasingly focus on its strategic functions and play the role of negotiator and facilitator with local actors, providing incentives for regions/places to develop proactive regional development strategies. The relationship with local actors should increasingly be a partnership. Poland has already moved in this direction through discussions across levels of government on the elaboration of regional operational programmes (see Section 3.4); but more needs to be done to enhance the ministry's strategic role. For example, it could provide more guidance on the development of regional innovation strategies. It is important to increasingly target a bottom-up approach, in which local actors can influence national policies for regional development. The MRD should move in the direction of incentives and calls for tender for place-based development approaches, and the process should not be entirely delegated to sectoral agencies. In addition to specific incentives to support territorial projects (agglomeration projects, rural projects, see Section 3.2.); the ministry could play a leading role in launching competitive selection processes to foster cluster development or innovative projects. As explained in Chapter 2, most programmes targeting clusters with an innovation focus in OECD countries use a competitive selection process, initiated by the central government. The advantage of competition and calls for tenders is that these allow information to emerge from the bottom up. The intervention of the central government to help reveal local assets would help regions/places to better understand that it is a win-win game; that the process is flexible enough for each region to make its own choice. At the same time it allows the national level to be better informed about local initiatives and make decisions on initiatives that can also be developed elsewhere (Box 3.13).

---

### Box 3.13. **Targets and incentives in regional innovation programmes in OECD countries**

While a competitive selection process can contribute to the importance of a "label", the number of projects selected must be limited. Programmes seeking to support leading regions or industries often impose a stricter selection process and fund fewer projects. The Norwegian Centres of Expertise specifically seeks to limit the number of selected clusters so that the label effect will be important enough to attract international attention. The Swedish VINNVÄXT programme in its first round selected only 3 full recipients and 7 partial recipients out of 150 initial applicants and selected 5 out of 23 in the second round. While France chose a very large number of poles, they developed a four-tier labelling system to distinguish between them: 6 were "international", 9 were "internationally oriented", 15 were "inter-regional" and 37 were "regional".

The capability and credibility of the bodies that make selections play a role in public perception and hence in the effectiveness of the label. The involvement of private actors appears to be an important source of credibility. The Georgia Research Alliance in the United States, for example, serves as an expert body for selecting the most relevant research projects to support the state's growth. While state legislators allocate the funding to the Georgia Research Alliance, its Board members are representatives from universities (many are private entities) and industry. Most countries have selection committees comprised of both public and private actors. In cases where the selection process is performed entirely by civil servants, the process is more subject to debate. In France, for example, the lack of private-sector involvement in the selection committee has been noted by the policy's critics. However, France does have a committee to ensure the integrity of the pole label. In Sweden, the fact that the programme designation was national, and not simply regional, was considered in evaluations to play an important role in cluster legitimacy.

---

---

Box 3.13. **Targets and incentives in regional innovation programmes in OECD countries** *(cont.)*

One additional benefit of competitive selection procedures is that sometimes, even for candidates that are not selected, the process results in network building and action plans. Sweden's VINNVÄXT programme accepted only a small fraction of the applications received. When Sweden's subsequent Visanu programme was introduced, many groups that had already worked together on a VINNVÄXT application applied to Visanu and were selected. Some networks have also worked together to reapply for subsequent VINNVÄXT funding rounds. In Germany as well, unsuccessful applicants to the BioRegio and InnoRegio programmes have gone on to develop their projects on the basis of other funding mechanisms. The momentum generated by the BioRegio competition led to the expansion of support to biotechnology via the BioProfile programme to a larger number of regions, many of which had been unsuccessful applicants for BioRegio.

*Source:* OECD (2008b).

---

The Ministry of Regional Development may have to engage in experimentation, undertake pilot projects, and try different institutional tools for various regions. In Poland, some industrial regions with developed social capital (such as Silesian regions) do not necessarily need the same institutional tools as rural regions, with their less developed public-private co-operation. Governance is not a science but a continuous learning process, and different answers are needed in different types of regions and institutional settings (OECD, 2005). The ministry should increasingly play the role of initiator and launch pilot projects in different places. For example, Finland has tested greater autonomy at the regional level and reinforcement of inter-municipal co-operation in certain areas. These various institutional experiments are tools for progress in governance (OECD, 2005).

## 4. Building stronger capacities at sub-national government level

Efforts to tailor central government policies to different local needs cannot be separated from related initiatives at the sub-national level. Building stronger capacities at the sub-national level is particularly important in the Polish context, both in the short term and in the long term:

- *In the short term*, the kick-off of the EU 2007-13 programming period has opened the way to an unprecedented budget and an exceptional variety of programmes devoted to regional development that must be managed over the next few years (16.5 billion EUR for the Regional Operational Programmes). While much attention has been devoted so far to the sub-national level's capacity to fulfill the immediate requirement to absorb EU funding in a given period of time, the magnitude of the tasks to be carried out during the current programming period calls for a broader impulse to upgrade regional capabilities beyond the simple absorption capacity.

● *In the long term*, the massive injection of EU funds constitutes a decisive but not everlasting factor for governance reforms in Poland. The large scale and scope of Poland's allocation of Structural Funds in 2007-13 do not mean that a comparable amount of external funding will be available permanently. Regions were created relatively recently in 1999, but their first experience in the design and management of EU programmes between 2000 and 2006, combined with the overall process of institutional modernization currently underway in Poland, already suggests valuable paths for durable improvement of policy-making practices. Present efforts to enhance regional capacities are therefore likely to influence an important part of Poland's future development, and the 2007-13 momentum needs to be fully exploited in view of an in-depth transformation.

### 4.1. *Programming and managing capacities of regions*

Regional capacities will mainly be tested via the forthcoming implementation of Regional Operational Programmes (ROPs) in the 2007-13 period. Compared with the previous 2004-06 period, the elaboration of ROPs already represented a major turning point in building regional capacities. While regions had little say in the elaboration of the Integrated Regional Operational Programme[28] (one single programme covering all regions) and focused on the management of funds,[29] they played a proactive role in the preparation of the ROPs. First, the ROPs were largely based on the preexisting "regional development strategies", *i.e.* broad-ranging documents in which each region set its own long-term vision for development up to a 2015 or 2020 time horizon. Second, although the Ministry of regional development issued strategic guidelines for the ROPs *(e.g.,* no more than 40% of total funding should be allocated to transport infrastructure projects), regions were given extensive flexibility and autonomy to prepare their ROPs.

The ROPs resulting from this new distribution of labour across levels of government suggest that further progress could be achieved to enhance the effectiveness of regional policy. Most regions have carefully followed the central government's guidelines and their ROPs are obviously keen on targeting Lisbon-related objectives (competitiveness and employment creation). Overall, 24% of total ROP funding was allocated to innovation and entrepreneurship projects; which means just a little less than the 25% allocated to transport infrastructure projects (see Annex 3.A5). Some regions – such as Dolnoslaskie (Box 3.14), Wielkopolskie, and Malopolskie – have developed promising ROPs focusing on metropolitan development, transport connections, innovation and SME networks, and social infrastructure. Yet it seems that most ROPs could have been better differentiated according to specific regional needs, based on a deeper analysis of regional comparative advantages. For example, it is unclear to what extent the strong financial support currently devoted by the Eastern regions' ROPs

Box 3.14. **ROP of Dolnoslaskie**

The ROP of Dolnoslaskie was negotiated with the Ministry of regional development in early 2007, then negotiated with the European Commission starting from June 2007, and validated in August 2007. It represents of total of about 1.2 billion EUR and a first audit is scheduled to be completed by the end of April 2008. The ROP focuses on the following ten priorities:

1. Development of local enterprises (25.54%).
2. Development of information society (8%).
3. Development of transports (18%).
4. Dimprovement of natural environment (anti-flood protection) (10%).
5. Development of energy infrastructure (3%).
6. Tourism and cultural potential (8.94%).
7. Education infrastructure (8.16%).
8. Health infrastructure (4.35%)
9. Degraded urban areas (8%) – this priority was included in the ROP as a result from public consultation.
10. Technical assistance.

The ROP was elaborated after an extensive one-year consultation process, which involved gminas and powiats as well as private stakeholders through the regional steering committee and sub-regional working groups. In the implementation phase, *gminas* and *powiats* account for 30% of the monitoring committee (whose main task is to approve the criteria to select projects and to supervise the implementation of the selected projects).

to innovation transfers can be expected to foster development in these regions where networks of SMEs are quite weak, and the scientific and technical base is insufficient. In some places basic education needs could be more targeted.

Both the general concentration of the ROPs on Lisbon-related objectives and their uneven relevance in light of different regional realities reflect the level and variety of institutional capacities across Polish regions. While regional public officials tend to share an overall lack of experience due to the short history of decentralisation in Poland, some regions (such as Slaskie) have traditionally enjoyed a relatively higher degree of institutional autonomy, whereas other regions (especially those in the East) have long remained locked in a passive attitude *vis-à-vis* the central government. Given that institutional capacities resulting from historical legacies cannot be changed easily at this stage, there are at least two ways to ensure that the implementation of regional policy is more closely tailored to regional needs in the future: by reinforcing public-private collaboration, and by strengthening local public employment itself.

## 4.2. Enhancing public-private collaboration

A key factor to increase the effectiveness of regional policy lies in improving collaboration between policymakers and the private sector. Lessons from EU countries show that EU funds are most effective when they are implemented in a bottom-up approach with active involvement of local and private actors (see comparative research in *The Economist*, 2006). In the case of Poland, it seems that the lack of collaboration between public and private actors has been an obstacle to the absorption of EU funding. Although absorption can fluctuate rapidly over time[30] and does not reflect the long-term impact of projects on regional competitiveness, it offers an informative indicator on implementation of EU projects. Absorption rates (defined as the share of payments to final beneficiaries) vary significantly across Polish regions (ranging from 40% in Warminsko-Mazurskie to 60% in Malopolskie) (Figure 3.7). Due to the high complexity of administrative procedures (see Section 3.5), there are clear advantages for firms and municipalities to collaborate on a smaller number of large joint projects rather than present a higher number of small individual projects. Yet, the surprisingly lower absorption rates in large urban areas (such as Mazowiekie,[31] Dolnoslakie, Slaskie) suggest that co-operation between actors has been difficult to achieve, especially in infrastructure, human capital and entrepreneurship projects for which administrative procedures are already more complicated than for rural development projects for example.

Figure 3.6. **Payments made as percentage of the 2004-06 IROP allocation**
Total: 4.1 billion EUR

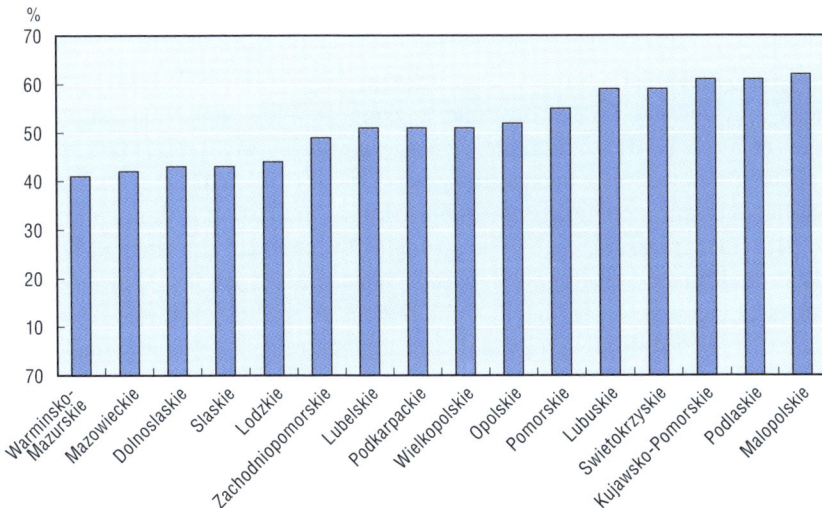

*Source:* Ministry of Regional Development, 2007.

Going beyond the need to increase absorption rates, the mismatch between utterly competitiveness-oriented ROPs and existing regional assets in practice is often due to the lack of information sharing between the local public officials in charge of drafting the programmes, the firms driving the local economy, the universities generating local human capital, and the civil society as well as all stakeholders who contribute to shaping the local social environment. In this respect, Poland needs to overcome several specific obstacles to public-private collaboration:

First, it is not easy to change a long-established tradition of mutual mistrust between public administration and the private sector. On the one hand, Polish public administration has long cultivated a climate of suspicion vis-à-vis the private sector and thereby reinforced a risk-adverse attitude. In Poland as in many post-socialist countries, any kind of co-operation with the business sector is easily interpreted by citizens as corruption or clientelism (Swianiewicz 2001). On the other hand, the business sector and NGOs have shown little interest in being more closely involved in local development policies, which indicates a lack of trust in collective local government actions.[32] Weak public-private co-operation in Poland is partly explained by the dominance of individual entrepreneurship, strong patterns of individualisation, and refusal of collective obligations. Although the collapse of the communist regime in 1989 was largely driven by the civil society (especially unions such as Solidarnosc),[33] social stakeholders were paradoxically unable to play a strong role in the institutional system's transformation since then. This has resulted in an unexpected fragmentation of the private sector (e.g., weak chambers of commerce, weak unions) and the absence of a powerful intermediary able to speak a single voice on behalf of the private sector and to take the leadership in public-private dialogue.

Second, earlier attempts to improve public-private collaboration have not been conclusive so far. For example, Regional Development Agencies (RDAs)[34] were created in order to promote economic growth by facilitating public-private collaboration; yet it has been a tricky assignment to make them strong enough to effectively promote horizontal and vertical co-ordination without falling prey to particular interests, but not so strong as to "capture" the issue of regional policy and thereby disempower voivodships or municipalities. Their influence varies in fact across regions, in some regions they play a key role to support regional economic development and attractiveness (in Dolnoslaskie for example), while in others they play a much less proactive role for development. Evaluations on the use of funds in 2007-06 also indicate that there were deficiencies in the co-operation among public and private actors under the IROP management system (Grosse, 2007). Regional Steering Committees[35] were established to associate non-public actors to the selection of projects under the IROP, but their impact on the outcome of the debates and the final choice of projects seems to have remained marginal (Dabrowski, 2007).[36] In 2006, a broad assessment (conducted by the Silesian economic agency) on the selection of regional development projects in the 16 Polish regions led to the following three main conclusions: i) criteria to select projects are often unclear; ii) experts involved in the selection process are sometimes not qualified enough; and iii) civil society representatives are not invited to participate in the different steps of the selection process.

Building mutual trust between public and private actors in Poland is crucial for the absorption of 2007-13 EU funds, but also in a much broader perspective for regional development. Bringing civil society and private sector closer to policymaking yields both democratic and economic advantages by reducing information asymmetries in increasingly complex and inter-dependent policy areas such as regional development. This is the reason why the European Commission has promoted partnerships with private actors and civil society since the early stages of EU cohesion policy, and even enhanced this focus in the 2007-13 framework. The current reinforcement of regional powers and especially of the marshal's responsibilities[37] offers an opportunity to bolster public-private collaboration. Two ways could be highlighted: increasing public-private collaboration in planning processes, and enhancing public-private partnerships.

*Public-private collaboration in planning processes* remains very formal and legalistic in Poland. Even though some municipalities organise public consultations and discussions, public participation is very often recognised as a simple optional procedure. The case of Warsaw is particularly interesting as both the Warsaw city authorities and existing NGOs are reluctant to co-operate. Several OECD countries tried to involve private actors more closely in planning processes (Box 3.15). Poland could draw inspiration from such experiences and combine it with promising efforts in some of its own regions, which used the new EU community initiative JESSICA to associate public and private actors in sustainable urban development measures for example.[38]

*Public-private partnerships (PPPs)* are not common in Poland, for different reasons: i) Poland introduced legislation on PPPs in 2005[39] but the legislative framework resulted in complex procedures, which are not appealing for private actors; ii) there is little knowledge about PPPs, especially in the public sector, and little attention is given to their potential benefits; iii) there is a lack of PPP co-ordination at the central government level. Very few PPP projects were developed so far *(e.g.,* A1 Motorway Gdańsk-Nowe Marzy (90 km), A2 Motorway Konin–Nowy Tomyśl (103 km), water management system in Gdansk). The government attempted to simplify the PPP procedure at the end of 2006 and adopted a project of a new act on PPP in July 2007, but political tensions interrupted the Parliament's work on this issue. The implementation of hybrid PPPs (*i.e.,* using EU funds) is currently under discussion with regard

Box 3.15. **Examples of public participation in planning processes in OECD countries**

Public participation varies from one country to another but it is usually recognised for bringing legitimacy to the final plan.

The **US** has a long tradition of civic leadership on spatial planning. In some areas including the Silicon Valley, civic coalitions have successfully promoted the adoption of urban growth boundaries. In other areas, different groups have adopted or prepared comprehensive regional plans.

In **Denmark**, the planning process starts with a public consultation, which then leads to a proposal to be re-discussed in public fora. However, citizens have progressively lost interest in this process. Officials in charge of the production of the plan are mainly civil engineers, architects or chartered surveyors who tend to focus more on land use tradition rather than on development and growth perspectives. Proposals remain bureaucratic and need to be simplified.

In **Japan**, advisory boards (Shinji-Kai) play a key role. They are composed of representatives from various institutions (chambers of commerce, resident associations, NGOs, academics, officials from upper levels of government). Since most of these stakeholders are appointed by the mayor, the composition of advisory boards may vary. However, given the relatively centralised nature of government in Japan and the dominant culture of consensus, debates do not have much impact on the society and controversial issues are mostly dealt with by the different levels of government involved in the planning.

In **France**, an important innovation of the 1999 National Planning and Sustainable Development Act was the mandatory creation of 'development councils' "conseils de développement". These councils are consultative bodies, bringing together major social and economic actors within a "communauté urbaine' or a communauté d'agglomération". Their main activities consist in approving the 'agglomeration project' and following up on the "agglomeration agreement" They were introduced as a tool to promote the involvement of civil society (economic actors, unions, non-profit assocations) in policy making and the elaboration of strategies at the area-wide level.

Based on the principle of participatory planning, Territorial Pacts in **Italy** bring together public and private actors to undertake ventures to promote local development at the sub-regional level. Territorial Pacts involve a large number of sectors, including industry, agriculture, services and tourism. Partners include local authorities and local development actors, although regions, provinces and financial institutions can be signatories. Territorial Pacts have fostered a learning process among stakeholders concerning common problems across all areas, and improved mutual understanding and dialogue between employers and trade unions, as well as communication with civil society.

*Source:* OECD, 2007b.

to the priorities of Operational Programmes co-financed with the Structural Funds and the Cohesion Fund.[40]

Poland has a particular need to enhance the use of PPPs. Not only can PPPs enhance the effectiveness of spending and achieve economies of scale that are important for regional development (Box 3.16), but they could also help fasten the implementation of the OP Infrastructure. Moreover, PPPs will help pool the additional resources that Polish public authorities will need in order to pursue infrastructure investment despite growing maintenance costs. Finally, PPPs will help finance the significant number of projects that still need to be implemented beyond the 2007-13 EU budgetary period (whose execution phase can be extended up to 2015) (OECD, 2008a). At the same time, PPPs entail a series of potential adverse effects to be taken into account. For example, experience in OECD countries suggests that governments tend to retain the majority of the risks, overprotecting private investors that participate in the projects, which undermines the PPP concept itself. A rigorous cost-benefit

---

**Box 3.16. PPPs and regional development**

The main financial advantage of PPPs is that they split the costs and risks of projects between the public and private sectors, tapping into the expertise and economies of scale available in the private sector that are rarely exploited for public policy. The principal risks of PPPs are linked to asymmetries of information and of commitment between the different parties of the agreements. These considerations have now to take into account more [ldquoe]inclusive' PPPs, to which the various local stakeholders of the development projects, profit and non-profit, may contribute. From the perspective of public policy, some outstanding issues include:

● Local public authorities need guidance and, as far as is practicable, standardised processes for selecting and operating PPPs. This help does not only concern respect of competition regulations but also the steps to be followed to identify the best partner, evaluate the effectiveness of the PPP option, and diffuse information to other local jurisdictions, among other things.

● Local firms should be involved in PPPs devoted to local development. As users of collective services, they have views on their needs in terms of infrastructure, training, etc. As suppliers of services, they will often be more attuned to improving outcomes than other actors that are less directly involved. Without infringing rules of competition, it would be worthwhile to provide them with the support and incentives necessary for them to participate in this way. This is particularly important with respect to SMEs. A similar logic should be applied with respect to citizen groups and other non-profit organisations.

Source: OECD (2005), Building Competitive Regions.

---

comparison of PPPs *versus* traditional procurement needs to be conducted, and PPPs should be subjected to at least the same scrutiny as traditional expenditures in the budget process.

## 4.3. Strengthening local public employment

The effective implementation of regional development policy requires a cadre of professionals and qualified support staff. This holds particularly true as regional development policy demands a strong capacity to manage complex and interdependent policy tools, in view of results that often occur only in the medium to long term. In Poland, challenges lie not only in the size of local public employment to cope with increased needs in terms of EU fund management, but mainly in reinforcing more systematically the capacities of local public officials by building a more standardised civil service system.

Poland has a relatively modest share of public employment. The OECD survey on Comparison of Employment in the Public Domain (CEPD) indicates that 13.3% of the total labour force in Poland is employed in government (OECD 2007n).[41] This is a similar proportion as Portugal, The Netherlands or Spain. This is well below France and Finland, which have more than 20% of their labour force employed in government, and Sweden and Norway, with almost 30% of their labour force employed in government. In Poland, 200 000 people were employed by the sub-national sector in 2005, which represents 55% of total public sector employees. Although total public employment increased significantly since 1999 (due to the creation of new layers of government and to EU accession),[42] the numerous additional tasks linked with EU fund management (*e.g.*, verification of applications for co-financing and payment claims, conclusion of agreements, control of expenditure, accounting, etc.) may require more manpower, in certain regions. Considering the significant wage gap between the public and the private sectors,[43] the current civil service system needs to offer more effective incentives in order to curb the exodus of public officials towards the private sector, to limit the loss of institutional memory and continuity in the public sector, and to attract qualified staff.

For this purpose, recruitment and promotion mechanisms need to be improved within a consistent and transparent civil service system. The lack of a standardized civil service system has generated risks of politicization of civil service, which seemed to be held down prior to EU accession but has returned two years afterwards, especially in the local public sector and at the senior management level (World Bank, 2006). Multiple attempts to rationalise public employment have translated into the successive adoption and abolition of legislation related to civil service, notably trying to introduce competition in the recruitment of senior civil service positions. However, such attempts were interrupted and the recent creation in 2005 of an alternative "*reserve*" of senior executives is unlikely to solve the need for enhanced professionalism and efficiency. The Polish government has recently stated as a key priority the need to introduce new regulations to build a more standardised civil service, at both central and local levels. Working on a less fragmented public employment framework, with clearer recruitment processes, career paths, promotion and mobility prospects, is an essential condition for an improved implementation of regional policy, at all levels of government.

Further improvement in local capacities could come from:

- *focusing training programmes on practical skills* (to facilitate day-to-day work on the planning and operational implementation of development strategies);
- *introducing performance management systems to better monitor individual and team performances.* At this stage, it is not recommended to introduce individual performance-related pay elements, but rather team bonuses or promotion incentives, to avoid risks of conflicts of interest;
- *enhancing staff mobility* (both nationally between central and local governments, and internationally between Poland and other EU countries);
- *exploiting ICTs and e-government tools to raise the efficiency of public service delivery* (the 47% increase in the number of e-public services between 2004 and 2007 is a promising start; plans to create fully integrated electronic platforms should be pursued).

The three priorities set up by the central government for employees in charge of EU funding management are already going in the right direction: i) secure enough positions inside public administration; ii) increase wages for employees working on EU Structural Funds (wage increases started in 2006, and the EU budget for technical assistance rather than national funds will be used to finance them); iii) provide appropriate training for these employees (Box 3.17).

---

## Box 3.17. **Training policy related to the management of EU funding**

Under the 2004-2006 Community Support Framework, the integrated strategy for promotion and training activities aimed at developing and co-ordinating training activities related to the management of EU Structural Funds. The training process was composed of two main axes: i) training for central and regional administration involved in the process of management, implementation, monitoring and evaluation of Structural Funds; ii) training for beneficiaries of particular operational programmes.

Training activities for the administration involved in the process of funds implementation were carried out mainly through twinning agreements, but also technical assistance components in Operational Programmes, and the *Technical Assistance* Operational Programme. Management authorities are in charge of preparing, implementing and monitoring the different training plans.

---

Box 3.17. **Training policy related to the management of EU funding** (*cont.*)

Using the opportunity to collaborate with experts from Germany, France and the United Kingdom under twinning agreements, the Community Support Framework managing authority carried out a training series covering issues such as project assessment and preparation, cost eligibility, information and promotion, and public aid. By the end of 2004, approximately two thousand employees had been trained. At the same time, employees were offered a further possibility to follow up with foreign experts. In November 2004, a series of training sessions (both general and specialist) was validated for employees of the CSF managing authority, *Technical Assistance* OP managing authority, monitoring and control unit, and other institutions listed in the *Technical Assistance* OP.

## 5. Enhancing efficiency and monitoring performance for regional development

Poland faces the twofold challenge of absorbing large inflows of regional development funding in a relatively short time, optimising the use of the money and improving the monitoring of performance to ensure the most effective accountability. EU funds provide both a major window of opportunity for institutional change (better co-ordination at the central level and across levels of government) and an opportunity to enhance the effectiveness of public spending and public administration. This section addresses the question of accountability as a tool for improving the effectiveness of regional development policy. First, the possibilities for simplifying the administrative and regulatory framework are explored. Second, the opportunities for better monitoring performance and reforming budget procedures are analysed.

### 5.1. Simplifying the administrative and regulatory frameworks

Poland's absorption of EU funds in early 2008 presents a rather positive picture. In May 2008, 85.6% of total structural funds allocated to Poland for the 2004-06 financial period had been absorbed (*i.e.* paid to final beneficiaries). After a slow start in 2004, the absorption rate has improved regularly since 2006, with faster progress in 2007 and 2008. The first phase of absorption was slow, as for example at the end of 2006 the transport programme had only spent 15.8% of the allocated budget. Some programmes – such as the one for rural development – had a more successful start. In mid-2007, Poland had absorbed half of the structural funds allocated for 2004-06, more than the Czech Republic and Hungary, but less than smaller countries such as Estonia, Lithuania and Latvia (Figure 3.8). Although absorption of structural funds made good progress, the situation was more challenging for the absorption of Cohesion Fund, with only 27% absorbed in June 2007. Anyway, significant

Figure 3.7. **Absorption of EU funds by new member states (June 2007)**
**(Percentage of funds used)**

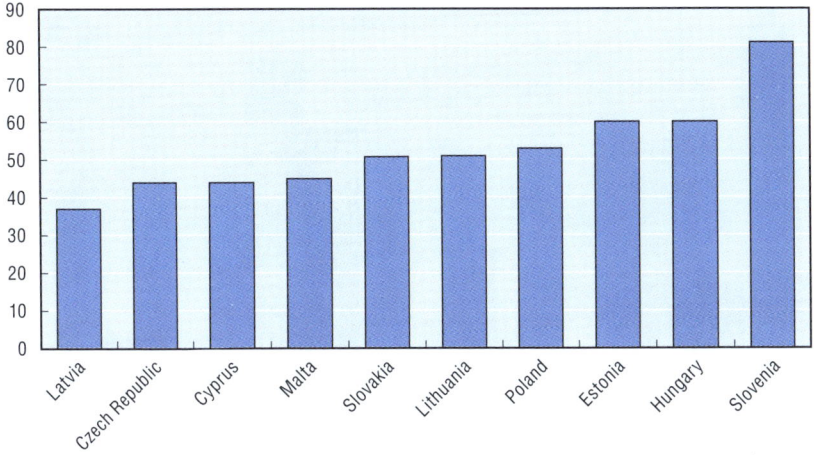

*Source:* Ministry of Regional Development, 2007.

Figure 3.8. **New member states' ERDF absorption 2004-06**
**(% of funds used)**

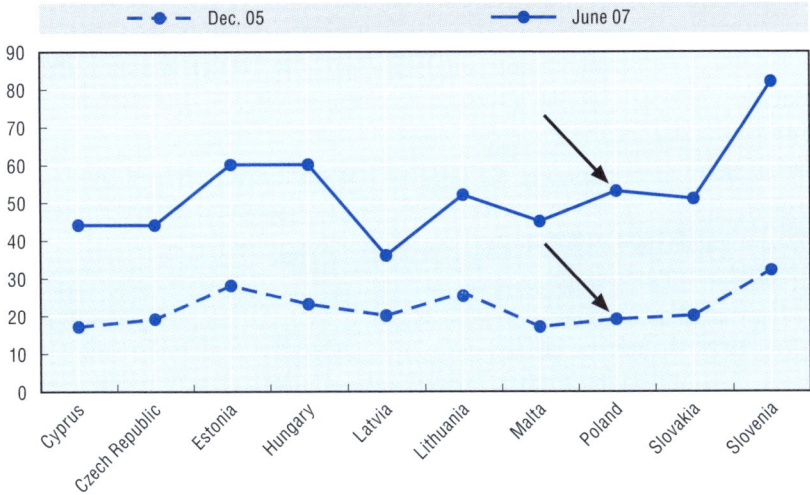

*Source:* "The structural funds' implementation in Poland – Challenges for 2007-13", Presentation to the European Parliament committee on budgeting control, 12 September 2007.

progresses were made in one year for the absorption of the Cohesion Fund, as the proportion of the fund absorbed reached 42.7% in May 2008 (Ministry of Regional Development, 2008).

Figure 3.9. **ERDF and Cohesion Fund absorption (% of funds used)**

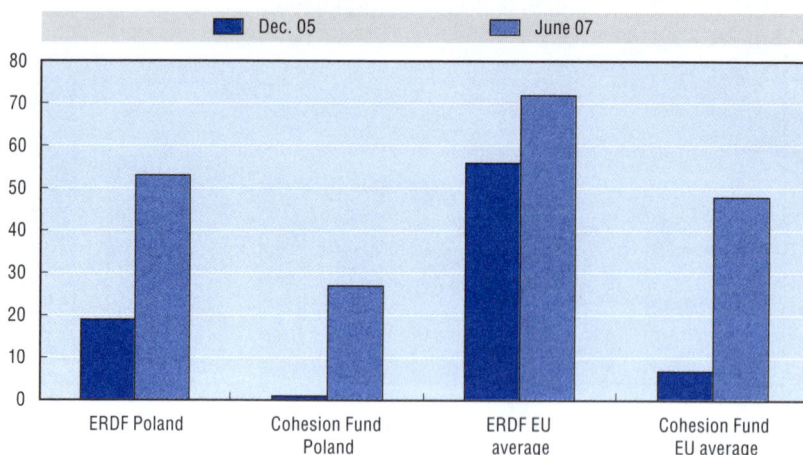

Source: "The structural funds' implementation in Poland – Challenges for 2007-13", Presentation to the European Parliament committee on budgeting control, 12 September 2007.

Although Poland has made significant progress for the absorption of EU funds, some major challenges remain, considering the size of the allocation for 2007-13 (much higher than for 2004-06) and the short delays for absorption. There are three main types of obstacles to using funds effectively: the availability of co-financing, the supply of eligible projects and administrative capacity.[44] A fourth type is linked to services, workforce, capacity and skills shortages in key sectors (construction):

- **Availability of co-financing.** So far, this has not proven to be a problem in Poland. However, some experts have warned that rural *gminas* in eastern Poland may face difficulties for co-financing after 2010, owing to their limited fiscal autonomy.

- **Supply of eligible projects.** Poland is doing well in terms of preparing the programmes that the EU agrees to finance, with a high and rising rate of project submissions from local governments and private companies. In Poland, applications from municipalities for local infrastructure projects have been extremely numerous, and only 40% of eligible projects were able to receive financing. The number of applications was twice the number of signed contracts in 2004-06, and is likely to increase in 2007-13.

- **Administrative capacity.** Implementation of projects and payment to final beneficiaries are much slower, even if improvements were noticeable through 2006. Following the creation of the Ministry of Regional Development, the pace of absorption increased; 9% of the global envelope for 2004-06 had been paid at the end of February 2006. The main implementation problems are linked to insufficient capacities at the local level to manage large number of projects (insufficient staff, inappropriate training) and complex bureaucratic procedures and inflexibility in the use of funds which have slowed the process. In addition, the rules relating to the funds vary, and some are more rigid than others. For example, as the European Social Fund is more complex to manage, and there absorption of funds under this scheme is low.

- **Skills shortages in key industries and restricted availability of supporting services.** Limited services capacity and skills shortages (planners, architects, engineers, environment experts, legal personnel, accountants) as well as the availability of construction firms also slow the absorption of funds, mainly for infrastructure development.

### Lengthy administrative procedures

Lengthy administrative procedures have constituted major obstacles to the implementation of co-financed EU projects. The main problems appear to be an uncertain and constantly changing legal framework, difficulties for access to finance and slow public procurement. Public procurement procedures are too lengthy and over-regulated, despite improvements in the past few years. The 2004 law on public procurement aims at ensuring EU companies equal access to the Polish public procurement market. It simplified procedures for public procurement for orders below EUR 60 000 (no appeals and claims). An amendment voted in 2006 further simplified procedures by increasing from EUR 6 000 to EUR 14 000 the threshold above which the act applies. Public procurement legislation should be further reformed, notably to limit the abuse of appeal procedures and to simplify the delivery of building permits and environmental impact assessments (OECD, 2008a).

Reducing the administrative burden relating to public-private collaboration in Poland is a priority, as little deregulation has taken place since EU accession. Administrative barriers remain high in comparison to other countries of Central and Eastern Europe. Similarly, it takes much longer than elsewhere in the region to obtain licences, register property or enforce a contract (Economic Forum CEEC, 2007). According to the World Bank's 2006 *Doing Business* report, the minimum capital requirement for starting a business in Poland is almost four times higher (relative to per capita income) than in the rest of the region. The quality of regulation at local level can also be improved. In addition to reducing regulatory burdens, in particular for small businesses, strengthening accountability and transparency mechanisms will reduce the risks of corruption.

Bureaucratic procedures have considerably lengthened the process of absorbing EU funds. To apply for funding implies submitting an exorbitant number of attachments. For instance, an NGO applying for funding for a training programme must submit about ten attachments and if the project is conceived in a partnership, all partners must submit the same number of attachments (Dabrowksi, 2007). Therefore, preparing documentation for an application is a real challenge, especially for small SMEs and NGOs. In addition, the process is frequently blocked as a result of a rule according to which an objection can result in a trial which can take several months (Dabrowski, 2007).

Finally, the system of management and control of the structural funds has contributed to delays in the delivery of funds. Although Poland meets the requirements set by the European Commission, the system was criticised in 2004-06 for its complexity: the procedures for management and financial control adopted for operational programmes were heavy and introduced duties that were not required by Community law (NKU, 2006). This, in practice, resulted in delays in the use of structural funds by the final beneficiaries.[45]

### State aid

Lengthy decision-making processes for the preparation of the state aid plan, which determines the amount of regional aid, have also been criticised. As mentioned in Chapter 2, Poland, the largest of the new member states, also spends the most on state aid as defined by EC competition policy, although it is decreasing.[46] State aid is one of the most complicated components of Polish public expenditure. The intensity of state aid varies across regions from 40 to 50% (for the Mazowieckie region, the maximum will be reduced to 30% after 1 January 2011). However, both for the first financial period (2004-06) and for the current one (2007-13) there have been delays in the preparation of state aids plans. For 2004-06, activities that contain elements of state aid were identified relatively late. The need to prepare aid programmes[47] to regulate the granting of state aid, their notification to the European Commission, and finally lengthy procedures of acceptance of aid programmes by the European Commission, all delayed the initiation of activities, and therefore the implementation of projects involving state aid. For 2007-13, the state aids plan is not yet available. As a consequence, it is impossible for firms and private investors to plan investments, and call for tenders are delayed. This results in lengthy delays in investments, with strong repercussions on the local economy. Some local authorities have mentioned this problem as the main obstacle to the implementation of co-financed EU projects. Another important problem is linked to the administrative crowding that will occur when the state aid legal framework is ready and tenders are launched.

### 5.2. Enhancing accountability for results and performance

Removing administrative obstacles is important, but needs to be accompanied by trust building, a key element in public-private co-operation. Because of the complex nature of regional policy and the many relationships required to achieve its goals, accountability can be challenging (OECD, 2007e). To enhance accountability, OECD countries have increasingly moved towards systems of *ex ante* and *ex post* monitoring and evaluation of regional policy.

Monitoring the performance/impact of regional policy is a key tool for sharing information across levels of government, for helping local actors to reveal their knowledge, and for building trust. Although many countries have developed increasingly sophisticated performance monitoring systems – for regional policy and other policy areas – it is important to keep in mind that there is no single model of performance monitoring, and that some flexibility is needed in implementation. Expectations from such systems have to be managed, and it is important to remember that "the journey is as important as the destination" (OECD, 2008d).

### From monitoring and control to focus on performance and impact

Poland has made significant progress since 2004 in developing infrastructure for performance monitoring, for both sectoral and regional programmes.[48] The monitoring and evaluation system for regional development policy is based on the elements required and recommended by the European Commission (EC) for monitoring and evaluating structural and cohesion funds. With the overwhelming majority of funds for regional development coming from the European Union, it makes sense for the structure and functioning of the monitoring and evaluation system to provide information that can be used to ensure accountability at the EU level. All evaluations under the NSRF and the operational programmes are conducted by independent external evaluators. The EC's key priority is the ability to measure on an annual basis progress towards targets: it is not to provide sanctions or rewards if targets are not met.

The EC evaluation system for 2007-13 has evolved towards a slightly more flexible system compared to 2000-06. Significant modifications have been introduced for evaluations carried out by member states during programme implementation. A shift from a concept of mid-term evaluation towards more demand-driven (on-going) evaluation – flexible in terms of thematic scope, methodological design and timing – reflects these changes. The aim is to better integrate evaluation results into decision-making. The main purpose of ongoing evaluation is to follow, on a continuous basis, the implementation and delivery of a programme and changes in the external environment, in order to better understand and analyse outputs and results achieved and progress towards longer-term objectives, as well as to recommend, if necessary, remedial actions. An evaluation carried out when there is a significant departure from the goals initially set may come too late to inform decision making. Therefore, the EC recommends establishing an evaluation plan and evaluating programmes on a regular basis.

As the largest recipient of EU structural and cohesion funds for 2007-13, Poland appears to recognise its obligation to demonstrate performance. It is moving to strengthen its monitoring and evaluation system, and is one of the most advanced EU member states in organising and planning evaluation for 2007-13, *e.g.* in terms of establishing evaluation units and drafting evaluation plans. Technical assistance funds have been used to train regions and beneficiaries of project funds to enhance their understanding and capacity in this area. Poland has also received assistance from the Public Investment Evaluation Unit (UVAL) of Italy's Ministry of Economic Development.

The monitoring and evaluation system for regional development in Poland has two major elements:

- Programme monitoring focuses on attaining strategic and interim objectives specified in the programme (monitoring of delivery) and full absorption of EU allocated funds (financial monitoring). Progress and effectiveness of implementation are measured by means of physical and financial indicators specified in the different programmes. Emphasis is placed on output and results indicators. Monitoring of programmes co-financed by the structural and cohesion funds is performed by the managing authorities and monitoring committees appointed for each programme. The SIMIK IT system (Informational System for Monitoring and Controlling Structural and Cohesion Funds) is supposed to be used to monitor the financial and physical progress of programme implementation.

- Evaluation of regional development co-financed by EU structural and cohesion funds takes place at two levels: the National Strategic Reference Framework (NSRF) for 2007-13 and the operational programmes. Evaluation of the NSRF is the responsibility of the National Evaluation Unit, while the evaluation of the different operational programmes is performed by the evaluation units of the respective managing authorities. In the current programming period (2007-13), as a result of decentralisation of the implementation system for structural funds in Poland, the competencies related to evaluation have been delegated to the regional level[49] (16 managing authorities for the regional operational programmes).

Poland's monitoring and evaluation system has both top-down and bottom-up elements. The national government has taken the lead in selecting indicators and targets for the NSRF and co-ordinating data collection from national and regional operational programmes. The regional level generates data, selects indicators and establishes targets for the ROPs. In some regions, monitoring processes are undertaken in collaboration with managing authorities to enhance the quality and relevance of data and targets. In other regions, programme managers have been less involved.

The introduction of a performance reserve may provide incentives for better performance, but clear criteria are required to define the conditions under which it will be allocated to successful programmes. There are plans to implement a 3% performance reserve in Poland linked to programme evaluations to be carried out in 2011. Best performers would be identified. However, it is not yet entirely clear whether specific evaluations will be carried out, and no *ex ante* criteria for distribution of the reserve have been established, so the conditions of allocation are unclear. Actors need to know in advance the rules of the game, otherwise the incentive dimension of the reserve is likely to be limited. Poland should clarify the criteria for good performance. Experience in the EU with the performance reserve introduced between 2000 and 2006 also indicates that, although it may help increase transparency and comparisons among different projects, it may also add further bureaucratic requirements with the result that the costs may outweigh the benefits (Box 3.18).

---

### Box 3.18. **EU experience: The Community Performance Reserve (2000-06)**

Introduced for the first time in the 2000-06 programming period, the Community Performance Reserve scheme aimed at better programme management and effective expenditure of funds. Performance was gauged according to three sets of criteria reflecting different aspects of the implementation of a programme: effectiveness, good management, and financial implementation.

The mechanism consisted in retaining a proportion (4%) of the total budgetary resources at the disposal of a programme (those both of the Community and the national co-financing) and using this to reward the most successful programmes, assessed on the basis of physical and financial performance indicators reflecting the above criteria.

Four stages characterised the implementation of the scheme: the selection and quantification of performance indicators, annual monitoring, identification of successful programmes, and allocation of the performance reserve.

While assessment was the responsibility of member states working in close co-operation with the Commission, the actual allocation, as of 31 March 2004, was placed under the responsibility of the European Commission, and was carried out with the help of member states.

General assessments of the scheme are difficult, as it was received and managed quite differently across member states. However, it apparently succeeded in acting as an incentive for capacity building in good management practices, albeit in a rather fragmented and uncertain way. It induced regions to ensure that money was spent, that evaluations were carried out (on time), and that monitoring and financial control systems were established. Also, it also helped make the process of project selection increasingly transparent. Another positive achievement was the contribution of the scheme to strengthening the partnership between the Commission and member states (regions were not directly involved). The European Commission welcomed the positive attitude of member states towards the linking of financial allocation to performance (CEC, 2004b).

Positive assessments by some managing authorities (*e.g.* Sachsen Anhalt, United Kingdom) approved the contribution of the scheme to stronger performance through increased transparency and comparisons between different interventions. By contrast, the underlying philosophy of the scheme was discussed in Austria (*Niederosterreich*) where it was considered that promoting competition among programmes did not quite fit Austria's traditional consensus-based approach to policy making.

---

---

Box 3.18. **EU experience: The Community Performance Reserve (2000-06)** *(cont.)*

Regarding practical conditions of implementation of the scheme, some objections were voiced by the regions about the selection of indicators and targets. Regions often encountered difficulty in defining clear and measurable indicators. Financial indicators, in particular, were seen as duplicating the objective of the De-commitment Rule. As to management indicators, they were deemed unsophisticated and too easy to achieve. Finally, effectiveness indicators, although useful in principle, were sometimes too difficult to assess because the process occurred too early in the programming process. Various examples illustrate the importance of securing agreement on selected indicators and targets in advance.

In general, the scheme's lack of flexibility was often criticised. According to some observers, it was an innovative instrument but also created uncertainty. For example, the fact that the scheme resulted in many different versions, with different indicators and targets depending on programmes and priorities, might have challenged the objective of transparency promoted by the European Commission. Complexity might have been the single most important drawback of the scheme, again a factor potentially undermining transparency.

*Source:* CEC (2004) in OECD (2008e).

---

Looking ahead, Poland faces a variety of challenges for establishing and using an effective monitoring and evaluation system.

- *Target-setting* – Like many countries, Poland has had some difficulty in establishing realistic targets for regional policy. Target setting is likely to improve with time, as more and better data become available and as managers and planners gain experience with programming.

- *Lack of capacity* – At the outset of the last programming period (2004-06), little infrastructure existed for monitoring and evaluation of regional development policy. The system that exists today is thus relatively new. Data production, collection, utilisation and evaluation capabilities are still developing at both the national and regional levels.

- *Co-ordination between levels of government* – While monitoring and evaluation responsibilities are assigned at different levels of government, the top-down and bottom-up strategies are not always co-ordinated. NSRF targets, for example, are not necessarily connected to regional targets.

- *Data availability* – Regional offices face challenges for getting data from the national statistics office as some data, such as an economic census, do not exist. This makes tracking the performance of certain investments difficult (*e.g.* tourism as a percentage of the regional economy).

● *Data utilisation* – Data produced for the monitoring of regional policy are used as the basis of discussions, but otherwise seem to have little feedback effect on decision making, and are not included in the budgetary process as informative elements (check with local team).

A major problem in the monitoring system is linked to the difficulties Poland has experienced in launching the IT system SIMIK for the monitoring of funds by the Ministry of Finance. The introduction of SIMIK started in 2002 but the system was not yet functioning in 2005, although EU funds had already been allocated. This resulted in an additional cost for the institutions involved in the implementation of the operational programmes. For example, the Polish Agency for Enterprise Development (PARP) developed a substitute system in order to monitor co-financing applications submitted by beneficiaries, which cost PLN 394 000. Further delays in implementing SIMIK may have an impact on the funds allocated to Poland for 2007-13, because to pay out funds, the European Commission requires a positive evaluation of the operation of the management and control systems of the different operational programmes, to which the IT system contributes.

The cohesion policy has acted as a major incentive for the introduction of evaluation and monitoring systems. While these systems remain concentrated on public policies linked to the EC cohesion policy, they should be gradually expanded to all individual public policies in Poland, not only the spheres financed within the framework of the European cohesion policy.

## 5.3. *Effectiveness of spending and multi-year budgeting*

In addition to monitoring performance linked to EU funds, Poland should increase its focus on outcomes and the quality of services provided by local governments, in particular in health and education. This would enable local governments to develop more cost-effective managerial approaches. In the education sector, for instance, school performances could be better monitored and results could be included as information in the budget process, and achievements in terms of quality could be rewarded. In instances where national standards are deemed important, performance grants could be instituted conditional on reaching certain levels of service or improvements in performance. Among various tools used by OECD countries, indicator systems for measuring and monitoring sub-central service delivery have gained prominence. The choice of the objectives that the indicator system will serve (*e.g.* benchmarking performances, promoting best practices, improving the quality of services, promoting accountability, etc.) determines the type of indicators used (OECD, 2008e).

In addition, the impact of financial transfers from the EU depends not only on a country's capacity to absorb the funds efficiently, but also on how effectively they are spent. EU funds should be subject to the same discipline as other government resources, by clearly defining objectives and prioritising needs (OECD, 2006b). Since there is no multi-year budget in Poland, the use of EU funds has been decided separately from that of government resources in the NSRF with the co-operation of the European Commission. As a result, some expenditure that has been decided may have relatively low priority, given the overall budget constraint (OECD, 2006b). Funds subject to "additionality" should be used to finance high-priority new expenditure. The fact that expenditure is financed by EU funds and that some funds cannot be used to finance existing expenditure should not be a reason to undertake spending that is not of high priority or that has unclear goals (OECD, 2006b).

The Polish authorities need increasingly to move towards a multi-year budgeting framework. There is no multi-year budget in Poland, apart from limited provisions of multi-annual budgeting for EU funds introduced in 2006 (three-year perspective). These multi-year budgeting provisions are not translated at the regional level, so the question of how best to combine the central budgeting system and local governments' budgets remains. Co-ordination of the budget planning process among different levels of government needs to be improved.[50] Not only will multi-year budgeting reduce uncertainty in the planning process, it can help to ensure continuity over the medium and long term, particularly for municipalities with short election cycles. It can also enhance the likelihood that projects whose outcomes will accrue in the future can be adequately monitored and evaluated, thereby enhancing the role of evidence-based planning and investments. Compared to the huge challenges linked to EU funds inflows, the change in the system of public finance in Poland appears to be too slow.

Finally, enhancing the effectiveness of the implementation of regional policy implies improved public-private co-operation, simplification of the administrative and regulatory framework, in particular public procurement and public-private partnerships. The focus should not be concentrated only on the rapid absorption of funds but also to a higher degree on monitoring performance and the impact of regional policy. Poland has made good progress in that direction, as it has developed for 2007-13 a sophisticated infrastructure for performance monitoring. However, its impact will largely depend on the appropriate setting of targets and co-ordination across levels of government, as well as on improved data collection. The impact of performance indicators will also depend on the way they are used in the decision-making process, which so far appears limited. In addition, although the introduction of a performance reserve may appear as a positive element, its impact depends greatly on making criteria for its use transparent. Finally, there is a need to move to multi-annual budgeting for regional policy, as provisions are too limited in the current context, and to better co-ordinate central budget process and local ones.

## Notes

1. In this chapter (and throughout the review), the terms voivodship and region, and municipalities and gminas, are used as synonyms. Unless mentioned explicitely, the term voivodship refers to regional government, and not to the voivod (prefect) office.

2. These include education up to college, social welfare, local public utilities and networks, basic public health care and housing.

3. There are 307 urban gminas (gminy miejskie), 580 urban-rural gminas (gminy miejsko-wiejskie) and 1 591 rural gminas (gminy wiejskie). The autonomy of gminas is established in the Polish constitution.

4. Budgetary entities, appropriated funds, cultural institutions and independent sub-national health-care facilities.

5. 31.8% according to DEXIA if fees and sales are taken into account.

6. Earmarked grants represent 15% of sub-national revenue.

7. The biggest differential with OECD countries in terms of taxes is linked to social security spending, much higher in Poland than in the rest of the OECD.

8. There are eight local taxes on real estate, agriculture, forests, means of transport, dogs, inheritance and gifts, personal income lump-sum and civil law contracts. All income from these local taxes goes to communal budgets. The remaining two sources of taxes, personal income tax and corporate income tax, are state taxes which are shared between the state and all local governments. As of 1 January 2004, the shares going to local government budgets have risen significantly.

9. This, combined with a relatively high minimum wage and generous early-retirement and disability benefit programmes, contributes to low employment rates, in particular among low-skilled workers. The system also relies heavily on consumption taxes, whereas relatively little revenue is collected from such bases as environment externalities, inheritances and, in particular, property (OECD, 2008).

10. In Denmark, Finland or Japan, the size of equalisation is above 3% of the GDP.

11. Municipalities have access to equalisation grants when their tax revenue is lower than 90% of the average (instead of 85% in the previous system); those with revenue higher than 150% of the average must contribute to the financing of the grant. An additional part is paid to municipalities with low population density. Counties and regions have access to the equalisation grant when their tax revenue per capita is lower than the average, and they contribute to the fund when it is higher than 110%. An additional part is paid to counties having an unemployment rate higher than average and to regions having less than 3 million inhabitants (DEXIA, 2007).

12. According to the algorithm, 80% of funds are allocated proportionally to population of the voivodships, 10% to the voivodships with average GDP per capita of less than 80% of Poland's average GDP per capita and 10% to powiats with an average unemployment rate in 1999-2001 higher than 150% of the national average. The same algorithm was used for the regional allocation of EU funding.

13. This is a general trend in the EU. In 2005, 64% of public investments in the EU were conducted by local governments.

14. On the basis of article 3 of the Law of 16th December 2005 on land transport infrastructure financing (JoL No 267, pos. 2251), task concerning financing of construction, modernisation, repair, maintenance, protection and management of roads are financed by: the minister responsible for transport through General Director of National Roads and Motorways as the national roads are concerned, voivodship local government as voivodship roads are concerned, powiat (county) local government as county roads are concerned. Tasks concerning the communal roads are financed by communities. Cities with the rights of counties (urban counties) are responsible for all roads on their territory with the exception of motorways and expressways.

15. Public health services and facilities beyond the municipality territorial boundaries (specialised regional hospitals, organisation of public health transport services and supervision of regional public health funds).

16. Decentralised responsibility for provision of compulsory school education has passed to two levels. Gminas, with a mean population of around 7 300, are responsible for primary and lower secondary (gimnazjum) education, while powiats (mean population about 75 000) look after upper secondary, post-secondary non-tertiary education and public special schools.

17. Warsaw has a special statute since the adoption of the Act on Organisation of the Capital City Warsaw adopted in March 2002. Up until then, the city was organised into 11 municipalities. It is now one city divided into 11 city districts. With this Act, the city also took on the statute of county (Dexia, 2007).

18. Amalgamation reforms were mainly conducted in Korea, Japan, Canada and Denmark; while countries such as France, the Netherlands, Switzerland, Spain and the United States have not adopted policies towards mergers.

19. Financial support for municipal co-operation is also provided in Norway, which promotes co-operation by providing economic support for new approaches to co-operation, by spreading examples of successful strategies through conferences and a database, and through laws and regulations.

20. In the course of its municipal reform, from 1999 to 2002, the provincial government of Quebec was aware of the fact that heavily urbanised areas, rural areas and mixed urban/rural areas each required their own special strategy. The government's preference went to consolidating municipalities in urban and metropolitan areas, strengthening the intermediate regional structure in rural areas, and stepping up inter-municipal co-operation in mixed rural/urban areas. This differentiating strategy takes into account the fact that these three types of municipal environments have different skills and utilise these skills in different ways (OECD, 2006a).

21. The "pays" are as "project territories" which purpose is to transcend administrative boundaries so that territorial strategies can be formulated. The underlying logic of the "pays" is to base territorial action on synergies between willing local players and at the same time to match the boundaries for these unifying projects to functional areas. When co-operation and local dynamics work well, these "pays" can offer a genuine means of unblocking the system's complexities through local action, especially when facilitated by the competences of local actors. They do however appear to suffer from structural difficulties in terms of resources at their disposal.

22. The question is whether one or several medium-sized cities of eastern Poland should be included in the metropolitan policy, even if they fall below the threshold of 500 000 inhabitants. The definition of metropolitan development could

comprise functional criteria, and not only quantitative threshold in terms of population, in order to allow Eastern cities to benefit from new institutional arrangements for metropolitan areas.

23. The minister in charge of regional development is responsible for the co-ordinating the implementation of the cohesion policy. The minister is responsible for the organisation and proper functioning of the management, implementation, monitoring, reporting, control and evaluation of operational programmes (NSRF, p.112).

24. One of the six NDS priorities is: "Regional development and enhancing territorial cohesion", which determines the horizontal dimension of the policy, its goals and main areas of operation as well as selected implementation indicators.

25. Under the Act on the principles of regional development policy making, assessments have been carried out since 2007 on compliance of the sectoral strategies with the National Development Strategy for 2007-15.

26. Their competences often overlap, such as in the case of evaluation of projects applying for funding as part of IROP which is organised in 4 stages taking place in 3 different institutions (Dabrowski, 2007).

27. The main goal of the Committee would be to monitor the co-ordination of the activities implemented under the Cohesion Policy, Common Agricultural Policy, Common Fisheries Policy, the Lisbon Strategy as well as the EEA Financial Mechanism, the Norwegian Financial Mechanism and the Swiss Financial Mechanism and other financial instruments (in the case of undertakings covered by the Cohesion policy), by monitoring the implementation of particular operational programmes.

28. During the 2007-06 2004-2006 period, the Integrated Regional Operational Programme (IROP) represented a total amount (including private funds) of EUR 4.08 billion, among which EUR 2.53 million came from the European Regional Development Fund and EUR 438.5 million from the European Social Fund. Three priorities were planned: i) development and modernisation of infrastructure enhancing regions' competitiveness; ii) enhancement of development of human resources in regions; iii) local development.

29. Under the IROP, management competencies were divided between the Voivod (prefect) (in charge of controlling the spending) and the Marshall (head of the region), which sometimes resulted in a confusing institutional equilibrium, as some of their competences concerning the selection of projects were overlapping (Dabrowski, 2007).

30. Absorption of funds has changed significantly between the beginning of the period and the year 2007. In a region like Dolnoslaskie for example, significant progress was made in the second half of 2006.

31. The relatively low absorption of funds in the capital region Mazowieckie also highlights the problem of achieving co-operation at the metropolitan scale, due to the difficulties to reach agreements among municipalities (see Section 3.2).

32. For example, only 9% of Polish NGOs have applied for EU funding during the 2007-06 2004-2006 period (MRD, 2007). Financial institutions are little involved in local development strategies (in particular for rural development) and micro-credit initiatives remain rare. However, regional variations exist in terms of social capital. For instance, private actors seem to be more involved in regional strategies in Southern regions (Silesia) than in Northern-Eastern ones.

33. The transition was democratically led in Poland, and the Round Table organised between April and June 1989 has become recognised worldwide as a model for peaceful negotiations.

34. Regional Development Agencies (RDAs) aim at supporting the development of small and medium-sized enterprises at the voivodship level. They provide subsidies or loans for business development as well as advisory services, and they organise training courses. An important part of their mandate consists in promoting information sharing. RDAs work in collaboration with central and sub-national government authorities, as well as with national and international institutions of a similar profile of activity. In a number of cases the RDAs also perform the role of regional financing institutions and act as agencies transferring EU funds to entrepreneurs.

35. Regional Steering Committees were composed of representatives from regional and local authorities, social stakeholders, business associations, universities and NGOs (Dabrowski, 2007).

36. Besides, some conflicts of interest were noticed in the selection of members of the Regional Steering Committees, as the Marshall could choose the members based on his own selection criteria (Dabrowski, 2007).

37. In 2006, the Polish central government had proposed to give a much stronger role and notably the veto power to its own representatives in the regions (the voivod), but the European Commission opposed. Now the voivod has no management functions but only regulatory and supervisory functions, while the marshal gained new responsibilities. Regional Steering Committees were abolished and replaced in 2007 with monitoring committees, which are placed under the chairmanship of the marshal and are composed of various stakeholders (including 30% of central government representatives, but also local government representatives and socioeconomic representatives).

38. Joint European Support for Sustainable Investment in City Areas (JESSICA) is an initiative of the European Commission in co-operation with the European Investment Bank and the Council of Europe Development Bank, in order to promote sustainable investment, growth and jobs in Europe's urban areas *http://ec.europa.eu/regional_policy/funds/2007/jjj/jessica_en.htm*). The region of Wielkopolskie (Poznan) is working towards the establishment of a single urban development fund (UDF) under this community initiative, and other regions are also thinking about implementing the JESSICA initiative.

39. Public-private partnerships in Poland are regulated by the law of 28 July 2005 supplemented by three Decrees issued in June 2006. The main fields of a possible application of PPP formula include: road and rail infrastructure, public transport, waste and water management systems, health, education, housing, sports and leisure, revitalization activities.

40. For example, the managing authority recommended the use of hybrid PPPs in the OP Infrastructure and Environment, as well as on the level of ROPs. In July 2007, the Ministry of Transport disclosed a new ambitious plan for the 2007-2015 period, according to which it 443 km out of 1213 km of new motorways are expected to be built via PPPs.

41. "Government" refers to the "General Government" sector in the System of national Accounts. General Government includes core ministries, departments and agencies, non market publicly owned hospitals, public schools, social security organisations etc. It includes units at all levels of governments including regions, provinces and municipalities.

42. The number of civil servants involved in the management of EU funds increased by 41% at the central level and 80% at the local level between 2003 and 2004. It must be noted, however, that the initial number was already quite low (3384 employees in total in 2005).

43. Compared to the rapid rise in wages in the private sector in Poland (12% increase in 2006), average public sector wages have remained at a much lower level and general government expenditure on wages (compensation of employees relative to GDP) has declined, especially in 2003-2005. Despite a few exceptions, wages are even lower at the sub-national level (in 2004, the average monthly gross salary in the sub-national public sector was PLN 2 553, compared with PLN 3 296 in the central government). This may accelerate the loss of qualified employees in rural regions which have little financial capacity.

44. See *The Economist*, 2006.

45. *www.nku.cz/seminars/eurosai-prague-2006/documents/SZPAKOWSKI_Summary_Internal ControlOfTheStructuralFunds.pdf* (Supreme Audit Office, Czech Republic).

46. For Poland, the negotiations on state aid ended with some transitional arrangements, especially as regards fiscal aid schemes to attract foreign investment and measures to restructure the ailing steel industry. Although vertical state aid (especially to coal mining and shipbuilding) has been reduced substantially, state aid remains an important source of attraction for foreign investments. A regional aid map was developed to define the areas of the country where the granting of regional aid is acceptable and the maximum levels of the aid intensity for such areas. The decree of the Council of Ministers of 1 September 2004 on the establishment of a map of regional aid was published in the Journal of Laws No. 200, item 2050.

47. Aid programmes regulating the granting of state aid were prepared for the SOP Human Resources Development, SOP Increased Competitiveness of Enterprises, Integrated Operational Regional Development Programme and SOP Transport.

48. For the regional programme, every beneficiary has been obliged to present a report on the implementation of the operation every six months and after winding up the operation, together with the application for final payment.

49. For more information, see: *http://ec.europa.eu/regional_policy/sources/docoffic/working/ sf2000_en.htm*.

50. Not all countries include sub-national governments under the Medium Term Economic Framework. However a number of OECD countries found that the MTEF on a general government basis improves fiscal planning and control. For example, Austria, where a substantial amount of transfers are provided to sub-national governments, uses the MTEF to improve overall spending control. In Germany where fiscal decentralisation is substantial, the MTEF is used as an instrument to reach agreement on the distribution of deficit targets between the different levels of government (OECD, Managing public expenditures in Poland, 2003) *http:// unpan1.un.org/intradoc/groups/public/documents/UNTC/UNPAN012395.pdf*.

# ANNEX 3.A1

# *Allocation of Functions Among Tiers of Local Governments in Poland*

| | Municipality *(gminas)* | County *(powiats)* | Region *(voivodships)* |
|---|---|---|---|
| Strategic and physical planning | ✓ Plans for local development<br>✓ Local physical master plans<br>✓ Granting building permits | ✓ Plans for county's development<br>✓ Building inspection | ✓ Strategic regional planning (including International economic relations and regional promotion)<br>✓ Regional development<br>✓ Contracts with central government<br>✓ Water supply and sewerage<br>✓ Waste collection and disposal |
| Roads and communal infrastructure | ✓ Street cleaning<br>✓ Street lighting<br>✓ Parks and green areas<br>✓ Conservation<br>✓ Central heating<br>✓ Local roads<br>✓ City public<br>✓ Transportation | ✓ County road network | ✓ regional work network<br>✓ Water management (flood protection) |
| Public order and safety | ✓ City guards<br>✓ Voluntary fire brigades | ✓ Public order and security (police)<br>✓ Civil defence | |
| Education | ✓ Kindergartens and primary schools | ✓ Secondary school education | ✓ Some higher education facilities |
| Health | | ✓ Public health and sanitary services | ✓ Regional hospitals |
| Welfare | ✓ Social services, such as housing benefits, services for elderly, social welfare benefits | ✓ Unemployment measures and fighting,<br>✓ Care for homeless people | |
| Housing | ✓ Construction of social housing<br>✓ Management of municipal housing | | |
| Culture, sport and leisure | ✓ Local libraries,<br>✓ Theatres, cultural<br>✓ Institutions | | ✓ Regional cultural facilities |
| Misc. | ✓ Civil act registration | ✓ Land registry and surveying | ✓ Protection of the environment |

*Source:* Swianiewicz, 2002.

ANNEX 3.A2

# Structure of Sub-national Revenue by Type in 2005

| | Total sub-national government | | Municipalities[1] | | Counties | | Regions | |
|---|---|---|---|---|---|---|---|---|
| | Million EUR | % | Million EUR | % | Million EUR | % | Million EUR | % |
| **Tax revenue** | **9 627.5** | **37.6** | **8 177.9** | **40.1** | **471.2** | **13.8** | **978.5** | **55.7** |
| *Own local tax revenue* | *3 962.8* | *15.5* | *3 962.8* | *19.4* | *–* | *–* | *–* | *–* |
| *Shared tax revenue* | *5 664.,7* | *22.1* | *4 215.0* | *20.7* | *471.2* | *13.8* | *978.5* | *55.7* |
| **Grants** | **11 937.1** | **46.7** | **8 898.5** | **43.6** | **2 422.3** | **70.8** | **616.3** | **35.1** |
| *General grants* | *8 067.6* | *31.5* | *6 066.6* | *29.7* | *1 665.3* | *48.7* | *335.7* | *19.1* |
| *Earmarked grants* | *3 869.5* | *15.1* | *2 831.9* | *13.9* | *757.0* | *22.1* | *280.6* | *16.0* |
| **Other, among which** | **4 016.3** | **15.7** | **3 327.1** | **16.3** | **527.5** | **15.4** | **161.7** | **9.2** |
| *Asset sales* | *1 077.4* | *4.2* | *1 009.2* | *4.9* | *52.3* | *1.5* | *15.9* | *0.9* |
| *Fees* | *520.0* | *2.0* | *520.0* | *2.5* | *n.a.* | *n.a.* | *n.a.* | *n.a.* |

1.  Including towns with county status
Source: Ministry of Finance and *Statistical Yearbook*. Data are not consolidated, in Dexia 2008.

ANNEX 3.A3

# Allocation of EU Funds for Polish Regions 2007-13: Regional Operational Programmes (ROP)

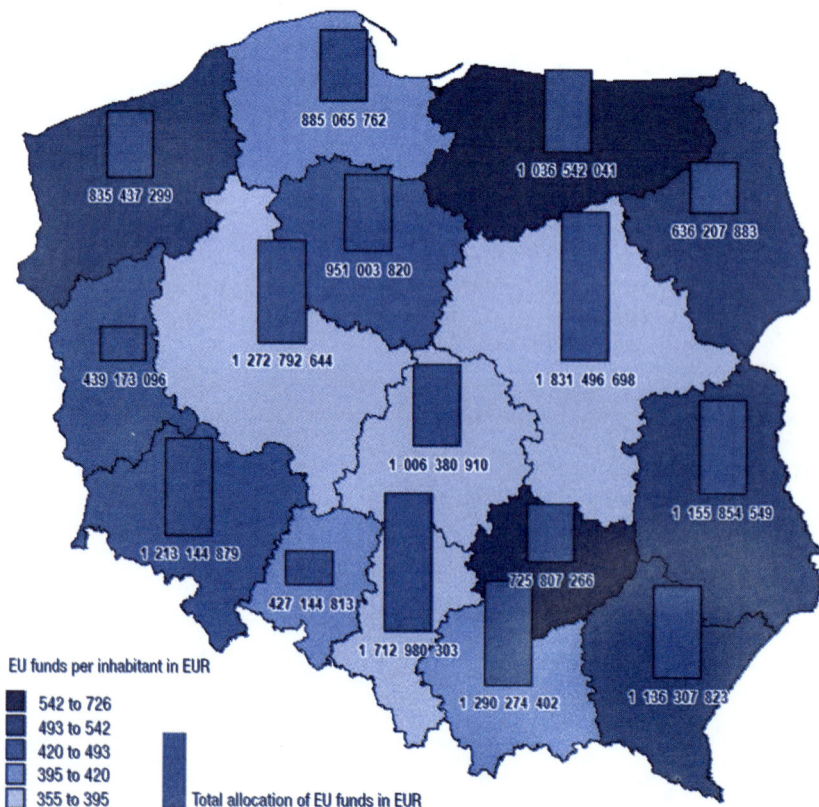

885 065 762

1 036 542 041

835 437 299

636 207 883

951 003 820

439 173 096

1 272 792 644

1 831 496 698

1 006 380 910

1 155 854 549

1 213 144 879

725 807 266

427 144 813

1 712 980 303

EU funds per inhabitant in EUR

- 542 to 726
- 493 to 542
- 420 to 493
- 395 to 420
- 355 to 395

Total allocation of EU funds in EUR

1 290 274 402

1 136 307 823

Source: Ministry of Regional Development, 2007.

ANNEX 3.A4

# Grants and Taxes for Polish Local Governments

**Grants**

The *general grant* was EUR 8.1 billion in 2005. Municipalities received 75%, counties 21% and regions 4%. It constitutes the main grant for sub-national governments (68% of all grants received by municipalities, 69% of those received by counties and 55% of those allocated to regions).

The general grant was significantly modified by the 2004 Act. Several parts of the grant (the part received by regions and counties for roads and the compensatory payments received by municipalities) were removed. Two new parts were created: i) a balancing part, aimed at covering social expenditures by municipalities and counties (EUR 226 million in 2005); ii) a regional part (EUR 78 million in 2005), which is calculated for each region on the basis of the unemployment rate, GDP per capita, area of public roads per capita, and regional railways expenditure.

Two other parts of the grant were maintained under the new Act. Unlike the balancing and regional parts, they concern the three tiers of sub-national government. They are: i) the education part for covering educational expenses, which is by far the main grant to sub-national governments (EUR 6.5 billion, or 25.4% of total sub-national revenue in 2005); and ii) the equalisation part (EUR 1.2 billion or 4.6% of sub-national revenue in 2005).

*Earmarked grants* amounted to EUR 3.9 billion in 2005 (32% of all state grants), of which municipalities received 73%, counties 20% and regions 7%. Earmarked grants, which represent 15% of sub-national revenue, are divided into four types: grants earmarked to carry out state-delegated responsibilities: EUR 2.4 billion in 2005; grants earmarked to exercise specific responsibilities: EUR 957 million in 2005; grants earmarked to carry out responsibilities in conjunction with state organisations: EUR 57 million in 2005; grants from special funds: EUR 156 million in 2005.

**Taxes**

*Own local tax revenue.* In 2005, municipalities' own tax revenue generated almost EUR 4 billion, representing 48.5% of municipal tax revenue and 19.4% of all municipal revenue. The primary source of tax revenue for municipalities is the property tax. Introduced in 1991, it generated EUR 2.9 billion in 2005, representing 35.5% of municipal tax revenue and 14.2% of all municipal revenue. Municipalities can levy other taxes (dog tax, tourism tax, market tax, etc.), but all together they only generated around EUR 660 million in 2005.

*Other own local taxes:* One is the agriculture tax, with a rate set by law which depends on the size of the farm and the average purchasing price of wheat. It generated EUR 240 million in 2005 and represented 2.9% of municipal tax revenue and 1.1% of total municipal revenue. Municipal councils have the right to lower the rates of this tax. The other is the tax on vehicles, with rates set by the municipal council within the limits fixed by law and updated every year by the Ministry of Finance. It represented 2% of municipal tax revenue and 0.8% of total municipal revenue.

*Shared tax revenue* comes from retrocession of a share of receipts from two national taxes: the personal income tax and the corporate tax (increased in 2004 to compensate for the decrease in grants). In 2005, shared tax revenue brought in EUR 5.7 billion for sub-national governments, with the lion's share going to municipalities (74.4% of all shared revenue) and more specifically to towns with county status (44.9% of all shared tax revenue). It represented 51.5% of municipal tax revenue and 20.7% of all municipal revenue, as well as the totality of county and region tax revenue.

*Source:* DEXIA, 2008.

OECD TERRITORIAL REVIEWS: POLAND – ISBN 978-92-64-04926-0 – © OECD 2008

ANNEX 3.A5

# Allocation of Expenditures of Regional Operational Programmes (2007-13)

As a % of total allocation

| Voivodship | R&D, enterpreneurship | Information society | Transport | Energy | Environmental protection | Culture and tourism | Human resources development | Social infrastructure | Territorial development | Institutional and administrative potential |
|---|---|---|---|---|---|---|---|---|---|---|
| European Union | 16.89 | 3.75 | 24.50 | 2.50 | 15.00 | 3.10 | 23.00 | 5.50 | 2.50 | 1.70 |
| Poland | 17.07 | 5.77 | 35.53 | 3.46 | 13.44 | 3.27 | 13.00 | 4.24 | 2.58 | 1.66 |
| ŚWIĘTOKRZYSKIE | 14.05 | 3.91 | 42.98 | 1.03 | 13.39 | 4.18 | 10.97 | 5.74 | 2.02 | 1.74 |
| WARMIŃSKO-MAZURSKIE | 14.50 | 4.73 | 41.72 | 6.91 | 7.22 | 4.47 | 10.74 | 5.02 | 2.51 | 2.18 |
| PODKARPACKIE | 14.77 | 4.83 | 46.61 | 2.90 | 9.44 | 1.57 | 10.49 | 5.31 | 2.66 | 1.42 |
| PODLASKIE | 16.80 | 5.69 | 39.04 | 5.30 | 6.66 | 3.99 | 10.86 | 6.87 | 2.55 | 2.24 |
| LUBELSKIE | 14.02 | 4.54 | 43.27 | 3.28 | 7.09 | 4.86 | 13.29 | 6.28 | 1.74 | 1.65 |
| MAZOWIECKIE | 15.92 | 11.63 | 36.15 | 1.77 | 14.73 | 3.12 | 12.25 | 2.88 | 0.68 | 0.87 |
| ZACHODNIOPOMORSKIE | 15.25 | 4.12 | 37.35 | 10.48 | 9.42 | 4.23 | 11.16 | 3.11 | 2.80 | 2.08 |
| LUBUSKIE | 16.11 | 4.92 | 34.06 | 1.41 | 14.80 | 2.50 | 13.18 | 3.98 | 6.24 | 2.80 |
| DOLNOŚLĄSKIE | 22.17 | 4.90 | 27.56 | 3.37 | 15.73 | 4.09 | 12.32 | 4.42 | 3.71 | 1.72 |
| POMORSKIE | 15.46 | 5.26 | 32.78 | 5.85 | 14.56 | 4.25 | 14.43 | 2.70 | 2.98 | 1.72 |
| ŁÓDZKIE | 17.62 | 4.78 | 37.77 | 2.24 | 11.73 | 2.66 | 15.37 | 3.69 | 2.45 | 1.70 |
| WIELKOPOLSKIE | 17.86 | 4.14 | 38.59 | 2.32 | 14.38 | 1.81 | 14.46 | 3.69 | 1.23 | 1.52 |
| KUJAWSKO-POMORSKIE | 19.95 | 4.13 | 34.77 | 2.65 | 10.25 | 2.90 | 15.66 | 4.57 | 3.02 | 2.10 |
| MAŁOPOLSKIE | 20.75 | 3.67 | 30.24 | 1.41 | 15.49 | 3.77 | 15.16 | 4.91 | 2.65 | 1.94 |
| OPOLSKIE | 21.32 | 4.88 | 23.33 | 4.53 | 19.20 | 2.46 | 14.19 | 3.12 | 3.73 | 3.24 |
| ŚLĄSKIE | 18.17 | 5.71 | 22.30 | 4.23 | 23.42 | 2.25 | 14.03 | 3.64 | 5.01 | 1.23 |

Legend: ▉ Maximum. ▊ Minimum.

Source: Ministry of Regional Development, May 2008.

ISBN 978-92-64-04926-0
OECD Territorial Reviews: Poland
© OECD 2008

# Bibliography

Bafoil, François (2006), "Europe centrale et orientale. Mondialisation, européanisation et changement social" (Central Europe: Globalisation, Europeanisation and social change), Les Presses de Sciences Po, Paris.

Bafoil, François (2009), "Eastern and Central Europe: Globalisation, europeanisation and social change", Palgrave.

Bafoil, François (ed.) (2007), "La Pologne (Poland)", Fayard-Ceri, Paris.

Bañski J. (2006), "The development of rural areas" [in:], M. Degórski (ed.) *Natural and human environment of Poland. A geographical overview*, Polish Academy of Sciences, Polish Geographical Society, pp. 193-210, Warsaw, *www.igipz.pan.pl/zpz/banski/PDF/5_The_development.pdfm*.

Bienkiewicz, Maciej (2007), *CSR and competitiveness, European SMEs good practices*, National Report Poland, Lodz.

Boldrin, M., F. Canova (2003), *Regional Policies and EU Enlargement*, C.E.P.R. Discussion Papers 3744, *www.cepr.org/pubs/dps/DP3744.asp*.

Bourdeau-Lepage, Lise (2002), "Marché du travail et disparités regionales en Pologne", Revue Régions et développement, No. 15-2002, *www.regionetdeveloppement.u-3mrs.fr/pdf/R15/R15_Bourdeau_Lepage.pdf*.

Bradley, J. (2005), "Has EU regional policy been effective? The debate on Structural Funds", Congress of the European Regional Science Association, Amsterdam.

Braunerhjelm, P. *et al.* (2000), "Integration and the Regions of Europe: How the Right Policies can Prevent Polarisation", Centre of Economic Policy Research, London, March 2000, pp. 115.

Bury, Piotr and Swianiewicz, Paweł (2002), "Grant Transfers In Financing Local Governments In Poland", short version of the paper presented at the NISPAcee Annual Conference, Kraków, April 24-27, 2002, *http://unpan1.un.org/intradoc/groups/public/documents/NISPAcee/UNPAN004538.pdf*.

Bury, Piotr, "Rural Areas and Local Finance in Poland", University of Lodz, Lodz, *http://unpan1.un.org/intradoc/groups/public/documents/NISPAcee/UNPAN005088.pdf*.

CEE Bankwatch Network and Friends of the Earth Europe (2007), "EU funds for public and environment-friendly transport", *www.foeeurope.org/publications/2007/EUfunds4Transport.pdf<*.

Centre for European Regional and Local Studies (2005), *Regional Development and Urban Revitalization Project. A Feasibility Study*, Warsaw, 2005.

Churski, Pawel (2005), "Problem areas in Poland in terms of the Objectives of the European Union's Regional Policy", *European Planning Studies*, Vol. 13, No. 1, January 2005, pp. 45-72.

Dabrowski, Marcin (2007), "Implementing Structural Funds in Poland: Institutional Change and Participation of the Civil Society", *Political Perspectives EPRU 200*, Issue 2 (5).

Dabrowski, Marcin (2008), "Structural funds as a Driver for Institutional Change in Poland", *Europe – Asia Studies*, vol. 60, No. 2, March 2008, pp. 227-248, *www.informaworld.com/smpp/section?content=a791605783&fulltext=713240928*.

Department for Transport (1999), "SACTRA: The Standing Advisory Committee forTrunk Road Assessment", *www.dft.gov.uk/pgr/economics/sactra/ sactrathestandingadvisorycom3140*.

DEXIA (2008), *Sub-national governments in the European Union: Responsibilities, organisation and finances*, Dexia Editions, 656 pages.

Djordjevic, Masa (2006), "Politics of Urban Development Planning: Building Urban Governance in Post-Socialist Warsaw?", First Annual Doctoral Conference of the Department of Political Science at CEU, 13-14 April 2006.

Dzun, Wlodzimierz (2005), "Panstwowe gospodarstwa rolne w porcesie przemian systemowych w Polsce" (The state agricultural units (exploitations) during the systemic change in Poland), Institut rozwoju wsi i rolnictwa polskiej, Akademii Nauki, Poland.

EBRD (2006), *Transition Report 2006: Finance in transition*, European Bank for Reconstruction and Development, London.

Economist Intelligence Unit (2007), *Country Profile on Poland*, London, June.

European Commission (2007), *Growing Regions, Growing Europe, Fourth Report on the Economic and Social Cohesion*, European Commission, Brussels.

European Commission (2004), *Third report on the Economic and social cohesion*, European Commission, Brussels.

European Commission (2006), *Annual Innovation Policy Trends and Appraisal Report*, European Trend Chart on Innovation, European Commission, Brussels.

European Commission (2007), *Fourth report on the Economic and social cohesion*, European Commission, Brussels.

European Commission, (2007), "Territorial Agenda of the European Union, Towards a more competitive Europe of diverse regions", European Commission, Brussels.

Maastricht Economic Research Institute on Innovation and Technology (MERIT) and the Joint Research Centre (Institute for the Protection and Security of the Citizen) of the European Commission (2006), *European Innovation Scoreboard: comparative analysis of innovation performance*, 2006

Ferry, Martin (2003), "The EU and the Recent Regional Reform in Poland", *Europe Asia Studies*, Vol. 55, No. 7, pp. 1097-1116.

Ferry, Martin (2007), *Policy developments in Poland*, Regional policy developments in member states and Norway: country reviews in 2006-07, EPRC European Policies Research Centre, University of Strathclyde, Glasgow.

Ferry, Martin, Mc Caster, Irene (2005), "Implementing Structural Funds in Polish and Czech regions: Convergence, Variations, Empowerment?", *Regional and Federal Studies*, Vol. 15, No. 1, March 2005, pp. 19-39.

Furmankiewicz, Marek (2002), "The Effects of Co-operation between Territorial Self-Governments In Local And Regional Associations In Poland", *Przekształcenia*

*Regionalnych Struktur Funkcjonalno-Przestrzennych Vii Wrocław*, University Of Wrocław, Poland.

Gdansk Institute for Market Economics (IBMGR) (2007), "Investment Attractiveness of Polish Voivodships and Regions".

Gdansk Institute for Market Economics, Marcin Dabrowski et alii, Jan red. Jan Fazlagic (2008), *Edukacja dla modernizacji i rozwoju* [Education for modernisation and development], III Kongres Obywatelski [Third Citizens Congress], Gdansk.

Gorczyca, Katarzyna and Kotuła, Łukasz (2006), "Land-use planning and public participation in Norway and Poland", Institute of Urban Development, Krakow, Poland.

Gorzelak, G. (2003), "Bieda i zamożność regionów (założenia, hipotezy, przykłady)", [Poverty and exclusion of the regions (hypothesis and case studies)], *Studia Regionalne i Lokalne*, Poland.

Gorzelak, G. (2004), "Polska polityka regionalna wobec zróżnicowań polskiej przestrzeni" (Polish regional policy based on the differentiation of Polish territories), "Studia Regionalne i Lokalne", Poland.

Gorzelak, G., M. Smętkowski (2005), "Metropolia i jej region w gospodarce informacyjnej" (Metropolitan cities and their regions in the information economy), Wyd. Naukowe Scholar, Warsaw.

Gorzelak, G., Tucholska, A. (dir.) (2007), "Rozwoj, Region, Przestrzen, Euroreg" (Development, region, Territories), MRR Warszawa.

Gorzelak, Grzegorz, Blachter, John, Kasprzyka, (dir.) (2004), "Wspolpraca transgraniczna unii europejskiej. Doswiadczenia polsko – niemieckie" (Trans-border co-operation in the Europe Union. German-Polish experiences), Uniwersytet Warszawski, Scholar, Warsaw.

Grosse Tomasz G. (2002), "Ocena systemu polityki regionalnej w wybraych wojewodztwach" (Assessment of the system of regional policy in some voivodships), *Studia regionalne i Lokalne*, No. 4 (10), pp. 5-22.

Grosse Tomasz G. (2007), "Save Public assets. Monitoring corruption threats in the distribution of structural funds. The case of IROP in Poland", *Institut of Public Affairs*, February 2007.

Grosse Tomasz G., Bobinska L. KOLARSKA (2008), "New Modes of Governance in new Member states", *Institute of Public affairs*, Policy Brief, No. 25.

GUS (Central Statistical Office, CSO) (2005), *Statistical Yearbook for Poland*, Zakład Wydawnictw Statystycznych, Warsaw.

GUS (2006), *Statistical Yearbook for Poland*, Zakład Wydawnictw Statystycznych, Warsaw.

GUS (2007), *Regions of Poland*, Zakład Wydawnictw Statystycznych, Warsaw.

Halamska, Maria (1998), "Dekolektywizacja rolnictwa w europie srodkowej i jej spoeczne konsekwencje" (De-collectivisation of the agriculture in Central Europe and its social consequences), Institut rozwoju wsi i rolnictwa polskiej, Akademii Nauki, Warsaw.

Hansen, Malin and Böhme, Kai (eds.) (2001), "Spatial Planning in the Baltic Sea region, Implications of European Spatial Development Perspectives", European Regional Development Fund, European Community, Brussels.

Hughes, James, G. Sasse, C. Gordon (2001), "Centres and Peripheries in the New Europe: EU Enlargement and the Dynamics of Regionalisation in Central and Eastern Europe", ECPR Joint Session.

Izdebski, H., A. Nelicki, I. Zachariacz (2007), "Land use and development. Polish regulatory framework and democratic ruleof Law standard", *Sprawne Panstwo*, Ernst and Young.

Izdebski, Hubert (2000), *Administration publique en Pologne, ISBN 83-7206-051-7, LIBER, 2000.*

Intervention of Prof. Grzegorz Grzelak (2003), "Quelles sont les chances des régions polonaises dans une Europe intégrée", Conférence "Une Stratégie polonaise pour les années 2004-2015 après l'adhésion à l'Union", Warsaw.

Jakubowska P., A. Kuklinski, P. Zuber (2008), "Probematyka przyszlosci regionow. W poszukiwania nowego paradygmatu" (The future of regions. Towards a new paradigm), Tom I, Ministerstwo Rozwoju regionalnego, Warsaw.

Keating, Michael (2003), "Regionalisation in Central and Eastern Europe: The Diffusion of a Western Model ?", in Keating Michael, Hughes, James (eds.), *The Regional Challenge in Central and Eastern Europe, Territorial Restructuring and European Integration*, Bruxelles, P.I.E. Lang.

Ketels, Christian, O. Sölvell (2006), "Innovation clusters in the 10 new members states of the European union", Europe Innova, Paper 1, European Commission, Directorate General Enterprise and Industry.

Konecny, Martin, CEE Bankwatch Network/Friends of the Earth Europe (2007), *EU funds for public and environment-friendly transport*, Comparison of transport measures and allocations in the draft Operational Programmes of CEE countries for the 2007-13 period, Brussels.

Kowalczyk, Andrzej (2003), "Local government in Poland", World Bank, from the book by Tamas M.Horvath "Decentralization: Experiments and Reforms, Budapest", *www1.worldbank.org/wbiep/decentralization/ecalib/poland.pdf.*

Kulesza, Michal (2001), "Methods and techniques of managing decentralization reforms in CEE countries, The Polish Experience", Warsaw University, Warsaw.

Lendzion, Jacek and Lokucijewski, Krzysztof (2001), *Poland*, Compendium of Spatial Planning Systems in the Baltic Sea Region, *http://vasab.leontief.net/countries/poland2.htm#3.*

Lepesant, Gilles (2006), "La mise en œuvre de la politique régionale en Pologne", Janvier 2005, *www.ceri-sciencespo.com/archive/jan05/artgl.pdf.*

Lepesant, Gilles (2006), "The European Union and its Neighbourhood: Towards a New Contract", Politique étrangère 4/2004 Volume 69, pp. 767-780.

Marcou, Gérard (2002), "L'adaptation des structures territoriales face à la politique régionale communautaire", *Revue d'études comparatives Est/Ouest*, Vol. 33, No. 3 (septembre 2002), pp. 131-167.

Marcou, Gérard (2002), "Un échelon faible promis à un rôle important: les régions polonaises", in *Marcou, Gérard, Hellmut, Wollmann (2004), Réforme de la décentralisation, réforme de l'État, Régions et villes en Europe: Annuaire 2004 des collectivités locales*, 24e édition, Centre National de la Recherche Scientifique –C.N.R.S., Paris. Marek Furmankiewicz (1997), "Major Tendencies and Structural Problems of Major Polish Cities in the New Economic Context", University of Wroclaw.

Ministry of Economy (2007), "The Impact of Economic Emigration on the Polish Economy", February 2007, Ministry of Economy, Warsaw.

Ministry of Regional Development (2004), "Improvement of the Competitiveness of Enterprises", Ministry of Regional Development, Warsaw.

Ministry of Regional Development (2005), "Integrated Regional Development Operational Programme", March 2005, Ministry of Regional Development, Warsaw.

Ministry of Regional Development (2007), Background Report, Answers to the OECD Questionnaire.

Ministry of Regional Development (2007), "National Strategic Reference Framework", Poland.

Ministry of Regional Development (2007), "Operational Programme Eastern Poland Development", Ministry of Regional Development, Warsaw.

Ministry of Regional Development (2007), "Operational Programme Human Capital", Ministry of Regional Development, Warsaw.

Ministry of Regional Development (2007), "Operational Programme Infrastructure and Environment", Ministry of Regional Development, Warsaw.

Ministry of Regional Development (2007), "Operational Programme Innovative Economy", Ministry of Regional Development, Warsaw.

Ministry of Regional Development (2007), "The Assessment of Poland's Progress on the Way to Cohesion with the EU", Synthesis, August 2007, Ministry of Regional Development, Warsaw.

Ministry of Regional Development (2007), "The Assessment of Poland's Progress on the Way to Cohesion with the EU", August 2007, Ministry of Regional Development, Warsaw.

Ministry of Regional Development (2006), "Examining reasons for differences in levels of payments made within the scope of Irop on the regional level", Report summary IROP, October 2006 (Wyg international), Ministry of Regional Development, Warsaw.

O'Dwyer, Connor (2006), "Reforming Regional Governance in East Central Europe: Europeanisation or Domestic Politics as Usual ?", East-European Politics and Societies, Vol. 20, No. 2, pp. 219-253.

OECD (1993), Regional Problems and Policies in Poland, OECD Publishing, Paris.

OECD (2002), OECD Reviews of Regulatory Reform, Poland: From Transition to New Regulatory Challenges, OECD Publications, Paris.

OECD (2003a), Managing Public Expenditures in Poland, Economics Department, Working Papers No. 346, OECD Publishing, Paris.

OECD (2003b), Territorial Review of Hungary, OECD Publishing, Paris.

OECD (2005), Building Competitive Regions, OECD Publishing, Paris.

OECD (2006a), Competitive Cities in the Global Economy, OECD Publishing, Paris.

OECD (2006b), Economic Survey of Poland, OECD Publishing, Paris.

OECD (2006c), PISA (Programme for International Student Assessment), OECD Publishing, Paris.

OECD (2006d), Poland's Education and Training: Boosting Innovation and Human Capital, ECO Working Paper No. 495, OECD Publishing, Paris.

OECD (2006e), *Policy-mix for Innovation in Poland*, OECD Publishing, Paris.

OECD (2006f), *Territorial Review of Finland*, OECD Publishing, Paris.

OECD (2006g), *Territorial Review of France*, OECD Publishing, Paris.

OECD (2006h), *The New Rural Paradigm*, OECD Publishing, Paris.

OECD (2006i), "Workshop Proceedings: The Efficiency of Sub-Central Spending", Paris May 2006, OECD Network on Fiscal Relations across Levels of Government

OECD (2006j), *Metropolitan Review of Randstad-Holland*, OECD Publishing, Paris.

OECD (2007a), *Baltic Partnerships: Integration, Growth and Local Governance in the Baltic Sea Region*, LEED, OECD Publishing, Paris.

OECD (2007b), *Competitive Cities: A new Entrepreneurial Paradigm in Spatial Development*, OECD Publishing, Paris.

OECD (2007c), *Fiscal Equalisation in OECD Countries*, OECD Publishing, Paris.

OECD (2007d), *Innovation OECD/DSTI*, OECD Publishing, Paris.

OECD (2007e), *Monitoring Review on Mexico*, OECD Publishing, Paris.

OECD (2007f), *OECD Regions at a Glance*, OECD Publishing, Paris.

OECD (2007g), *OECD Reviews of Regional Innovation, Competitive Regional Clusters: National Policy Approaches*, OECD Publishing, Paris.

OECD (2007h), *Rural Review on Mexico*, OECD Publishing, Paris.

OECD (2007i), *Rural Review on Scotland*, OECD Publishing, Paris.

OECD (2007j), *Rural Review on Finland*, OECD Publishing, Paris.

OECD (2007k), *OECD Reviews of Regional Innovation, Competitive Regional Clusters: National Policy Approaches*, OECD Publications, Paris.

OECD (2007l), *Business Clusters: Promoting Enterprise in Central and Eastern Europe*, LEED, OECD Publishing, Paris.

OECD (2007m), *OECD Factbook 2007*, OECD Publishing, Paris.

OECD (2007n), *Employment in Government in the Perspective of Production Costs of Goods and Services in the Public Domain*, November, Paris.

OECD (2008a), *Economic Survey of Poland* , OECD Publications, Paris.

OECD (2008b), *Territorial Review of Portugal*, OECD Publishing, Paris.

OECD (2008c), *OECD Factbook, 2008*, OECD Publishing, Paris.

OECD (2008d), "Performance Budgeting: a Users's Guide", *Policy Brief*, March, Paris.

OECD (2008e), *Linking regions and the central government: Indicators for performance-based regional development policy*, Paris.

Piasecki, Ryszard (2006), "Regional Policy of Poland", Report prepared for CIFE (Turkey), Warsaw.

Rapacki Rychard (2006), "Polan economi developmen leve in comparative perspective 1950-2005", paper presented in International conference in memory of Georges Blazyca, "Reinventing Poland", Glasgow, University of Paisley, 10-11 November.

Rodriguez-Posé and R. Crescenzi (2006), "R&D, spillovers, innovation systems and the genesis of regional growth in Europe", OECD paper, *www.oecd.org/dataoecd/23/28/37618122.pdf.*

Rodriguez-Posé, Andres (2000), "Economic convergence and regional development strategies in Spain: The case of Galicia and Navarre", EIB Papers, Vol. 5, 2000.

Rodríguez-Pose, Andrés and Fratesi, Ugo (2003), "Between development and social policies: the impact of European Structural Funds in objective 1 regions", Working Paper No. 28.

Rosner Andrzej, dir. (2007), "Zroznicowanie poziomu rozwoju spoleczno-gospodarczego obszarow wiejkskich a zroznicowanie dynamiki przemian" (The differentiations of the level of socio-economic development of rural areas and of dynamics of changes), Institut rozwoju wsi i rolnictwa polskiej, Akademii Nauki, Warsaw.

Smetkowski (Maciej), "Delimitacja obszarow metropolitalnych w Polsce Nowe spojrzenie" in *Rozwoj, region polityka* (Delimitating metropolitan areas in Poland: a new approach), in *Rozwol region przestrzen* (Gorzelak and Tucholska dir.), pp. 215-233.

Swianiewicz, Pawel (2002), "Reforming Local Government in Poland: Top-Down and Bottom-Up Processes", paper prepared for the Joint Conference of IPSA's RC05 and the German Political Science Association Workgroup on Local Government Studies, "Reforming Local Government: Closing the Gap Between Democracy and Efficiency", Stuttgart, 26-27 September.

Szafraniec, Krystyna, (dir.) (2006), "Kapital Ludzki i zasoby spoleczne wsi. Ludzie, spolecznosc lokalna, edukacja" (Human Capital and social resources in rural areas. People, local society, education), Institut rozwoju wsi i rolnictwa polskiej, Akademii Nauki, Warsaw.

Szlachta, Jacek (2001), "Politique du développement régional de la Pologne comme élément du processus d'intégration européenne" (Regional Development policy in Poland as part of the process of EU accession), Département de l'aide extérieure, des fonds et des programmes communautaires du Comité d'intégration européenne (Department of Community Programmes of the Committee of European Integration), Warsaw.

The Economist (2005), "Accessing EU funds in the new member states: best practice from around Europe", Briefing paper, Economist Corporate Network, March, *The Economist Newspaper.*

Wilkin *et al.* (2005), "Multifunctionality of Agriculture: Comments, Case Studies and Areas for Further Research", *European Network of Agricultural and Rural Policy Research Institutes, Policy Brief* No. 5.

World Bank (2006), "Administrative capacity in the New Member States: The Limits of Innovation ?", *Study, Poverty Reduction and Economic Management Unit Europe and Central Asia,* Report No. 36 930-GLB, December, World Bank, *www-wds.worldbank.org/external/default/WDSContentServer/WDSP/IB/2007/03/07/000020953_20070307140723.pdf*

World Bank (2007), "Labour Markets in EU8+2: From the Shortages of Jobs to the Shortage of Skilled Workers", World Bank EU8+2 Regular Economic Report: Part II: Special Topic, September, World Bank, *http://siteresources.worldbank.org/INTECA/Resources/RER_ST_FINAL_26-09-2007.pdf.*

Yoder, Jennifer A. (2007), "Leading the Way to Regionalization in Post-Communist Europe: An Examination of the Process and Outcomes of Regional Reforms in Poland", *East European Politics and Societies*, Vol. 21, No. 3, pp. 424-446.

OECD PUBLICATIONS, 2, rue André-Pascal, 75775 PARIS CEDEX 16
PRINTED IN FRANCE
(04 2008 07 1 P) ISBN 978-92-64-04926-0 – No. 56381 2008